THE SOCIAL SCIENCES
AND BIBLICAL TRANSLATION

Society of Biblical Literature

Symposium Series

Christopher R. Matthews, Editor

Number 41

THE SOCIAL SCIENCES
AND BIBLICAL TRANSLATION

Edited by
Dietmar Neufeld

THE SOCIAL SCIENCES AND BIBLICAL TRANSLATION

Edited by
Dietmar Neufeld

Society of Biblical Literature
Atlanta

THE SOCIAL SCIENCES
AND BIBLICAL TRANSLATION

Copyright © 2008 by the Society of Biblical Literature

Library of Congress Cataloging-in-Publication Data
The social sciences and biblical translation / edited by Dietmar Neufeld.
    p.   cm. — (SBL symposium series ; no. 41)
Includes bibliographical references and index.
ISBN 978-1-58983-347-0 (paper binding : alk. paper)
1. Bible—Translating. 2. Bible—Criticism, interpretation, etc. 3. Social sciences. I. Neufeld, Dietmar.

BS449.S63 2008b
220.501—dc22   2008008004

15 14 13 12 11 10 09 08   5 4 3 2 1
Printed in the United States of America on acid-free, recycled paper
conforming to ANSI/NISO Z39.48-1992 (R1997) and ISO 9706:1994
standards for paper permanence.

CONTENTS

ABBREVIATIONS

AA	*American Anthropologist*
AB	Anchor Bible
ABR	*Australian Biblical Review*
AcT	*Acta theologica*
AE	*American Ethnologist*
AGP	*Archives of General Psychiatry*
AMP	Amplified Bible
ANRW	*Aufstieg und Niedergang der römischen Welt: Geschichte und Kultur Roms im Spiegel der neueren Forschung.* Edited by H. Temporini and W. Haase. Berlin, 1972–
AQ	*Anthropological Quarterly*
ASV	American Standard Version
BDAG	Bauer, W., F. W. Danker, W. F. Arndt, and F. W. Gingrich. *Greek-English Lexicon of the New Testament and Other Early Christian Literature.* 3rd ed. Chicago, 1999
BDB	Brown, F., S. R. Driver, and C. A. Briggs. *A Hebrew and English Lexicon of the Old Testament.* Oxford, 1907
BGU	*Aegyptische Urkunden aus den Köiglichen Staatlichen Museen zu Berlin, Griechische Urkunden.* 15 vols. Berlin, 1895–1983
Bib	*Biblica*
BibInt	*Biblical Interpretation*
BJS	*Brown Judaic Studies*
BT	*The Bible Translator*
CA	*Current Anthropology*
CAD	*The Assyrian Dictionary of the Oriental Institute of the University of Chicago.* Chicago, 1956–
CBQ	*Catholic Biblical Quarterly*
CEV	Contemporary English Version
ConBNT	Coniectanea biblica: New Testament Series
CP	*Classical Philology*
CQ	*Classical Quarterly*
CurBS	*Currents in Research: Biblical Studies*
CurTM	*Currents in Theology and Mission*
DISO	*Dictionnaire des inscriptions sémitiques de l'ouest.* Edited by Ch. F. Jean and J. Hoftijzer. Leiden, 1965
DJD	Discoveries in the Judaean Desert
DSD	*Dead Sea Discoveries*
EDNT	*Exegetical Dictionary of the New Testament.* Edited by H. Balz and G. Schneider. ET. Grand Rapids, 1990–93
EncJud	*Encyclopaedia Judaica.* 16 vols. Jerusalem, 1972

ETL	*Ephemerides theologicae lovanienses*
EvQ	*Evangelical Quarterly*
ExpTim	*Expository Times*
HAR	*Hebrew Annual Review*
HNTC	Harper's New Testament Commentaries
HTR	*Harvard Theological Review*
HUT	Hermeneutische Untersuchungen zur Theologie
ICC	International Critical Commentary
IDB	*The Interpreter's Dictionary of the Bible*. Edited by G. A. Buttrick. 4 vols. Nashville, 1962
IG	*Inscriptiones graecae*. Editio minor. Berlin, 1924–
Int	*Interpretation*
ISBE	*International Standard Bible Encyclopedia*. Edited by G. W. Bromiley. 4 vols. Grand Rapids, 1979–88
JAAR	*Journal of the American Academy of Religion*
JAOS	*Journal of the American Oriental Society*
JB	Jerusalem Bible
JBL	*Journal of Biblical Literature*
JETS	*Journal of the Evangelical Theological Society*
JPA	*The Journal of Psychological Anthropology*
JPS	Jewish Publication Society
JPSP	*Journal of Personality and Social Psychology*
JSNTSup	Journal for the Study of the New Testament Supplement Series
JSOT	*Journal for the Study of the Old Testament*
KJV	King James Version
L&N	*Greek-English Lexicon of the New Testament: Based on Semantic Domains*. Edited by J. P. Louw and E. A. Nida. 2nd ed. New York, 1989
LCL	Loeb Classical Library
LTJ	*Lutheran Theology Journal*
NAB	New American Bible
NASB	New American Standard Bible
NEB	New English Bible
NJB	New Jerusalem Bible
NICNT	New International Commentary on the New Testament
NIGTC	New International Greek Testament Commentary
NIV	New International Version
NRSV	New Revised Standard Version
NTS	*New Testament Studies*
OGIS	*Orientis graeci inscriptiones selectae*. Edited by W. Dittenberger. 2 vols. Leipzig, 1903–5
OTL	Old Testament Library
PA	*Practicing Anthropology*
REV	Revised English Version
RevQ	*Revue de Qumran*
RSV	Revised Standard Version
RSR	*Religious Studies Review*
RTR	*Reformed Theological Review*

RV	Revised Version
SBLSP	*Society of Biblical Literature Seminar Papers*
SBLSymS	Society of Biblical Literature Symposium Series
SEG	Supplementum epigraphicum graecum
SNTSMS	Society for New Testament Studies Monograph Series
STDJ	*Studies on the Texts of the Desert of Judah*
SV	Scholar's Version
SVTP	Studia in Veteris Testamenti pseudepigraphica
TBT	*The Bible Today*
TDNT	*Theological Dictionary of the New Testament.* Edited by G. Kittel and G. Friedrich. Translated by G. W. Bromiley. 10 vols. Grand Rapids, 1964–76
TEV	Today's English Version
THAT	*Theologisches Handwörterbuch zum Alten Testament.* Edited by E. Jenni, with assistance from C. Westermann. 2 vols., Stuttgart, 1971–76
ThWAT	*Theologisches Wörterbuch zum Alten Testament*
TynBul	*Tyndale Bulletin*
VT	*Vetus Testamentum*
WTM	*Das Wörterbuch über die Talmudim und Midraschim.* J. Levy. 2nd ed. 1924
WYC	Wycliffe New Testament

INTRODUCTION

> The Bible is not a Western Book. To be sure, it has generated ideas and attitudes that can be found everywhere in Western cultural and religious history. But the plain fact is that it was written by, for, and about people in the ancient Mediterranean world whose culture, worldview, social patterns, and daily expectations differed sharply from those of the modern West. The simple reality is that in spite of our fondest personal hopes, and even our religious aspirations, the Bible was not written for us. (Rohrbaugh 2007, ix)

It is my great privilege to edit a volume on the social sciences and biblical translation. I have been a member of the Context Group (CG) for twelve years, attending both its annual meetings in the United States and its international meetings in South Africa (2001), Scotland (2004), Russia (2005), and Spain (2006). While the history of the CG has evolved through several developmental stages, it was in the spring of 1990 that the group, newly named "The Context Group: Project on the Bible in Its Cultural Environment," convened its first meeting in Portland, Oregon. The modus operandi of the annual CG meeting centers on providing rigorous critique of papers in progress toward both presentation at the annual meetings of the Society of Biblical Literature and publication. Members of this group have presented the results of their research through the auspices of the Society of Biblical Literature, within the program unit of Social-Scientific Criticism in the New Testament Section—of which I am now chair with my collaborator, Richard E. DeMaris.

The scholars contributing to this volume for many years have focused their research on the ancient Mediterranean world and its culture, worldview, social patterns, values, and daily expectation. The CG believes in the usefulness of social-scientific ideas and insights as a foundation in exploring and ultimately translating the biblical texts. They also deem it necessary to read the Bible with eyes attuned to honor and shame, patron-and-client associations, androcentric gender relations, group orientation, envy and the evil eye, purity/impurity issues, and health and sickness in the ancient world. Furthermore, they believe that a cross-cultural reading of the Bible is not a matter of choice (Rohrbaugh 1996, 1). The meanings that the writers of the New Testament exchanged with their contemporary audiences were rooted in the social systems that enveloped them. This volume has grown out of the concern that North American religious sensibilities, cultural and social values, political views, ways of reading and understanding the biblical texts, and lived experiences have all too often been imposed upon the Bible without regard for its original social and cultural context. Reading the Bible from a North American perspective has emasculated it of its foreignness. The Bible was written by, for, and about people whose worldview, culture, social values, and aspirations differed radically from those of the modern reader (Rohrbaugh 2007, ix).

1

This volume, therefore, intends to deal, in part, with the issue of interpreting or translating specific sets of Greek and Hebrew texts from the perspective of cultural anthropology and the social sciences. Each of the essays deals with fundamental methodological issues with the purpose of enabling readers to take note of the differences in translation and meaning when words, sentences, and ideas, are part of ancient social and cultural systems that shape meaning. These issues, which in modified form guide the approach of the CG, are offered as models to be tested in interpretative practice. The use of social-scientific models generated by anthropologists permits the translator to shuttle back and forth between model and data to establish meaning. In the words of Philip Esler, "Models of phenomena such as identity, ethnicity, religion, sect, kinship, time, honor and shame, patron and client, collective memory, and so on allow us to interrogate these issues in biblical texts in helpful and socially important ways" (Esler 2006, 4). The CG does not claim to be immune to charges of manipulation or claim to have found the final, definitive interpretation of the Bible and its texts. It recognizes that rewriting suppresses, distorts, and contains, but that in an age of ever increasing manipulation, being sensitive to and attempting to mitigate, not eliminate, the forces of manipulation through the use of the insights from cultural anthropology is important (Gentzler 1993, ix; Horden 2000, 485–641).

Books and articles on the Bible and translation continue to consider issues of gender in translation, cultural identity, sex bias in language, the politics of transmission, translation and empire/power, and the merit of "dynamic equivalence" translations (Prickett 1986, 10; Robinson 1997; Mazid 2007). Any one of a dozen methodological approaches (feminist criticism, autobiographical criticism, reader-response criticism, semiotics, ideological criticism, ritual studies, cultural studies, and post-structuralist epistemologies) have been developed to deal with the many difficulties of transposing an ancient "source language" into a modern "metropolitan target language." As will be discovered in the course of this volume, a social-scientific approach considers the role of anthropological concepts in interpreting the Bible.

While much sophisticated work has been done on the development of the theories of translation and practices in anthropology/ethnography, translating ancient Mediterranean texts is fraught with potential pitfalls. Translators and interpreters speak of "boundary crossing" and of creating "a monster," that is, the violence often done to ancient texts when they are made to cross the border from the ancient to the modern world in the translation process (Dingwaney 1995, 4). The process of translation is intended to make the ancient Mediterranean world accessible and comprehensible to Western readers but, in the process, it involves a specific exercise of power, be it colonial or gender, as "it seeks to constitute the Mediterranean world as an object of its study" (Dingwaney 1995, 4). The act of translation carries an ideological weight—because translation is always first interpretation, it will therefore be caught up in relationships of cultural dominance and subordination. In addition, there are the institutional beliefs of sponsoring ecclesial bodies and the inertia of religious traditions for which the translations are prepared that determine the translations undertaken. There is also the issue of the asymmetrical power relationship between the culture of the Mediterranean world and the culture of one studying the Mediterranean world—in which for example, strange cultural forms, practices, and concepts are "recuperated via a process of familiarization (assimilation to culturally familiar forms or concepts or practices) whereby they are denuded of their foreignness, even, perhaps, of their radical inaccessibility" (Dingwaney 1995, 5). Bassnett-McGuires avers that "to attempt to impose the value system of the source language onto the target language is dangerous ground, and the translator should not be tempted by the school that pretends to determine the original intentions of the author on the basis of a self-contained text" (1980, 23).

In other words, translation is not simply linguistic transfer. "No two languages are ever sufficiently similar to be considered as representing the same social reality. The worlds in which different societies live are distinct worlds, not merely the same world with different labels attached" (Sapir 1956, 69). Any word, by itself, captures multiple ideas. For instance, *table* can refer to currency, kitchen furniture, hydrology, Robert's rules of order, chart, and topography. Modern dictionaries list the range of meanings that words have in social systems and update that range of meanings in living languages. To update the semantic range that words have in Hellenistic Greek or Hebrew is more problematic. James Barr (1961) and others have demonstrated that theological dictionaries of the Bible, in the attempt to define the meaning of words used in circum-Mediterranean cultures, frequently base the study and determination of the meanings of words in isolation. The limited range of meanings assigned to words in these lexica is woefully inadequate and misleading and therefore leads to translation muddles (Barr 1961; Nida 1992).

Joshua A. Fogel points to the fascinating new developments that have taken place in translation theory in the past two decades. We are now in a "cultural turn" (1993, 3) in which the important unit of translation is not merely a series of words or sentences between languages or even of texts moving from one culture to another but rather words and sentences in their cultural and social contexts—each has a distinctive cultural and social universe. Translators, therefore, no longer simply speak of a "source language" or a "target language" but of source and target cultures (Fogel 1993, 1–3). This has led to the investigation of such variables as social class, education, gender, age, values, and the social minutiae that make up the lives of ancient Mediterranean people (Pöchhacker 2002, 391). Translation is, then, not simply the transference of meaning from one language system to another with the use of dictionaries and grammars. Language is at the heart of a social context and gives it voice so that translators now see the source text as embedded in its social/cultural universe (Rohrbaugh 2007; Malina 2001). Language is regarded as a guide to social reality, and it is recognized that to some extent humans are held captive by the language of their social group. How one understands and experiences the world is largely the result of the language habits of the community of which one is a part: "No two languages are ever sufficiently similar to be considered as representing the same social reality" (Bassnett-McGuire 1980, 13; Engler et al. 2007, 299).

Frantz Fanon observes that "to speak a language is to take on a world, a culture" (1967, 38). Language cannot be isolated from the social context or world within which it is embedded. Thus, when seeking to transport the meaning of words and sentences from one language to another, the translator cannot simply search for word equivalents in the target language to render the meaning of the source. The translator must attend to the cultural and social context of the ancient Mediterranean world from within which the words and sentences arise. As Mary Snell-Hornby notes, "Translation is more an act of cultural transfer than linguistic: the act of translation is no longer simply transcoding from one context into another, but an act of communication. Texts are part of the worlds they inhabit and cannot be neatly ripped from their surroundings" (1990, 81–82). Translation then becomes an act of cross-cultural transfer where the translator must be both bicultural as well as bilingual.

In recent years, therefore, translation theory and practice have turned both to source and target cultures as things that require careful study before the work of translation can begin. In translating words and sentences in the language of the ancient Mediterranean world into the English of the West, the work of anthropologists and social scientists in sorting out the social context of the source language takes on crucial significance. Translation is the vehicle through which not only the language but also the social and cultural values of the ancient Mediterranean world are made to travel—transported, or borne across to and recuperated by audiences in the West.

As mentioned, however, in the attempt to recuperate the meaning of the original languages, North American translations tend to denude the Bible of its foreignness and distance. This is due to translators not being critically self-aware of the influences of their own culture on them (target culture): an acculturated blindness. Egregious examples of acculturated blindness abound. Back in the 1970s and 1980s it was Hal Lindsey's best-selling *Late Great Planet Earth* that inspired the likes of Ronald Reagan:

> That [a coup in Libya] is a sign that the day of Armageddon isn't far off. . . . Everything is falling into place. It can't be long now. Ezekiel says that fire and brimstone will be rained upon the enemies of God's people. That must mean that they'll be destroyed by nuclear weapons. (Boyer 1992, 142)

Speaking to a lobbyist for Israel in 1983, Reagan says:

> You know, I turn back to your ancient prophets in the Old Testament and the signs foretelling Armageddon, and I find myself wondering if we're the generation that's going to see that come about. I don't know if you've noted any of those prophecies lately, but believe me, they certainly describe the times we're going through. (Boyer 1992, 142)

For Reagan as well as many of his contemporaries, the prophecies of the Bible always describe contemporary times, whether in the first or twenty-first centuries C.E., and therefore may be used to read the signs of the times.

Translations of the Bible that fail to take into account the problem of social distance will suffer from ethnocentric and theological myopia. In part, this myopia is attributable to the assumption that the North American social and cultural milieu, if not the same as the ancient Near Eastern cultural and social milieu, is at the very least similar to it. In one of a recent series of feature articles on translation and the Bible in the *Religious Studies News/SBL Edition*, Walter Harrelson writes:

> I am passionate about Bible translation because I have gained insight into virtually all aspects of what it means to be a responsible and free human being through the

literature, imagery, and thought of the Bible. I have never been able to draw a firm line between "then" and "now," because the world I know today has so many similarities—in matters that count—with the biblical world. That frequently makes me an oddity in contemporary settings, but I can't help but draw much of my understanding of politics, ecology, social relations, and moral perceptions from the strange mix of biblical literature and thought. (2002, 5–6)

While not necessarily wishing to imply that Harrelson is unable to make the requisite hermeneutical shift, the casual reader of Harrelson may get the impression that it is easy to do so. The Cotton Patch version of the New Testament gives the impression that it is easy to make the hermeneutical shift between then and now. It hails itself as a "colloquial translation with a Southern accent" (Jordan 2004) and so offers this translation of Luke 1:5: "In the days when Ole Gene was governor of Georgia, there was a preacher by the name of Zack Harris. His wife was a very aristocratic woman named Elizabeth. They were both strict church members and were careful to observe all the rules and regulations of the Lord. They had no children, since Elizabeth was barren and by now they were both quite old" (Jordan 2004). This colloquial translation is clearly a flagrant example of the failure to draw the line between the world of the New Testament and modern culture.

Failure to draw a firm line between the world of the Bible, the Dead Sea Scrolls, and the contemporary world unfortunately promotes the assumption that all cultures function similarly. When the modern reader encounters in the biblical text the notions of forgiveness, barrenness, disease, healing, heart, homosexuality, conscience, grace, righteousness, and deviance, the tendency is to project onto them modern sensibilities. These notions are held hostage to the commonplace theological understandings of Western Christian belief and practice and derive from Westerners' peculiar cultural adaptations of the Bible and the Dead Sea Scrolls.

Moreover, industrial and technological revolutions impair the ability of modern readers to understand the Bible and the Dead Sea Scrolls. Contemporary social forms and values, coupled with new technologies, have brought about permanent changes in vast areas of human experience. Novel modes of perception and the formulation of new worldviews have led to radically different interpretations of human experience, and have fundamentally altered ways of constructing interpretations of reality. The outlook of an earlier era, preindustrial and agrarian, however, is markedly different from today's world and affects the capacity of moderns to read and understand the biblical texts and the Dead Sea Scrolls. While much study has been done on the time-and-place boundedness of the biblical texts and Dead Sea Scrolls—the product of a small group of people living in the eastern Mediterranean region—that study has basically been calculated in historical terms, in terms of the flow of events or ideas that might account for what the biblical texts describe. These accounts, while sensitive to the historical vagaries of time and geography, have not accounted for the social distance that stands between the ancient world and the world of modern Bible translators/readers. Social distance includes differences in social structures, social roles, values, and other cultural features. It involves being socialized into a different understanding of the self, of others, of nature, time and space, and of God.

To mitigate the forces of social distance, the CG has set itself the task of first understanding and describing the social context of the biblical texts by using Mediterranean anthropology and then, armed with this information, to interpret and provide new translations of a selection of biblical texts and Dead Sea Scrolls. Each of the following essays proceeds by a close analysis of particular passages selected from within an ancient context understood by the use of social-scientific ideas and insights. The stated aim of each of the essays is to understand what meanings these passages would have had to their original, ancient audiences.

Richard L. Rohrbaugh ("Foreignizing Translation") addresses the problems inherent in the dynamic equivalence theory of translation and the literal or formal correspondence theory of translation. Each is found deficient because neither makes an effort to understand the cultural values that are implicit in the source language. Rohrbaugh therefore promotes what he calls a *foreignizing translation*—"a deliberate attempt to stage a culturally alien reading experience that avoids the prevalent ethnocentrism common in Western translations." This means understanding the social systems that the language of the New Testament encodes—such as, for example, ancient kinship patterns, cultural values, systems of hierarchy, and patriarchy.

Zeba A. Crook ("Grace as Benefaction in Galatians 2:9, 1 Corinthians 3:10, and Romans 12:3; 15:15") tackles the term *grace*—a word heavily influenced by the thinking of Augustine and Luther and reflected in all English translations of it—to argue that grace is best understood within the context of patronage, benefaction, and reciprocity. Marshaling evidence from inscriptions, papyri, literary and historical writings, and Hellenistic Jewish sources, Crook demonstrates that Paul did not use the term differently from his contemporaries. He did not use the word *grace* to refer to a pleasing quality or to gratitude for having received an unearned gift but rather to the concrete act of generosity in the system of benefaction. Hence, when translating the term *grace*, words such as *benefaction, beneficence*, even *favor*, will catch the tone and meaning of *grace* in Pauline usage.

Richard E. DeMaris ("Contrition and Correction or Elimination and Purification in 1 Corinthians 5?") investigates what Paul could have meant when he appeared to enjoin the removal of a sexual deviant from the assembly in Corinth. Noting that modern sensibilities have distorted Paul's intent, DeMaris turns to ritual theory—particularly execration rituals—to seek clarity on 1 Cor 1:1–5. Because ritual is the way communities achieve and maintain purity and how they negotiate bodily matters, he turns to the problem of the sexual deviate in the Corinthian community. Paul's foremost concern was to unite a splintered community. He thus advised the community to engage in an execration ritual—to pronounce a curse against this person's behavior that threatened public welfare and to enact the community execration—the purpose of which was to bring it back to health, order, and wholeness.

Dietmar Neufeld ("Sins and Forgiveness: Release and Status Reinstatement of the Paralytic in Mark 2:1–12") tackles the concepts of sin and forgiveness in Mark's narrative of the healing of the paralytic. He argues that the notions of sin and forgiveness play themselves out in the key of honor and shame and in the social structure of patronage and brokerage. As such, rather than the paralytic being forgiven for sins, the result of his innate depravity in the Augustinian sense, the offer of forgiveness from Jesus refers to release from the shame of his affliction, the establishment of his well-being in the community, and to the restoration of his honor in his home. In his encounter with Jesus, he was released from the stigma of his illness and the erroneous public perception that sin was at the root of it, commanded to stand up and go home—"Son, you are released from the bondage of your paralysis and free to go home."

Alicia Batten ("The Degraded Poor and the Greedy Rich: Exploring the Language of Poverty and Wealth in James") asserts that current translations of πλούσιος and πτωχός do not reflect the moral and social connotations of the words. Taking into account how ancient economies worked in the context of limited good, Batten concludes that "the rich," are by definition avaricious and "the poor" dishonored and lowered. She thus translates the terms to read "the greedy rich person" and the "degraded poor person." James, reflecting both the Jewish prophetic traditions concerning the poor and Hellenistic moral teaching with its suspicion of usury and love of wealth, denounces the greed of the rich because it was detrimental to the well-being of the poor and the community.

John H. Elliott ("God—Zealous or Jealous but Never Envious. The Theological Consequences of Linguistic and Social Distinctions") engages in a thorough analysis of the dispositions involved in zeal, jealousy, and envy. He traces the use of the terms in Greek and Roman literature, the Old and New Testaments, and the Septuagint. Elliott observes that most English translations of the Hebrew and Greek terms are socially implausible and conceptually misleading because they have not taken into account the different social situations, social relations, and social dynamics involved. His research concludes that the insidiousness of envy as distinct from jealousy and zeal made certain that ancient Israelites and the early church never spoke or conceived of God as envious. God was capable of jealousy, zeal, ardor, or anger but not of envy.

John J. Pilch ("The Usefulness of the 'Meaning Response' Concept for Interpreting Translations of Healing Accounts in Matthew's Gospel") comments that current translations of the Greek word θεραπεύω render it as "cure" and "healing" without distinction. Such imprecise translations characterize the entire semantic field of health, sickness, and related terms in the Bible. The risk of promoting misunderstanding and misinterpreting the Bible because of imprecision in translation is especially acute for Western readers who have a sophisticated understanding of health and sickness issues. Turning to medical anthropology, Pilch picks up the concept of *meaning response* and argues that it will help to ameliorate the propensity of modern Western readers for medicocentric translations. A meaning response describes the way that humans interact with the total context in which they experience a therapeutic intervention. Using the healing stories in Matthew as a test case, Pilch shows the usefulness of the concept to promote a more respectful and plausible interpretation of Matthew's sickness and healing reports.

Carolyn Leeb ("Translating the Hebrew Body into English Metaphor") addresses the difficult Hebrew idiom "speak to the heart." While in many instances the metaphorical usage is self-evident and easily translatable, in others it is not. Especially problematic is the use of the idiomatic expression in the context of sexual violence committed against women where both God and humans are the perpetrators. She notes that in seven different Old Testament narratives invariably the idiomatic expression is translated by phrases like "speak tenderly," "speak gently," "placate," or similar expressions that indicate empathic speech, directed at the emotions, which Westerners tend to locate in the heart. This language of tenderness is used to translate these words even when, for example, in Gen 34, Judg 19, Hos 2:16–17, and Isa 40:1–2, these words are placed in the mouth of a putative rapist or abusive husband. The result is that Western readers form a positive identification with the speakers of these words and misunderstand the tone of these stories. A social-scientific examination of the ancient Israelite understanding of the body reveals that in their world the heart was understood to be the seat of reasoning, not of feeling, and that a better way of translating this phrase would be "argued with" or "reasoned with." Since there is asymmetry of power between the speaker of this expression and its target, a proper translation changes the dynamic of the narrative entirely.

Rob Kugler ("Relexicalizing Leviticus in 4QMMT: The Beginnings of Qumran Anti-language?") sends out a test probe for a different approach to understanding the legal-rhetoric reasoning of 4QMMT. He proposes to assess 4QMMT's legal reasoning in its own right in comparison with scripture without resorting to the specific comparative evidence adduced from later Jewish groups' models of legal reasoning. Kugler adopts a generic interpretative framework useful in examining linguistic phenomena across time periods and cultures and which is responsive to and coherent with the specific, scripture-based legal rhetoric of 4QMMT. Using the socio-linguistic concept of anti-language, he works with "the idea that developing an anti-language, although apparently a matter of interpretation, is more akin to translation, at least from the standpoint of the community that develops the anti-language." The point is, "not only is all translation interpretation, but at least some interpretation is also merely translation."

John Sandys-Wunsch stands well positioned to write the final chapter of this volume. In his book *What Have They Done to the Bible? A History of Modern Biblical Interpretation*, he points out the difficulties inherent in translating ancient texts: "accurate translation is not a simple task. The French saying *traduire, c'est trahire* sums up the matter and is itself appropriately only translatable as the much less effective "to translate is to betray," where the nuance carried by the pun is lost (2005, 10). Translation of ancient texts is not a simple matter because words often have a spectrum of meanings, and it is not always readily evident which meaning the context requires (2005, 10). Additional complications arise when a word in one language does not have an equivalent word in the target language. He concludes that "it is not possible to render the Bible into modern English in a way that we as products of our culture can understand without the sort of explanation methodologically that should accompany any honest translation that is willing to admit its inadequacies" (p. 146).

This Symposium volume highlights the importance of culturally sensitive translations of the Bible and Dead Sea Scrolls, indeed, of any ancient documents for that matter. The Bible and Dead Sea Scrolls are not products of the Western world but of the Mediterranean one in which culture, worldview, social patterns, and daily expectations and lived experiences shaped the meaning of the words that each author used (Rohrbaugh 2007, ix). While the cultural gap is significant, it is nevertheless possible to traverse it. As each of the authors has attempted to demonstrate, with the requisite cultural models at hand it is possible to narrow the gap between then and now and to open the writings of the Bible and Dead Sea Scrolls in new ways—even if at times this means deliberately staging a culturally alien reading experience for modern readers when the gap cannot be narrowed.

FOREIGNIZING TRANSLATION

Richard L. Rohrbaugh

It has become a commonplace in New Testament studies to say that there are two alternatives when it comes to biblical translation: so-called literal or formal correspondence (between source language and target language) on the one hand, and functional or dynamic equivalence on the other (Porter 2001, 353). Translations such as the NASB and RSV claim adherence to the former, while those like the TEV and the NIV are examples of the latter. Unfortunately, neither addresses the issue of the cultural otherness of the Bible. By contrast, this essay proposes and illustrates a "foreignizing" translation—a deliberate attempt to stage a culturally alien reading experience that avoids the prevalent ethnocentrism common in Western translations.

DYNAMIC EQUIVALENCE TRANSLATION

The distinction between these two types of translation, and the case for the dynamic equivalence approach, is usually traced to the seminal work of Eugene A. Nida. Nida argued that strict word-for-word replacement would produce an unintelligible translation. Since a clearly understood Bible was central to Nida's personal evangelistic agenda, the English readability of the translated text became the byword of his dynamic equivalence theory (Venuti 1995, 22).

Throughout his career Nida argued that the translator's task is one of uncovering the essential message—what he calls the "underlying kernel"—beneath the linguistic form of the source language and then rendering the result in the "natural" idiom of the target language (Porter 2001, 355).[1] He characterizes this "dynamic equivalence" approach to translation as one in which "message" takes priority over form or style (Nida and Taber 1969, 33–55). While Nida himself has restated and refined this method many times over the last thirty years, he remains committed to the way he first described it in 1964:

> A translation of dynamic equivalence aims at complete naturalness of expression and tries to relate the receptor to modes of behavior relevant within the context of his own culture. (159)

---

1. For a good summary and analysis of Nida's concept of an "underlying kernel" and his most frequently used example, see Porter (1999).

11

As Lawrence Venuti has pointed out, it is this dynamic equivalence approach that remains the dominant one in contemporary Anglo-American translation (1995, 21).[2] That is not to say, however, that it is without serious problems. Brief comment on several items in Nida's statement will make that clear.

First, the notion of an "underlying kernel" that can be moved at will from language to language, and even from culture to culture or from one historical era to another, is built upon the dubious idea of a "transcendental" humanity that "remains unchanged over time and space" (Porter 2001, 370–71; Venuti 1995, 22; Rohrbaugh 2006, 12–13). Nida claims that messages in kernel form need only be given linguistic expression in whatever target language is at hand and they will be immediately understood because there is something in human nature that transcends time and culture. Yet few in the field of contemporary cultural anthropology would any longer acknowledge the notion of a "transcendental" humanity precisely because the notion of "humanity" is itself such a highly relative cultural construct (Barna 1998, 337).

Second, Nida's insistence on "naturalness of expression" inevitably results in what Venuti calls "domestication" of the text (1995, 21). What Nida wants is fluency. He advocates retaining the form of the original if possible, but translating idiomatically if necessary in order to achieve naturalness in the target language. The result is a cultural hegemony of the receptor language. Venuti comments:

> By producing the illusion of transparency, a fluent translation masquerades as true semantic equivalence when it in fact inscribes the foreign text with a partial interpretation, partial to English-language values, reducing if not simply excluding the very difference that translation is called on to convey. (Venuti 1995, 21)

The irony, of course, is that this kind of "ethnocentric violence" to the text, to use Venuti's term, puts into serious question the stated aim of the dynamic equivalence approach: generating a response in the reader of the translation similar to that produced in a reader of the original language.[3] We shall have occasion to see exactly that problem below.

Third, we note Nida's professed intent of trying, as he says, to "relate the receptor to modes of behavior relevant within the context of his own culture." As he put it elsewhere, "[T]he translator must be a person who can draw aside the curtains of linguistic and cultural differences so that people may see clearly the relevance of the original message" (Nida and de Waard 1986, 14). That says it rather clearly. Nida imagines the underlying kernel, the message, to be timeless and cultureless. He assumes time and culture are in the form but not in the essence. Of course, since New Testament writers were not really concerned with the relevance of their texts to twenty-first-century Americans, Nida can gain this relevance only by abandoning source-language features Americans do not understand and substituting English ones

---

2. This is true not only in biblical translation but in the translation of other literature as well. For a discussion of this Anglo-American preference and a variety of examples, see Venuti (1995, 25–38).

3. Venuti adds: "This relationship points to the violence that resides in the very purpose and activity of translation: the reconstitution of the foreign text in accordance with the values, beliefs and representations that preexist it in the target language" (1995, 18).

they do. But the glaring issue here is whether it is ever possible to leave the message intact with this kind of ethnocentric violence to the text.

Finally, and most importantly, as Nida says in a later work, "the receptors of a translation should comprehend the translated text to such an extent that they can understand how the original receptors must have understood the original text" (Nida and de Waard 1986, 36). Presumably they would then be able to replicate that same understanding in the mind of a contemporary reader by the skill with which they translate.

Unfortunately, however, in whatever measure such an agenda is even possible, serious study of the Mediterranean cultures of antiquity would seem to be the sine qua non for Nida's approach. To understand the original requires understanding the social system its language encodes. It requires understanding ancient kinship patterns, cultural values, social expectations, and the like. Yet that fact does not seem to have dawned on many Anglo-American translators. In fact, as we shall see below, ethnocentric translations that obscure the cultural difference between the Mediterranean world of the New Testament and contemporary America culture abound. Domestication is clearly the current rule.

While the alternative to dynamic equivalence translation discussed above is usually said to be "literal or formal correspondence," presumably giving weight to similarity of form and structure as much as meaning or message, the fact is that the literal strategy shares many of the same cultural liabilities inherent in the dynamic equivalence approach. Literal or formal correspondence may restrain some of the hegemonic tendencies inherent in the drive for English fluency, but it does nothing to ensure that the translator understands the cultural values implicit in the source language sufficiently well to make appropriate replacement choices. For example, the way the NRSV translates ἐὰν δὲ ὁ ὀφθαλμός σου πονηρὸς ᾖ (Matt 6:23), "if your eye is unhealthy," may qualify as formal correspondence, but the fact is it is painfully ethnocentric. It is clear to anyone studying ancient culture that the translators of the NRSV knew nothing of the Mediterranean belief in the evil eye (Elliott 1988, 42–71).

FOREIGNIZING TRANSLATION

Another alternative, therefore, one rarely discussed among New Testament translators, is what Venuti calls a "foreignizing translation." Here the issue is not the degree to which the translation attains English fluency; nor is it measured by its correspondence with the source language's form or structure. Rather it purposely aims to "develop a theory and practice of translation that resists dominant target-language cultural values so as to signify the linguistic and cultural difference of the foreign text" (Venuti 1995, 23). The significance of this approach can be seen quickly in a comment by Friedrich Schleiermacher, whom Venuti credits with first articulating the idea.[4] In an 1813 lecture on the roads open to the translator, Schleiermacher argues:

---

4. Andre Lefevere's historical collection of essays on "Germanizing" translation makes clear that Schleiermacher is building on earlier ideas in Johann Wolfgang Goethe's 1819 essay "The Three Epochs of Translation" (Lefevere 1977, 35–37).

> In my opinion there are only two. Either the translator leaves the author in peace, as much as possible, and moves the reader towards him; or he leaves the reader in peace, as much as possible, and moves the author towards him. (Venuti 1995, 20; Lefevere 1977, 74)

In other words, it is simply a question of who is going abroad, the author or the reader. Following Schleiermacher, Venuti opts to send the reader traveling. He argues for a foreignizing translation that is not a "transparent representation of an essence that resides in the foreign text and is valuable in itself," but rather a deliberately alien rendering that forces the reader to confront the cultural otherness of the text (1995, 20). Whereas fluent translation is inevitably imprinted with the values, codes, taboos, and intelligibility of English linguistic practice, foreignizing translation is valuable precisely because it disrupts these. As Venuti argues, foreignizing translation

> is highly desirable today, a *strategic* cultural intervention in the current state of world affairs, pitched against the hegemonic English-language nations and the unequal cultural exchanges in which they engage their global others. Foreignizing translation in English can be a form of resistance against ethnocentrism and racism, cultural narcissism and imperialism, in the interests of democratic geopolitical relations. (1995, 20; emphasis added)

While all that may a bit more than New Testament translators expect or wish to achieve, nonetheless sending the reader traveling has the benefit of resisting accommodation of the text to the cultural comfort level of the reader, something which threatens to make translated versions of the New Testament into a simple American cultural self-affirmation.

From a theological point of view one only need think of the near total inability of persons in American churches to distinguish between biblical values and American values in order to understand the strategic value of what Venuti is advocating (Rohrbaugh 2006, 1–17; Prothero 2003). By asking the reader to "go abroad" rather than requiring the author to come in our direction, a foreignizing translation creates a healthy "ethnodeviant pressure" that restrains the all too common tendency to force upon the New Testament cultural messages of our own creation. To put it simply, translation of this sort literally *stages* an alien reading experience as a means of preserving the cultural *otherness* of the original text.

SCENARIO THEORY

Before turning to New Testament examples of what we have been discussing, one more theoretical matter bears examination. Both the dynamic equivalence theory of Eugene Nida and the formal correspondence approach of the NASB presume what socio-linguists call the "propositional model" of reading (Malina 1991; Porter 2001, 364–66). The idea here is that the reader focuses on the sentences and words of a text in order to connect the series of propositions they contain into a procession of thought. Words, then sentences, are decoded for the ideas they contain and then fashioned into a stream of thought. The problem with this model, however, is that it cannot be verified experimentally. Nor, it turns out, is it what actually goes on in the mind of a person reading, simply because reading does not operate at the level of words in this fashion (Malina 1991, 13).

What can be verified experimentally, and what we wish to take into account in translating, is what is called the *scenario* model of the reading process. In this understanding the text sets forth a series of scenes, both explicit and implicit, which are thereby evoked in the mind of the reader. As reading proceeds, these scenes are altered or elaborated according to the directions given in the text (Malina 1991, 15). Especially important is that both writer and reader derive the scenarios they bring to their tasks from the social systems of which they are a part. Ancient Mediterranean persons bring scenarios from ancient Mediterranean society; modern Americans from modern American society. That is because language always encodes a social system. Or to put it another way, scenario theory is based on the fact that "every reader [or writer] has a full and verifiable grasp of how the world works" (Malina 1991, 15).

It is imperative to recognize that it is lived experience that is encapsulated in the scenarios conjured up by writer and reader. As we read, we picture what we know from experience. Of course some of the needed mental pictures are made explicit by a writer. They are spelled out. But many are not—simply because a text cannot say all that must be said. Much remains between the lines. The unwritten part, the implicit part, must be filled in by the reader from his or her own repertoire of experience. Thus, when an author mentions the name *Katrina* for an American audience, no more need be said. American readers can fill out the appropriate scenario with no difficulty whatever because it is part of their lived experience.

The problem, of course, is that readers from a different time or culture may not be able to fill in this particular scenario in an appropriate way. They may never have seen or experienced a hurricane. They may know nothing of the lay of the land along the Gulf Coast, or be aware of the North American practice of naming violent storms. Such foreigners would be unlikely to complete the scenario in the same way as an American reader.

Sociolinguists have demonstrated that all writing presumes this ability of the intended reader to fill out the pictures the text intends to evoke. But therein lies the difficulty for the New Testament translator. How do we choose terminology that will evoke scenarios in Anglo-American minds that are something like those that would have come to the minds of ancient Mediterranean readers? The lived experience in these two cultures is so sharply different, and the scenario repertoires available to persons in each culture so strikingly dissimilar, that the choice for the translator is very much like that posed by Schleiermacher above. Either the author is going abroad, in the direction of the reader, or the reader is going abroad in the direction of the writer. In the first instance the text is domesticated, often with considerable ethnocentric violence, as the translation evokes scenarios no ancient reader or writer could possibly have imagined. Or, alternatively, the translator stages an alien reading experience by leaving the scenarios in the unfamiliar world of the source language and expecting the reader to confront the otherness of the text's social world. Domestication, the approach advocated by Nida in order to make the result "relevant within the context of [the reader's] own culture," is one option available. The reader is left in peace. But foreignizing translation, in order to stage an alien reading experience that sends the reader abroad, is the other option. The author is left in peace (i.e., respected). It is this latter approach we intend to advocate. The difference in the translations these two options produce can be substantial and it is to the examination of that prospect that we now turn.

DOMESTICATING TRANSLATION

Examples of domestication are legion in contemporary English translations. So by contrast it is not difficult to identify opportunities for foreignizing the translation in order to stage an alien reading experience that respects the cultural otherness of the source language. A simple example can be found in John 1:47–48. The Greek reads as follows:

εἶδεν ὁ Ἰησοῦς τὸν Ναθαναὴλ ἐρχόμενον πρὸς αὐτὸν καὶ λέγει περὶ αὐτοῦ, Ἴδε ἀληθῶς Ἰσραηλίτης ἐν ᾧ δόλος οὐκ ἔστιν λέγει αὐτῷ Ναθαναήλ Πόθεν με γινώσκεις ἀπεκρίθη Ἰησοῦς καὶ εἶπεν αὐτῷ Πρὸ τοῦ σε Φίλιππον φωνῆσαι ὄντα ὑπὸ τὴν συκῆν εἶδόν σε.

From this the NRSV produces the following translation:

> When Jesus saw Nathanael coming toward him, he said of him, "Here is truly an Israelite in whom there is no deceit!" Nathanael asked him, "Where did you get to know me?" Jesus answered, "I saw you under the fig tree before Philip called you."

The domesticating phrase here is, "Where did you get to know me?" This way of putting it suggests something very modern—and Western: two people meeting and getting acquainted. That is exactly what would be necessary in our culture before making any kind of value judgment about a new acquaintance. Yet nothing in the narrative indicates that Nathaniel and Jesus have had this type of relationship. Rather, Jesus' answer justifying his judgment about Nathanael, "I saw you under the fig tree," conveys something nearly incomprehensible to speakers of English, and especially to Westerners unfamiliar with the ancient Mediterranean practice of stereotyping persons based on the geographical location from which they come.

The meaning of Jesus' seemingly cryptic reply to Nathanael is conveyed by the Greek term Πόθεν (literally: "from where"). Nathanael is asking about the geographical location that is the source of Jesus' knowledge about him. Therefore, in his reply Jesus specifies the precise location: "under the fig tree." When we learn (going abroad!) that "fig tree" is an OT idiom for one's home and place of origin, we understand that Jesus is indicating that, having seen Nathanael at home, he knows where he is from (Cana).

That is the critical information for Mediterranean readers because it reflects their practice of stereotyping persons depending on their place of origin. As Bruce J. Malina and Jerome H. Neyrey put it, the "defining characteristics of persons in antiquity were nearly always understood in terms of group of origin (generation) and place of origin (geography)" (1996, 3). Thus "Cretans are always liars, evil beasts, lazy drunkards" (Titus 1:12). Or as Virgil says, "to know one Greek is to know them all (*Aen.* 2.65; cited by Malina and Neyrey 1996, 4). The point is that if you know where someone is from, you know what kind of person he is and thus have all the information necessary to make value judgments about him.

A foreignizing translation of this clause in v. 48 might be, "Do you know where I am from?" That focuses the issue on geography and makes the reply of Jesus completely reasonable. It would, however, jog the sensibilities of a modern reader—staging an alien reading experience—who would be startled at the basis on which Jesus makes his judgment call. We do not stereotype people in this fashion. In other words, to put it in Schleiermacher's terms, to find out why Jesus did what he did the English reader would have to travel abroad and learn a little about the cultural otherness of the source language.

A similar, if somewhat more egregious example, can be found in Matt 1:18 (Luke 1:26–27). There Matthew is reporting on the relationship of Joseph and Mary. The Greek reads as follows:

Τοῦ δὲ Ἰησοῦ χριστοῦ ἡ γένεσις οὕτως ἦν μνηστευθείσης τῆς μητρός αὐτοῦ Μαρίας τῷ Ἰωσήφ, πρὶν ἢ συνελθεῖν αὐτοὺς εὑρέθη ἐν γαστρὶ ἔχουσα ἐκ πνεύματος ἁγίου.

The NRSV translation of that verse reads:

> Now the birth of Jesus the Messiah took place in this way. When his mother Mary had been engaged to Joseph, but before they lived together, she was found to be with child from the Holy Spirit.

The term that concerns us—μνηστευθείσης—is a term that the majority of English translations have rendered "betrothed." But perhaps sensing the outmoded character of that word in an American culture where that type of betrothal practice does not exist, the translators of the NRSV came up with the translation "engaged." Seemingly oblivious to the ethnocentric violence in this term, these translators invite us to conjure up American practices of self-initiated romantic attachment and an agreement between a couple that they will be married at some time in the future. It sounds like Joseph had given Mary a ring!

Marriage in antiquity, however, was not an amorous affair between individuals. Nor did it involve anything like our practice of engagement. Rather, it was an arrangement between two extended families that involved the transfer of property rights, inheritance rights, rights over children, and sexual rights. Moreover, it was designed to ensure economic equity between the two families being united. This type of marriage arrangement was the end result of a protracted negotiation in which the families, not the partners, were the principal agents (Hanson and Oakman 1998, 31; Deist 2000, 240). Most such marriages were parentally arranged, but even those arrangements in which the partners had some personal initiative were worked out in a formal agreement that was represented by a signed contract (or formal oral agreement) between the two extended families. We get the idea from a comment in the Laws of Eshnunna (ca. 2000 B.C.E.):

> If a man takes another man's daughter without asking the permission of her father and her mother and concludes no formal marriage contract with her father and her

mother, even though she may live in his house for a year, she is not a wife. (Pritchard 1969, No. 27, 162)

It is to this type of formal contract that the Greek term μνηστεύω directs us.

It is especially important to recognize that such a betrothal contract constituted a legally binding agreement that could only be broken by divorce (Matt 1:19). It would be followed at an appropriate point by a wedding, though the wedding was not the heart of the matter. The contract was. Weddings were primarily a time for celebration among family and villagers when the arrangements negotiated in the betrothal contract were finally fulfilled.

Unfortunately the English term engaged captures none of this, implying as it does the contemporary practices of English-speaking countries.[5] So if we were to suggest a foreignizing translation instead, we might render μνηστευθείσης with something like "contractually bound to marry." The line would then read: "Mary and Joseph, being contractually bound to marry, yet before they came together . . ."[6] Figuring out what that meant would automatically send the reader abroad—precisely the intent of a foreignizing translation.

A third example of domesticating translation illustrates how lack of knowledge of the cultural otherness of the source language can actually change the meaning of a phrase quite substantially. In the Greek of John 8:15 we read:

ὑμεῖς κατὰ τὴν σάρκα κρίνετε, ἐγὼ οὐ κρίνω οὐδένα

While many of the English translations of this verse are fairly literal, a number are not. Typical of the literal translations would be the RSV:

You judge according to the flesh, I judge no one.

That is very close to the form of the original Greek and will satisfy those who prefer that type of translation, even though it is not at all what we would call a foreignizing translation.

In contrast with the literal rendering, a number of translations offer dynamic equivalence alternatives that move into interpretation in the way domestication often does. In the NRSV that verse is translated:

You judge by human standards; I judge no one.

In the REV it reads:

You judge by worldly standards; I pass judgment on no one.

We must be careful here to understand correctly the issue under debate. The issue in this chapter of John is whether the judgment of Jesus is valid given the fact that he has only one witness (himself) instead of the two required in the Torah (Deut 19:15).

---

5. Unhappily the NRSV not only offers this translation of μνηστεύω in the New Testament, it does the same for the parallel word throughout the Old Testament.

6. Note that the REV uses the term "marriage contract" in Matt 1:19. It retains the term "betrothed" in v. 18.

While in 8:15 he says he does not make judgments, a verse later he argues that if he does make them he indeed has two witnesses: himself and the Father who sent him. In other words, the debate is over the number of witnesses Jesus claims.

Both the NRSV and the REV, however, introduce a word into John 8:15 that is not only absent in the Greek, but also one that subtly changes the issue Jesus is addressing. Both of these translations speak of standards, and in both cases the introduction of this word requires an adjective specifying what type of standards Jesus is accusing his opponents of using. In each case the adjectives chosen are the respective renderings of the Greek, κατὰ τὴν σάρκα. The NRSV's translation "human" implies a contrast with "divine." The REV's term "worldly" implies a contrast with "other worldly" or something like it. Moreover, both the terms "human" and "worldly" in this context suggest to English-speaking readers a theological, perhaps even pietistic, contrast being drawn between appropriate and inappropriate standards for judgment.

Apparently the translators assume there is an allusion here to 1 Sam 16:7 (". . . for the LORD does not see as mortals see; they look on the outward appearance, but the LORD looks on the heart") and thus consider it justifiable to introduce this kind of religious contrast in standards. As we shall see again, however, in John 8:15 the argument is not over standards of judgment, but number of witnesses.

As noted above, the Greek literally says, "according to the flesh." That recognizes an important cultural practice in the ancient Mediterranean world. The ancients normally made judgments on the basis of physical appearance (as 1 Sam 16:7 indicates). The science was called "physiognomy," and it is described thusly by Aulus Gellius:

> The word means to inquire into the character and dispositions of men by an inference drawn from their facial appearance and expression, and from the form and bearing of the whole body. (*Noct. att.* 1.9.2)

Polemo likewise considers this the proper way to form judgments about human character (*Physiog.* 31.236).

To put the matter graphically, the physique of a lion clarifies its character: courageous and aggressive. The physique of a mouse does the same: timid and fearful. Thus, if Jesus has physiognomy in mind, his statement is simply an ancient truism in which he is describing the usual social practice. But the point is that this too is a method of judgment with *only a single witness*: the observer. The opponents had accused Jesus of having only a single witness; he now does the same to them in return. There is nothing in this exchange about pietistic theologies contrasting human and divine, or worldly and otherworldly standards. There is only an argument about the number of witnesses. And Jesus reminds them that the usual social practice does the very thing they had accused him of doing: it offers judgments from a single witness. A culturally accurate translation would thus be quite simple: "You judge according to physical appearance; I judge no one."

Obviously domesticating examples such as these could be multiplied many times over, especially in the so-called dynamic equivalence translations. But perhaps the point is made: domesticating translation forces the author abroad, disrespects the cultural otherness of the text, and often creates messages that are sharply different from those conveyed by the original language. By contrast, foreignizing translation retains the cultural otherness of the text, indeed respects the social and cultural location of the text and author, and thereby expects the reader to be the one doing the traveling.

A READING SCENARIO EXAMPLE

Before drawing conclusions from our study it would be appropriate to illustrate the other assertion made above, namely, that English-speaking Westerners are unlikely to conjure up the mental pictures or scenarios needed to complete a text in the same way as would a reader from the ancient Mediterranean world. If this is in fact the way people read, and socio-linguistic research shows that it is, it is a factor that must be taken into account when we translate the New Testament. In this illustration, the verse we shall be addressing is Luke 1:36:

Καὶ ἰδοὺ Ἐλισάβετ ἡ συγγενίς σου καὶ αὐτὴ συνείληφεν υἱὸν ἐν γήρει αὐτῆς καὶ οὗτος μὴν ἕκτος ἐστὶν αὐτῇ τῇ καλουμένῃ στείρᾳ

It is translated in the RSV: "And now, your relative Elizabeth in her old age has also conceived a son; and this is the sixth month for her who was called barren." That is a fairly literal translation.

The phrase that interests us here is τῇ καλουμένῃ στείρᾳ ("who was called barren"). The question that reading scenario theory raises here is simple: What scenario came to the mind of an ancient reader when they encountered this phrase in the original language? And how might that compare with the scenario likely to be conjured up by a modern reader encountering its various translations?

BARRENNESS

While it may be true that having children is highly desirable for most people in the modern world, our reasons for wanting children vary sharply from those in antiquity. Our reasons today are primarily emotional: personal contentment, fulfillment, happiness, companionship, and the like. For modern Westerners, children fulfill deep-seated needs of this sort. Childlessness, however, is also a viable option in the modern world and, when it is a matter of personal choice, little social stigma is attached. Nor is it the source of significant social disgrace when it is unintended and involuntary. With the medicalization of childlessness in the modern West, those without children are often considered unfortunate persons and are often the subject of considerable sympathy, but they are not viewed as morally or spiritually culpable (Inhorn 2002, 5).

By contrast, in the patriarchal world of the New Testament, having children was a deeply serious social necessity. People had children for some of the same reasons we do, but as Marcia Inhorn points out, other factors were far more important. Having children was a matter of economic survival. It was a form of social power for women within patriarchal families and fulfilled a deeply rooted need for social perpetuity: keeping group structures, extended family systems, and ancestral memories alive (Inhorn 2002, 8). As Inhorn's work makes clear, in such societies the social mandate to bear children is emphatic, and the social, emotional, and psychological consequences of failing to bring forth children for the "husband, family, community, faith and nation" are intense (1996, 1).

Ancient authors agree. To Plato, childlessness was the cause of untold distress:

> The womb is an animal which longs to generate children. When it remains barren too long after puberty it is distressed and sorely disturbed: straying about in the body and cutting off the passages of breath, it impedes respiration and brings the sufferer into the extremest anguish and provokes all manner of diseases beside. (*Tim.* 91c; cited by Neufeld 2006, 135)

Especially in those parts of the ancient world with a popular belief in monogenesis, the consequences of childlessness for women could be severe.[7]

In the biblical world a woman's position in her husband's family was never really secure until she bore a son. Only then did she have a *blood* relationship that secured her place. Ancient stories of barren women thus describe an anguish of the deepest sort (cf. Gen 11:30; 25:21; 29:31; Judg 13:2; 1 Sam 1:2). In many cases that anguish was made all the worse by the mockery of other women in the community. The late-second-century *Infancy Gospel of James* (*Prot. Jas.*) provides a good example of the bitterness village ridicule of a barren woman could engender.

The story opens by describing how Mary's wealthy father, Joachim, is not permitted to be the first to offer his gifts at the temple because he is without offspring. After searching the genealogical records and discovering that he alone among the righteous is childless, he flees to the desert in self-reproach, returning only when given a divine message that his wife will conceive. Meanwhile, Anna, Mary's mother, bewails her barren condition: "my widowhood, my childlessness" (*Prot. Jas.* 3:1). Seeing a sparrow with its young in a nest, she sighs toward heaven and pours out her heart in a lengthy lamentation that begins:

> Woe to me, who begot me, what womb brought me forth? For I was born as a curse before them all and before the children of Israel, and I was reproached, and they mocked me and thrust me out of the temple of the Lord. (*Prot. Jas.* 3:1, cited from Schneemelcher 1991, 375)

As Anna's cry makes clear, a significant part of her anguish as a childless woman came from the mocking of the other women who "thrust me out of the temple of the Lord." Taunt songs and various other kinds of mockery aimed at childless women were common, especially around the wells where women came to draw water. Worse yet, barren women were often accused of possessing the evil eye. They were thought to have been inflicted with the βάσκανος demon or the φθόνος demon and therefore consumed with envy toward those who were mothers. Thus, when children became ill, mothers often accused childless women of injuring them with the evil eye out of

---

7. Monogenesis (or homunculus theory) is the notion that the sperm contains all the genetic material; the womb is simply the field in which it grows. Aristotle thought that while the female contributed some raw material, the male semen shaped and guided the entire growth process. The soul originated only in male semen. While the monogenetic theory was widely held in antiquity, the *duogenetic* theory of Hippocrates came to be promoted by Galen in the second century C.E. (Inhorn 1994, 57).

a hateful envy (Inhorn 1994, 205). Even today in the Middle East mothers will often hide their children from barren women out of fear of this kind of injury.

In sum, stigmatization and ostracism from the community of other women were all too often the childless woman's lot. The worst part of it was the public humiliation, regularly understood as the action of God (*Prot. Jas.* 2:5). In an honor-shame society such as ancient Israel, the consequences of such humiliation could be a heavy burden, frequently affecting an entire extended family. All would share in the shame visited upon their barren relative.

It is thus significant that in 1:36 Luke reports that Elizabeth was not only barren, her barrenness was a matter of public comment (τῇ καλουμένη στεῖρα). In other words this is not the private anguish of a woman hoping the curse will be lifted before her neighbors find out something is wrong. It is public humiliation. Luke tells us that Elizabeth's disgrace is known "among the people" (Luke 1:25 NRSV). In fact the author offers us an especially poignant clue in that regard by pointing out that when Elizabeth does conceive, when the Lord has finally "taken away the disgrace" of her childlessness, Elizabeth hides herself until the fifth month. Presumably by that time her pregnancy would show and her credibility would not be in doubt when she claimed to other women that she had finally conceived.

The important point in all this is that barrenness in antiquity was as much a social condition as it was a biological one. Accusations of having been cursed by God for some sin committed would have been common. Disgrace, shame, and above all blame for the failure would have been as hurtful to a family as the physical absence of children.

What then are we to make of an egregiously domesticating translation of this verse such as the one that appears in the Scholars Version (sv)?[8]

> Further your relative Elizabeth has also conceived a son in her old age. She who was said to be infertile is already six months along.

Note the comment of Marcia Inhorn cited above about the medicalization of childlessness in the modern world. The term *infertile* is a modern medical term. Moreover, it conjures up a scenario in the mind of a contemporary reader that is primarily medical in character. Drawing from our own experience we fill in between the lines with pictures of medical counseling, infertility clinics and the like. We might feel sympathy for Elizabeth as an unfortunate person. But we do not imagine her the object of public mockery, or going to the well and hearing taunt songs, or being accused of having the evil eye, or perhaps being thrown out of the court of the women at the temple. The scenario we bring to the story would be nothing like that engendered in the minds of ancient women. Nor would our modern scenario be anything they could have conjured up in their wildest imagination. The translation "said to

---

8. The translation produced by Robert W. Funk and the Translation Panel of the Jesus Seminar in 1993.

be" (also the NIV, NRSV, TEV: "it is said") only exacerbates the problem. It sounds as if Elizabeth's condition was a matter of casual comment.[9]

The commentary about their translation offered by the editors of the SV is both revealing and disturbing. They are very clear that in preparing the SV they made English readability the "final test of every sentence" (Funk and Hoover 1993, xvi). They claim they wanted a colloquial English translation that matches the colloquial quality of the original Greek, capturing if possible the "tone and tenor of the original" (1993, xvi). They are quite critical of literal or word-for-word translation, especially any that might sound "faintly Victorian" (or "politely religious"). Perhaps in their minds the term *barren* suggested that sort of stilted Victorian tone.

Yet at the same time they strongly assert that it was their intent to avoid translating "cultural anachronisms" out of the text. In their words, "the panel agreed at the outset not to translate out the social and cultural features of the text that are unfamiliar—worse yet, distasteful—to the modern reader" (1993, xvi). Instead, they claim that they tried to put those cultural features, "as alien and distasteful as they sometimes are, into plain English" (1993, xvi). Yet examining translations such as that cited here one is tempted to conclude that concern for social and cultural anachronisms played a far smaller role than the editors claim. The fact is they have domesticated the translation far more than they seem to be aware simply by encouraging modern scenarios in the mind of their contemporary readers.

CONCLUSION

As indicated above, it would not be difficult to multiply examples of domesticating translation or the evocation of inappropriate scenarios in most modern translations. They abound. The question then becomes one of deciding whether this matters, especially since domestication is so often the price we pay for English readability.

At the most basic level we have to decide who it is we are going to send abroad: the author or the reader. As Venuti described it above, a foreignizing translation is a strategic move designed to jar the reader with an alien reading experience. It is staged by the translator in order to convey source-language values and perceptions that readable English cannot. If the social and cultural features of biblical language actually matter to the sense of the text, as they almost always do, sending the reader abroad would seem to be the sine qua non of accurate translation.

By contrast, we must acknowledge that English fluency almost always involves domestication. It "masquerades as true semantic equivalence" when it in fact is not; it reduces, sometimes to nothing, "the very difference that translation is called on to convey" (Venuti 1998, 21). Unfortunately the editors of the SV, making readability as high a priority as they do, do not seem to understand the contradiction between that and their stated aim of retaining cultural anachronisms.

Finally, it is especially important to know that domestication has occurred when

---

9. Even worse is the Contemporary English Version: "Your relative Elizabeth is also going to have a son, even though she is old. *No one thought she could ever have a baby*, but in three months she will have a son." In this bizarre translation the matter of public comment is completely gone.

we in fact produce it. Without a thorough knowledge of ancient Mediterranean culture many translators simply domesticate the text unawares. We must acknowledge, of course, that there is much about ancient culture we will never be able to understand. Yet there is much that we do indeed know—thanks to the voluminous work in social-scientific criticism over the last thirty years. Even though respect for the cultural otherness of the biblical source language is only possible with that kind of cultural knowledge in hand, some translators remain without it. And without it, these translators will inevitably and unwittingly go on creating biblical messages in our own domestic image.

GRACE AS BENEFACTION IN GALATIANS 2:9, 1 CORINTHIANS 3:10, AND ROMANS 12:3; 15:15

Zeba A. Crook

Few words express and reflect the theological heart of Christianity more fully than does the word *grace*. Though Luther, inspired in large part by Augustine, emphasized the notion of divine grace as part of his own theology of protest, the concept plays no less significant a role in Catholic theology. Theologians reflect on grace as something that emanates from a superior God toward the inferior believer. The 'grace of God" refers to everything from a kindly and generous disposition on God's part to the claim that Jesus Christ himself is its incarnation. *The Encyclopedia of Religion* seems to presuppose that grace is an exclusively Christian concept when it claims that "God's grace is the gift of persevering, loving, purposeful generosity that becomes visible in a climactic way in the life, teaching, death, and resurrection of Jesus" (O'Meara 1987, 84). Luther's particular emphasis on justification by faith established the human's complete inability to effect God's grace. Thus, for many, grace is that quality of God that gives and loves utterly independently of human warrant.

Current Catholic theology tempers this somewhat extreme view: grace is the "patient, luminous, inviting presence of a transcendent and mysterious God intimately active in the pain and glory of life" (O'Meara 1987, 87). Catholic theological reflection on grace conflates it with *mercy*, adding to the sense that grace is a characteristic of God, as opposed to a concrete act. The *New Catholic Encyclopedia* defines grace as "a gratuitous supernatural gift of God to man" (Most 2002, 380). The concept of grace, theologians maintain, fills the pages of the New Testament, sustained by the fact that the very term appears throughout it. The history of scholarship on "grace in the New Testament" reveals, at times unwittingly, the extent to which it is impossible to read this New Testament term independently of several hundred years' worth of theological reflection on it. A. C. Piepkorn is to the point when he observes how difficult it is "to relate certain aspects of 'grace' as theologians have used the word to the biblical idea of 'grace' " (1965, 947).

When the word grace appears in the pages of an English Bible, it is most likely a translation of the Greek word χάρις. The translation is a natural choice for etymological reasons: the English word *grace* comes from the Latin *gra-* stem—*grace* in French, *grazia* in Italian, and *gracia* in Spanish. While the etymology might be self-evident, meaning is never limited to the etymology of a word. In fact, in Christian usage of the term, theology has eclipsed etymology. There are three problems with using grace to translate χάρις. First, the more theological and theologically abstract the definition becomes, the more separated we become from the reciprocal nature of the term χάρις. W. G. Most's definition of grace above as "gratuitous" (2002, 380), for example, suggests that it carries no reciprocal expectations, in addition to being unearned (free). But ancient χάρις could be earned, and it did come with explicit expectations of reciprocity and loyalty. The second problem is simply the theological weight that the English term *grace* carries. It is nearly impossible to divorce the term *grace* from the long and rich history of Christian theological reflection upon it. The third problem is that grace is actually a translation of a translation: the term translates the Vulgate's *gratia* and not really the Greek's χάρις. The question of how social-scientific criticism can help us translate biblical writings is, therefore, very usefully exemplified by the translation of the Greek word χάρις.

The need for such a discussion is evident in practically all work that was done on χάρις in the twentieth century. Since James Harrison shows in fine detail the limitations of these studies, I shall limit myself to one example (2003, 8–13). James Moffatt claims that when Christian writers used the term χάρις, they used it in a radically different manner than the manner in which it was used in the surrounding culture. Moffatt writes of the New Testament understanding of grace that "when sin or evil is omitted from the view of the world, the content of 'grace' as presented in the gospel is missed, no matter how belief in a friendly spirit or causal Reality within the universe may be stated in terms of grace" (1932, 6). Moffatt's theologizing continues when he claims that there were some aspects of pre-Pauline usage that were simply *unfit* for Paul to use, such as the Hebrew phrase "to find favour with/in the eyes of/before the Lord/God." According to Moffatt, Paul did not use this phrase because it suggests that humans could effect divine grace.[1] It goes without saying that Moffatt has come to this conclusion only by reading Paul through the lens of Luther.

Moffatt's desire to understand the meaning and usage of χάρις historically, that is in its ancient Mediterranean (and early Christian) context, is seriously impeded when he thinks of the term doctrinally, as *Grace*. When Moffatt associates the term χάρις with the Christian theological concept of grace, and when he assumes that Paul used the terms unlike other writers in the ancient world, he builds a fence around the term, as if its value would be diluted by allowing for parallels between Pauline and Greco-Roman usage. James Barr famously complained (of translation in general) that the "attempt to relate the individual word directly to theological thought leads to the distortion of the semantic contribution made by words in contexts; the value of the context comes to be seen as something contributed by the word, and then it is read into the word as its contribution where the context is in fact different. Thus, the word becomes overloaded with interpretive suggestion" (Barr 1961, 233–34). The first step, it seems, in understanding χάρις properly then is to translate it differently.

The Greek word χάρις is used in four semantic ranges: to describe something that

---

1. Likewise, Manson claims that the Christian usage of χάρις "involved a high ennoblement and extension of the Greek word" (1932, 34). See also Doughty (1973).

is beautiful or pleasing;[2] to express gratitude for a benefaction received;[3] to describe the quality of beneficence;[4] and to refer to the concrete gift or benefaction itself. Many examples of this usage will be offered below. Occurrences of χάρις across Greek writing are not distributed evenly across these four semantic ranges: the first usage is very rare, and the second is a common expression of gratitude, but its use is still limited. In the vast majority of cases, χάρις functions in the last two semantic ranges, either to refer to an *action* or *item* of generosity or to the *virtue* of generosity that leads people to give things. The translation of χάρις when it occurs in the first two semantic ranges is not a concern here; the more pressing issue is how to translate the term when it refers to the act or virtue of generosity, since it is in those instances that the English reader of the New Testament encounters the term *grace*.

If we are to translate χάρις properly, we need to recognize that the term is thoroughly embedded in the ancient system of patronage and benefaction, of which the primary characteristic is reciprocity: when something was received, something had to be reciprocated. The *form* of reciprocity (whether an action, general behavior, or something given in return) always mattered less than the *fact* of reciprocity. A translation that departs too far from this foundation is destined to miss Paul's meaning and to veer into post-Lutheran theologizing. This point is shared by James R. Harrison, whose book-length study of the term χάρις is peerless for its thoroughness, quality, and methodological rigor (2003).[5] In what follows, I carefully examine occurrences that situate χάρις in this system of reciprocity. These uses of χάρις occur in inscriptions, papyri, literary and historical writings, as well as in Philo and Josephus. After that I turn to some Pauline examples.

INSCRIPTIONS

Inscriptions are an important tool for understanding the ancient social world. All written sources are naturally elite in nature and not a reflection of the lower levels of society. This skews our perspective of the ancient world: it is impossible to be certain whether the daily concerns of non-elites can be derived from elite sources. But inscriptions might give us a way around this problem: they were placed in public places

---

2. When used this way, χάρις can describe precious metals and jewelry (Homer *Il.* 14.183), lovely portraits and art, impressive speech (Homer *Od.* 8.175; Luke 4:22), or the graceful movement of people.

3. Χάρις + the dative often expresses gratitude "to" someone. Papyri frequently use the verb ὁμολογέω (to acknowledge) with χάρις in a way that must refer to gratitude (*P.Grenf.* 92.9 and *P.Lips.* I 34.21 of a human patron, and *P.Oxy.* 939.6). Other papyri combine εἰδέναι + χάρις = "to know gratitude" (*P.Oxy.* 1021.17–18; see also Thucydides, *Pel.* 6.12; Theognis 1319; Herodotus, *Hist.* 4.136). The phrase εἰδέναι + χάριτας might have initially meant literally, "to know or acknowledge a benefaction," and it may have developed from there into an expression of gratitude (Joseph William Hewitt, "The Terminology of 'Gratitude' in Greek," *CP* 22 [1927]: 143–44, 149).

4. Thucydides tells us that Demosthenes agreed to attack the Aetolians in order to please, or to show a beneficent attitude toward, the Messenians who came up with the plan (*Pel.* 3.95.1). Hesiod predicts, rather apocalyptically, that "there will be no χάρις for those who keep to their oaths or who are just and good" (*Op.* 190).

5. My own research on the meaning of χάρις, while less expansive than Harrison's, resulted in the same conclusions (Crook 2004, 53–150).

with the intent that when people read about the deeds of a generous person, people would grant that person honor and the title of benefactor. So, while the giving of benefactions and the inscribing of stones reflect lives and concerns of the elite, it was an institution in which the awareness and participation of the masses was critical.

The reciprocal nature of χάρις is apparent when it occurs alongside εὐεργ- root words (εὐεργεσία, εὐεργετέω, εὐεργέτης, εὐεργετικός, εὐεργέτις). This happens, for instance, in *Syll³* 587. This honorary inscription is a public decree from the city of Peparethus: "In order both that the gratitude (εὐχάριστος) of our people might be apparent and that the apportioning of honours to good men and their benefactions (χάριτας) might be worthy of the good deeds (εὐεργετήμα) that have happened among us, the people and the council of Peparethus praise . . ." A second-century B.C.E. inscription from Pergamon reads: "In order, therefore, that the People may appear foremost in reciprocating a benefaction (ἐγχάριτος ἀποδόσει) and be conspicuous in honoring those benefiting the People and its friends voluntarily and in committing the goodness of their deeds to eternal memory . . ." (*OGIS* 248).[6] These inscriptions reveal a number of important things: the use of χάρις in a setting very clearly concerned with an act of benefaction and the overarching concern the people and their city councils had for reciprocity. Not only do the people want to reciprocate, they need the discharge of their reciprocity witnessed by all. The other inscriptions that reveal these same concerns are practically too numerous to count (Harrison 2003, 26–63).

We shall have many opportunities below to see that the institution of patronage and benefaction applied to interactions with the gods as much as with human patrons and benefactors. The gods were approached, addressed, and imagined as real and potential benefactors; human recipients were expected to respond with the same concern for reciprocity when the giver was a god. Human and divine patronage used brokerage, in which someone serves as intermediary between patron and client.[7] One second-century B.C.E. inscription from Megalopolis, discussed by Harrison, illustrates the function of a broker, namely, as mediator, bridge builder, and a go-between. He points out that this inscription honors a woman named Isidis Dionysia for her work as a priestess and promises that her work would bring continued benefactions: "and if you would seek a name, (it is) Dionysia, which blesses anyone who knows the divine benefactions (θείας χάριτας) which she received" (IG V² 472).[8] Another second-century inscription of the cult of Apollo contains the same manifesto clause we expect of honorary inscriptions set up for human benefactors: "In order, therefore, that the Council and the People may also manifestly watch closely not only the institutions of the ancestors, but also increase further both the sacrifices and honors well and loyalty (εὐσεβῶς), in order that they also may gain the appropriate benefactions (τὰς καταξίας χάριτας) proceeding from the gods" (*SEG* XXI 469).[9] And, finally,

---

6. Dittenberger (1903–5).

7. For a more sustained illustration of this claim, see Crook (2004, 72–84).

8. The reconstruction of the inscription is from Harrison (2003, 50), and this translation is a modest alteration of his.

9. This is another inscriptional reconstruction and most of a translation borrowed with gratitude from Harrison (2003, 55).

Hymn III inscribed in *I. Smyrna* 750 prays to Isis, "O most hallowed bestower of good things, to all men who are righteous, you grant great benefactions (χάριτας)."

Inscriptions reveal that χάρις functioned in the system of ancient patronage and benefaction, sometimes alongside terminology of good-works—εὐεργ- root words—but sometimes independently. The pattern will be repeated in other places where we find this term.

PAPYRI

Harrison finds much evidence of the reciprocal nature of χάρις in the writings of the epistolary theorists. Only one example he presents illustrates χάρις used to refer to a benefaction. Pseudo-Libanius offers the model of a diplomatic letter. The letter "is designed to remind the καλοκἀγαθός that he was constrained by honor to maintain munificence:"[10]

> We continue to enjoy the gifts your solicitude bestows on us. Hence now too, gentle-men, through these appeals do we make the following request which you have cus-tomarily granted as a benefaction (ἐχαρίσασθε) to those who make [the request]. Be constrained then to show in this matter how magnificently excellent you are.[11]

There are a number of interesting features in this passage. First, as Harrison points out, the writer is using honor and shame to cajole the recipient into maintaining the relationship of patron and client, since of course without benefactions there will be reduced honor to the elite. Clients were clearly susceptible to abuse from patrons, as Juvenal shows (*Sat.* 5.80–85), but they were not completely powerless, since they might remind potential patrons that their (continued) honor depended on giving. Also interesting in this passage is the use of the verbal form of χάρις: χαρίζομαι means here "to make a benefaction."

The verbal form χαρίζομαι is also found in actual letters of recommendation. Note for instance a letter dated 25 C.E. from Theon to Tyrannus that, like the previ-ous example, cites the recipient's concern for honor:

> Theon to his esteemed Tyrannus, many greetings. Heraclides, the bearer of this letter, is my brother. I therefore entreat you with all my power to treat him as your protégé. I have also written to your brother Hermias asking him to communicate with you about him. You will confer upon me a very great benefaction if Heraclides gains your notice. Before all else you have my good wishes for unbroken health and prosperity. Goodbye.[12]

Theon pulls out all the stops on behalf of his brother: he flatters Tyrannus, calling him τιμιωτάτωι; he elicits (threatens?) the support and pressure of Tyrannus's brother Hermias; he implies that any man of honor would confer such a benefaction.

P. Grenf. 68 presents an example of both the nominal and verbal form of our terms

---

10. Harrison (2003, 68).
11. Pseudo-Libanius, Ἐπιστολιμαῖοι Χαρακτῆρες, 76. Translation adapted from Harrison (2003).
12. Translation with alterations from Harrison (2003, 77).

appearing in a commercial papyrus. The writer offers to give away a quarter of his business through a deed of gift (ἀπόκτησις): "I agree to give to you as a benefaction (χαρίζεσ[θαι] σοὶ) by way of an unrevokable and unrepentant benefaction (χάριτι ἀναφαιρέτω καὶ ἀμετανοήτῳ) . . ."

As with inscriptions, papyri reflect the use of the term in the setting of divine patronage and benefaction. For example, an Egyptian papyrus decree honoring the emperor (*BGU* I 19.21) refers to benefactions of the emperor with the phrase προσφυγεῖν τῇ χάριτι τοῦ θεοῦ ἐπιφανεστάτου Αὐτοκράτορος (to flee into the refuge of the benefactions of the God manifest Emperor). A fragment, also from *BGU* (IV 1085.5), which is a royal decree, refers to τὴν χάριν τοῦ θεοῦ.

What is most revealing about these papyrus examples is that they reflect the same practices, expectations, and imagery of patronage and benefaction, and that such asymmetrical exchange can occur between humans as well as between humans and their gods. But importantly, when χάρις is used to refer to something received from a god, it does not have a different meaning than when it is used to refer to something received from a human: in both cases it refers to a benefaction, and in all cases it requires no less a concern for reciprocity. In other words, its usage in a setting of divine patronage and benefaction should not elicit unwarranted claims that its use is different from a secular usage. What is more, χάρις and εὐεργεσία are sometimes used more or less synonymously. When they appear not to be synonymous, it is rarely clear what the writer intends to communicate by using both terms.

LITERARY AND HISTORICAL WRITINGS

Χάρις as benefaction is reflected in the interaction between kings and a client state. Polybius relates that after the Roman consul Atilius Regulus (third century B.C.E.) had defeated the Carthaginians, he felt they should accept every concession he offered as if it were a benefaction (ἐν χάριτι). The Carthaginians, on the other hand, understand that to accept a benefaction from Regulus would permanently inscribe their inferiority to him, and so they refused even to hear his offer (Polybius *Hist.* 1.31.6). Likewise, when Polybius relates that Philip of Macedon restored Nicander's political position, the act of restoration is referred to as a χάρις (*Hist.* 20.11.10): this can only mean that the restoration was a benefaction to Nicander, and we can rest assured that Nicander would be in Philip's debt for a long time. Along the same lines, when patron-kings granted to their client-kings land and the income that the land generated, they were called benefactions.[13] Diodorus Siculus can use the term χάρις equally to refer to a praetor's willingness to hear the appeals of a noble (36.3.3) and to Nature's benefactions of food, vessels, homes, and ships (3.21.5).

In a reference to Dionysus by Diodorus Siculus he writes, "They say the god [Dionysus] came into the inhabited world bringing the regions into a cultivated state by way of cuttings, and making benefactions (εὐεργετοῦντα) to the people with great and valuable benefactions (χάρισι) for all time" (3.73.6; see also 1.70.6).

13. Polybius *Hist.* 30.31.7; Dionysus of Halicarnassus, *Ant. rom.* 5.21.3. See also Braund (1984).

Herodotus records that Pausanius requested that the Athenians send him their archers as a χάρις to him (*Hist.* 9.60.3).

Often the term χάρις can be translated as *favor*, reflecting that there is no concrete benefaction named. In this sense, χάρις can function as the indefinite version of εὐεργεσία. In this instance favor is definitely better than grace, and at times can be a better option than benefaction, but we should not confuse favor with kindness (in terms of a personal quality). To show favor is more than simply to show kindness; it is also and more importantly to bestow *something*, even if that something is unnamed. Favor should also not be confused with the modern sense of favor which does not by necessity inaugurate a relationship of dependence, though it may well result in expectations of reciprocity along the lines of gift exchange—a favor is a gift that is reciprocated with another favor of equal value, but is not a benefaction. In terms of translating the term, however, in a way that is sensitive both to its semantic context and to the prevailing cultural context of asymmetrical reciprocity, benefaction is to be preferred over gift, even though gift will often appear to make sense. Again, here one must be aware of the social status of those involved in the exchange, aware of the nature of the goods or services exchanged, and aware of the nature of the relationship that ensues as a result of the exchange. Language, of course, functions in semantic contexts, and it is those that we must consider when translating language. The contexts of gift and benefaction exchange are best not confused (Crook 2005b).

HELLENISTIC JEWISH SOURCES

Scholars have long assumed that because Philo and Josephus were Jewish, we could take for granted an Old Testament covenantal outlook for them on the relationship between God and humanity. But recently attempts have been made to take seriously that the Hellenization of Philo and Josephus extends beyond the language of their literary works. Philo and Josephus both do more than passively use the Greek language, some of which might incidentally overlap with benefaction terminology. Philo uses both the language and the imagery of patronage and benefaction to describe the Jewish God to his Greek readers, and Josephus replaces covenant with reciprocity terminology. Hellenistic Jews take over wholesale the language of divine patronage and benefaction to talk about the experience of their God. It was not a difficult transition for writers like Philo and Josephus: they knew, through their experience of Jewish history, that their God was a generous giver, and so the Greeks provided a conceptual framework and vocabulary not exactly present in the Hebrew language or Israelite culture.[14] Harrison writes of Philo that he was "intimately acquainted with the terminology and ideology of benefaction" (2003, 129; Borger, Fuglseth, and Skarsten 2000).[15] For Philo, creation was the one act of God that makes God the

---

14. I have argued elsewhere that the ancient Israelites understood asymmetrical reciprocity, but they were familiar with a form of it known as covenantal exchange. There is no evidence in the Hebrew Bible that they were familiar with patronage exchange; there seem to be parallels between the two because both covenantal and patronage exchange are types of asymmetrical exchange, and so they hold some aspects in common (Crook 2005a).

15. Philo uses words of the εὐεργ- root 156 times.

quintessential benefactor: "all things are a benefaction of God (χάριν ὄντα θεοῦ): earth, water, fire, sun, stars, heaven, all the plants and animals" (*Deus* 107). Philo's God is the supreme divine benefactor.

Philo discusses at some length the χάρις of God that Noah received (*Leg.* 3.77–78). The passage is worth presenting in whole, and in a translation that represents the language of patronage and benefaction:

> For if someone might ask why he [the prophet] says Noah found beneficence (χάρις) before the Lord God, having done, as far as they knew, no good deed first, we shall answer suitably that he has been shown to be of praiseworthy composition and birth, for Noah means "rest" or "righteous." It is necessary, when one has ceased from unrighteousness and sin, taken up the good, and lived together with righteousness, to find a benefaction (χάρις) from God. Now to find a benefaction (χάρις) is not only, as some think, equivalent to being well-pleasing, but also this: the righteous person investigating the nature of being finds this one excellent discovery: that absolutely everything is a benefaction (χάρις) of God, and there is no beneficence (χάρισμα) from nature because it has no possessions since all things are in possession of God, and therefore benefaction (χάρις) is his domain alone. At any rate, to those who investigate the beginning of creation the best possible answer might be given that it is the goodness and benefaction (χάρις) of God which he bestowed (ἐχαρίσατο) upon his people. For all things which are in the world and the world itself are a gift (δωρεά) and a benefaction (εὐεργεσία) and a beneficence (χάρισμα) of God. (*Leg.* 3.77–78)

Harrison's surprise that it took scholars so long to take seriously "Philo's wide use of benefaction terminology and reciprocity motifs" is wholly justified (2003, 115).

Although χάρις is normally translated as *grace*, and although the term is sometimes understood to refer to an unearned gift, the Greco-Roman context of patronage and benefaction reveals that χάρις can be a synonym of εὐεργεσία.[16] It is God and not nature who gives to humanity, and this God gives not abstract things like grace or favor but concrete goods. Philo refers to these concrete goods with the term χάρις. The phrase χάρις τοῦ θεοῦ also supports such a translation.[17] Philo believes that all things in the natural world are benefactions of God. God is a benefactor without parallel; there is nothing that another being (human or divine) could give because all things are God's alone to give. And there is no concern about the generosity of God: τῇ ἐλευθερίας χάριτι τοῦ εὐεργέτου (*Sacr.* 127).

What is interesting about Philo, however, is that while he makes extensive use of the Hellenistic language and imagery of patronage and benefaction to describe the Jewish experience with God, he shows occasional discomfort perhaps with the result-

---

16. Versnel agrees that "the term χάρις itself can be understood as 'favor' or something close to it" (1982, 48).

17. See the phrase εὐεργετεῖν χάρισι (*Opif.* 23, bis.). *Leg.* 3.215, *Ebr.* 32, and *Migr.* 73 also show χάρις (or χαρίζω) to be nearly synonymous with εὐεργεσία. The problem with translation is illustrated with the term εὐεργέτης; Colson and Whitaker (LCL) translate this term as "loving kindness!" No doubt, Philo understood these benefactions as signs of God's loving kindness, but as a translation this is another example of over-theologizing the term. Χάρις is best left in its original semantic context of patronage and benefaction.

ing parallels with Greco-Roman religion. It is a criticism of the institution of patronage we find among Greco-Roman writers as well (Dio Chrysostum, *Or.* 7.89), so we should not too quickly ascribe it to Philo's Jewishness or his ethical monotheism. Nonetheless, Philo does wish to distinguish his patron god from other patron gods.

> Look around and you will find that those who are said to make benefactions (χαρί ζεσθαι) sell rather than give away, and those who seem to us to receive them in truth buy. Those who give seek praise or honor as their exchange and look for repayment of the benefaction (χάριτος), and thus under the specious name of gift then in real truth carry out a sale, for the seller's way is to take something for what he offers. . . . But God is no seller, hawking his goods in the market, but a free giver of all things, pouring forth fountains of his free benefactions (χαριτῶν) and seeking no return. For he has no needs himself and no created being is able to repay his gift. (*Cher.* 122–23)

It would be naive to take Philo at face value here: he is clearly involved in some apologetics, since his claim that God (or the gods) does not require honor in exchange for benefactions is unequivocally wrong. Philo's god, as much as any other, expects gratitude, praise, and honor in exchange for all he gives. It is the only right response, and ἀχαριστία is as distasteful to Philo as it is to Seneca.[18] And not surprisingly, Philo knows that the cost of denying God rightful gratitude is high: were it not for God's proclivity toward pity, humanity would long ago "have been wiped out by reason of its ingratitude (ἀχαριστίαν) to God its benefactor (εὐεργέτην) and preserver (σωτῆρα)" (*Op.* 169). Philo is not being entirely forthright, then, when he suggests that God's benefactions are truly free of expectations and reciprocity.

There are many other passages in which Philo portrays God as a benefactor, though most of them rely on εὐεργ- root words rather than χαρ- root words. He does not, as far as I can tell, distinguish between the two word groups, reminding us that neither should we work too hard to distinguish between them.[19]

While Philo clearly makes extensive use of χαρ- root words in his depiction of God and the benefactions that come from God, Josephus differs slightly. For Josephus, God is every bit the benefactor that God is for Philo, but Josephus is more restrained in his use of χαρ- root words.

As mentioned above, Josephus avoids the covenantal land theology common in the Hebrew Bible. According to Harrison, "not only does Josephus unravel the covenantal threads of LXX fabric, he weaves in the new colours of benefaction ideology" (2003, 135). The only aspect of Josephus in this regard that Harrison under-emphasizes is that χαρ- terminology is used more sparingly than it is by Philo. Nonetheless, the difference between Josephus and Philo is one of degree, not one of kind. Like Philo, Josephus retells some of the Israelite stories using the revealing language of Greco-Roman patronage and benefaction. Of the story of the Israelites wandering

---

18. Seneca writes that "homicides, tyrants, thieves, adulterers, robbers, sacrilegious men, and traitors there always will be; but worse than all these is the crime of ingratitude" (*Ben.* 1.10.4).

19. Few other examples are as moving as Philo's description of God's generosity as τὸν ἀεὶ πλημμυροῦντα χειμάρρουν τῶν σῶν εὐεργεσιῶν—"the eternally overflowing swollen winter river of your benefactions" (*Her.* 32).

in the desert, Josephus claims it was a χάρις for God to sweeten the bitter waters of Marah (*Ant.* 3.7). In another episode, Josephus relates (*Ant.* 3.31) that there is a well he knows of that God gave as a benefaction to Moses (Μωυσεῖ χαριζόμενος). There are a few other uses of the term by Josephus, but overall it does not occur with the frequency we find in the inscriptions, in Philo, or in the New Testament.

Χάρις IN THE NEW TESTAMENT

Χάρις is, as we have seen, a term firmly grounded in the ancient system of patronage and benefaction. Danker is wholly correct when he states that χάρις is very nearly a "t.t. [technical term] in the reciprocity-oriented world dominated by Hellenic influence" (2000, 1979). The burden of proof, therefore, rests with those who would argue that Paul used this term differently than did those around him, that we should understand Paul's use of χάρις independently of the surrounding system of patronage and reciprocity. The far more reasonable position is that Paul used this term in a manner consistent with his cultural context. Tables 1 and 2 show the occurrences of χάρις in the New Testament, and in Paul's letters, and they illustrate that the term carries much the same semantic range in the New Testament as it does in non-Christian writings. Consistent with usage in non-Christian sources, χάρις refers least frequently to a pleasing quality and to gratitude, and most frequently either to the virtue or to the concrete act of generosity.[20]

A significant question to address is how translating χάρις as benefaction helps us to understand Paul better? In answer to the question, let us consider the repeated Pauline phrase "by the χάρις given to me" (Gal 2:9; 1 Cor 3:10; Rom 12:3; 15:15).[21] Since Paul clearly invokes something given to him by God, we are on firm footing to understand this as an item of generosity, and therefore to translate the phrase "By the benefaction given to me." This translation draws out from the passage that what Paul received was more likely a concrete good than an abstract theological virtue known ephemerally as grace.

There is no agreement among commentators as to what the χάρις in this phrase refers; what is worse, there is a fairly wide range of options. Some commentators see grace not as a cultural reference to a concrete good, which naturally requires an external referent, but as a virtue in and of itself, like faith, hope, or love.[22] Other commentators try to be more concrete when they explain what Paul means when he

---

20. Notably, I have chosen to translate χάρις in Paul's letter openings as "beneficence": "Beneficence and peace from God our father and the Lord Jesus Christ be with you." Since peace, however, is a concrete good conferred by God, one could just as easily translate χάρις here as benefaction. The benefaction Paul would be wishing for his communities would, of course, be his motivating desire for all his converts: resurrection in and reunion with Jesus Christ.

21. Gal 2:9 τὴν χάριν τὴν δοθεῖσάν μοι; 1 Cor 3:10 Κατὰ τὴν χάριν τοῦ θεοῦ τὴν δοθεῖσάν μοι; Rom 12:3 διὰ τῆς χάριτος τῆς δοθείσης μοι; Rom 15:15 διὰ τὴν χάριν τὴν δοθεῖσάν μοι.

22. Collins (1999, 155). Similarly vague is Barrett's claim that the χάρις was God's activity in Christ (1968, 86). A similar vagueness and abstractness attends the explanations of Fitzmyer (1993) and Achtemeier (1985).

Table 1. New Testament Usage (excluding Paul)

Virtue of Generosity (57x)	Act or Item of Generosity (16x)	Gratitude for Generosity (5x)	Pleasing Quality (11x)
Luke 1:30; 2:40; **John** 1:14, 16 (2x), 17; **Acts** 6:8; 11:23; 13:43; 14:26; 15:11, 40; 20:24, 32; **Eph** 1:2, 6; 2:5, 7; 3:2, 7; 6:24; **Col** 1:2, 6; 4:18; **2 Thess** 1:2, 12; 2:16; 3:18; **1 Tim** 1:2, 14; 6:21; **2 Tim** 1:2; 2:1; 4:22; **Titus** 1:4; 2:11; 3:7, 15; **Heb** 2:9; 4:16; 10:29; 12:15; 13:9, 25; **1 Pet** 1:2, 10, 13; 4:10; 5:5, 10, 12; **2 Pet** 1:2; 3:18; **2 John** 1:3; **Jude** 4; **Rev** 1:4; 22:21	**Acts** 4:33 (needs were met); 14:3 (signs, wonders); 18:27 (ability to believe); 24:27 (Paul jailed); 25:3 (person sent to Jerusalem), 9 (Paul tried); **Eph** 1:7 (redemption); 2:8 (salvation); 3:8 (Paul's ministry); 4:7 (gifts), 29 (pleasing speech); **2 Tim** 1:9 (Christ); **Heb** 4:16 (various); **James** 4:6 (2x; opposition of enemy); **1 Pet** 3:7 (life)	**Luke** 17:19; **Col** 3:16; **1 Tim** 1:12; **2 Tim** 1:3; **Heb** 12:28	**Luke** 2 52; 4:22; 6:32, 33, 34; **Acts** 2:47; 7:10, 46; **Col** 4:16; **1 Pet** 2:19, 20

refers to the χάρις given to him:[23] Betz says of Gal 2:9 that the χάρις is the *gospel* that Paul preaches (1979, 99);[24] a more common suggestion is that Paul refers to the *authority* he received from God;[25] another, and slightly related, item which some suggest Paul refers to can be called *task and ability*. This interpretation claims that it is not only, or even primarily, the apostolic office which Paul received (and which we shall consider shortly), but it was the *ability* to complete the task successfully that was the greater gift.[26]

Far more common is the claim that χάρις in this phrase refers to Paul's apostolic office, to his mission to the Gentiles.[27] Commentators who suggest that this is what

23. In this way, two commentaries which translate χάρις in this passage as *favor* are to be commended: Getty (1983, 26) and Pilch (1983, 13). Unfortunately, neither attempts to explain the meaning of the verse so, aside from the use of the word *favor*, they are of no help to us.

24. Betz is explicit that this meaning is appropriate only to this letter, and that in other contexts χάρις refers to other benefits (1979, see n. 389 on p. 99).

25. Cranfield (1979, 766); Black (1973); Käsemann (1980, 332–34); Byrne (1996, 368).

26. Fee (1987, 138); Orr and Walther (1976, 172); Collins (1999, 155).

27. Conzelmann (1975); Hays (1997); Schreiner (1998: 651); De Witt Burton (1921, 95). Käsemann (1980, 14); Kim (1978); Murphy-O'Connor (1998, 24). What is curious about Conzelmann's commentary is that when he discusses 1 Cor 3:10 in the commentary (75), he is unclear as to what χάρις refers. It is earlier in the book, when discussing 1 Cor 1:4 (26), that he says explicitly that χάρις refers to

Table 2. Pauline Usage

Virtue of Generosity (33x)	Act or Item of Generosity (25x)	Gratitude for Generosity (8x)
Rom 1:7; 4:16; 5:15, 20, 21; 6:1, 14, 15; 11:5, 6 (3x); 16:20; **1 Cor** 1:3; 16:23; **2 Cor** 1:2; 4:15; 6:1; 9:14; 12:9; 13:13; **Gal** 1:3, 6; 2:21; 5:4; 6:18; **Phil** 1:2, 7; 4:23; **1 Thess** 1:1; 5:28; **Phlm** 2, 25	**Rom** 1:5 (vision); 3:24 (justification); 4:4 (not wages); 5:2 (peace); 5:15 (justification), 5:17 (righteousness); 12:3 (vision); 12:6 (gifts); 15:15 (vision); **1 Cor** 3:10 (vision); 15:10 (3x; vision); 16:3 (collection); **2 Cor** 1:12 (holiness and godly sincerity); 1:15 (letter and Paul's presence); 8:1 (joy, liberality); 8:4 (participation in collection); 8:6 (collection); 8:7 (collection); 8:9 (richness); 8:19 (collection); 9:8 (everything); **Gal** 1:15 (vision); 2:9 (vision)	**Rom** 6:17; 7:25; **1 Cor** 1:4; 10:30; 15:57; **2 Cor** 2:14; 8:16; 9:15

Paul received from God are careful to point out the theological implications, namely, that the apostolic office was granted to Paul, and as such was unearned by him in any way, and was not of his own design. It is unlikely, however, that we are best served by thinking about Paul's mission to the Gentiles as a benefaction from God. The mission is not the benefaction from God; it is rather Paul's proper and honoring conduct as a client who has received a benefaction from a divine patron. Paul frequently draws attention to how hard he has worked in his mission to the Gentiles (1 Cor 9:1; 15:10). Both that Paul worked hard to honor his God, and that he draws attention to how he has discharged his duty, are fairly predictable when seen in the context of ancient Mediterranean patronage and benefaction. When clients of the healing god Asclepius leave *ex voto* offerings, they publicly proclaim the benefaction received from that deity (Edelstein and Edelstein 1975). When Isis appears to Apuleius in Lucian's *Golden Ass*, he joins in the parade of others who have been benefited by her. Together, they proclaim to on-lookers the benefactions they have received. Everyone does something a little different; the point is not that there is continuity in reciprocity, but that reciprocity is consistent (Crook 2004, 91–147).

That Paul's mission was his response to God's benefaction and not God's benefaction itself is suggested by 1 Cor 9:16: ἐὰν γὰρ εὐαγγελίζωμαί οὐκ ἔστιν μοι καύχημα· ἀνάγκη γάρ μοι ἐπίκειται· οὐαὶ γάρ μοι, ἐστιν ἐὰν μὴ εὐαγγελίσωαμι ("If I

Paul's apostolic office, by which we are presumably meant to understand that χάρις refers to this every time the word is used.

proclaim the gospel, this gives me no ground for boasting, for an obligation is laid on me, and woe to me if I do not proclaim the gospel" NRSV). Client reciprocity was not optional; it was an obligation. Failure to reciprocate adequately could dishonor a patron and benefactor, and the stakes were never higher than when that patron was a god: οὐαί μοι, as Paul says. Paul's language of being obligated to run his mission is paralleled in Seneca's depiction of client obligation to a patron or benefactor. Behind Basore's Loeb Classical Library translation "to place under an obligation" we find two different but equally evocative words. The first is *obliger* (*Ben.* 2.30.2; 2.17.7; 2.11.5; 3.8.2; 5.7.2), which carries a moral element, a sentiment no one is surprised to see come from Seneca. The second word is *debeo* (*Ben.* 2.19.2; 6.4.1), which implies that there is debt on the part of the client, but duty is also an element of this word. The debt of course is one of gratitude and reciprocity, as Seneca makes abundantly clear.

We can conclude therefore that the mission to the Gentiles was not the χάρις that Paul refers to having been given. It is not the case, however, that this conclusion contradicts Paul's testimony in Gal 1:16; there Paul claims that God revealed Christ in him ἵνα he "might proclaim him among the Gentiles." Paul does not claim he received the mission to the Gentiles from Christ, but rather he draws a causal link between his mission and the revelation of Christ in him. And here we arrive at the heart of the issue being considered in this essay. Paul implies a causal link between the vision and the mission that is clarified in his references to the χάρις given to him (1 Cor 3:10; Gal 2:9; Rom 12:3; 15:15).[28] The χάρις that Paul received is the vision of Christ in him, which then explains how the mission was a response to such a benefaction.[29]

In Gal 2, Paul relates his meeting in Jerusalem with James, Cephas, and John. He tells us that because they recognized the χάρις that had been given to Paul (2:9), they agreed to Paul's mission to the uncircumcised. They realized that Paul had seen the risen Jesus, and for them this was sufficient to prove the validity and authenticity of Paul's mission. What is more, in this letter Paul has already referred to his vision of Christ as a benefaction from God: in Gal 1:15 he claims that he was called through that benefaction. So, in Gal 2:9 the χάρις that was given to Paul is his vision of Christ.

In 1 Cor 3:10, Paul suggests that God gave him a χάρις, that this χάρις acted as a foundation, and that "that foundation is Jesus Christ" (3:11). The χάρις therefore here refers to the vision of Christ that Paul received. Paul's vision of Christ was not only authorizing, but it also provided a stable and unchangeable foundation. Throughout Paul's letters, his authority is contested: his opponents question whether he has any, while he himself believes he does. But it all goes back to his vision: the vision has given Paul authority.

The theme is repeated in the Romans occurrences of this phrase. At Rom 12:3, Paul's words might well have read, "By the authority vested in me." Here his vision,

---

28. At the end of his career, Paul seems to want to say more explicitly that he *received* the apostleship (Rom 1:5). The claim is without precedent in the Pauline corpus.

29. My own thinking on this issue has developed over the years. In Crook (2001–5, 9–26) (completed and accepted for publication in 2001), I argued that the χάρις Paul refers to in these passages is his apostolic office. In Crook (2004, 143), I was undecided.

the χάρις that was given to him, gives him the authority to instruct them on sober judgment. It is the authorizing power of the vision of Christ that Paul refers to as well at Rom 15:15: it allows Paul to speak boldly to people.

It can be difficult to separate authority and the apostolic office, and in some ways it may be unnatural to do so. What I have suggested here is that the mission, which results in Paul appointing himself apostle, is Paul's expression of reciprocity for the χάρις that he received from God: the vision of Christ. But, of course, the vision, his mission, and his authority are all intertwined. These are all together also expressed in 1 Cor 15:10, but here more than anywhere understanding χάρις as benefaction, and as the benefaction of the vision of Jesus Christ, brings the impact of this passage out. Here Paul writes, "By the benefaction of God, I am what I am, and his benefaction towards me was not in vain. On the contrary I worked harder than any of them—though it was not I but the benefaction of God that is with me." Paul received a benefaction from his god in the form of a vision of Jesus Christ, and he worked hard to ensure he honored God by reciprocating that benefaction, which he did through his mission to the Gentiles.

CONCLUSION

Grace can and should remain a core concept in Christian faith and theology. Translators, however, should have as their goal to render texts as closely to their original contexts as possible. This requires us not only to translate words from one language to another, but often from one culture to another. It also requires us to, as much as possible, translate texts free of theological reflection. Theological reflection, in other words, should be what people do *with* the translation, not what motivates the translation itself. To that end, I would recommend that we move away from the theologically charged language of grace when translating χάρις and adopt in its place language that reflects its first-century setting of patronage and benefaction: *benefaction, beneficence*, even *favor*, will all accomplish that.

Contrition and Correction or Elimination and Purification in 1 Corinthians 5?

Richard E. DeMaris

Modern translations of 1 Cor 5:1–5, a passage about the removal of a sexual deviant from the Pauline assembly in Corinth, almost universally misrepresent how Paul expected the Corinthians to respond to the deviant in verse 2 and what Paul expected to result from the expulsion he commanded in verses 3 through 5. Both modern sensibilities and contemporary theological considerations anachronistically projected back two millennia have contributed to the mishandling of this passage. A social-scientific approach to this passage highlights certain characteristics of ancient Mediterranean society that help properly to illuminate these verses: the central place of ritual in ancient society, especially in response to pollution or contamination, and the priority of the group over the individual. These features lead to a reading of 1 Cor 5:1–5 that differs subtly but significantly from modern English translations and that does greater justice to the Greek text than any of them.

What are these modern sensibilities and contemporary theological considerations? The former will become clear in the course of the essay. As for the latter, some attention to the disposition that contemporary biblical scholars bring to 1 Corinthians and Paul's other letters is needed before we look in detail at 1 Cor 5 and offer an alternative reading of it.

The Pursuit of Pauline Coherence

New Testament scholars studying the apostle Paul invariably face the problem of locating a coherent center in his writing and thinking (Meyer 1997; Achtemeier 1996; Hübner 1987; Beker 1980, 11–19). What prompted Paul to write accounts in part for this problem, for his letters were occasional in nature, sent to particular communities, and typically dealt with multiple, often unrelated, crises. Thus, their content depended to a great degree on the problems or issues troubling the communities Paul addressed. Even his letter to the Romans, which scholars judge the least occasional, does not constitute an organized or exhaustive presentation of his thought.

The makeup of a typical letter from Paul also rules against finding a coherent center. A lively debate surrounds some of Paul's letters over the issue of their literary unity. Second Corinthians, for instance, is widely thought to have a letter fragment, what is now chapters 10 to 13, imbedded in it (Meeks 1972, 48–49; Thrall 1994, 3–48, esp. 13, 43; Roetzel 1998, 93, 95). Also, most of Paul's letters contain exhortations and instructions set off from the rest of the letter, such as the final chapters (4 and 5) of 1 Thessalonians (Roetzel 1998, 66, 83). A once dominant view considered such paraenetical material an appendage to Paul's letters and not well integrated in them (e.g., Dibelius 1966, 239–41). Subsequent scholarship has sought to counteract this view by finding links between the theological and paraenetical sections of Paul's letters. Consequently, much of the scholarly discourse about the coherence and unity of Paul's letters has taken place in the language of theology and ethics (e.g., Bassler 1993; Cousar 1993). A recent contribution to that discourse, which now defines Pauline scholarship, has a subtitle that encapsulates the approach nicely. John Lewis's *Looking for Life: The Role of "Theo-Ethical Reasoning" in Paul's Religion* (2005) reviews two generations' worth of scholarship on the subject and seeks to advance this line of interpretation.

Scholars have come to assume that rooting Paul's ethical prescriptions in his theological formulations will make the case for his coherence. This assumption clearly operates in Richard B. Hays's important study of New Testament ethics, *The Moral Vision of the New Testament: Community, Cross, New Creation*. Quite understandably, Hays devotes a great deal of attention to Paul. When he approaches Paul's ethics, he understands his task to be twofold: once he has identified and characterized Paul's ethical discourse—Paul did not, after all, write a manual of discipline or book of church order—he must demonstrate how it grew out of, and was grounded in, his theology (1996, 16–19). Accordingly, Hays offers the following remarks:

> The ethical norm, then, is not given in the form of a predetermined rule or set of rules for conduct; rather, the right action must be *discerned* on the basis of a christological paradigm, with a view to the need of the community. (1996, 43)

Hays seeks to join Pauline theology and ethics together under the rubrics of community, cross, and new creation, hence the subtitle of his book. So at this point in his chapter on Paul, Hays tells us that Paul encouraged moral discernment informed by a christological paradigm (i.e., the cross) and community need. He then reflects on the failure of this recommendation among the Corinthians:

> Paul's reluctance to specify narrow behavioral norms was perhaps one of the factors that led to trouble in the Corinthian community. Acting in light of their own spiritual discernment, some of the Corinthians were conducting themselves in ways that Paul found deeply objectionable. In 1 Corinthians 5:1–5, for example, he condemns an incestuous relationship between a man and his mother-in-law as "sexual immorality of a kind that is not found even among the Gentiles." Here he gives no reason for his rejection of this behavior; he merely pronounces condemnation. He formulates his moral indignation in a manner ("not found even among the *Gentiles*") suggesting that this particular normative judgment is rooted in Jewish cultural sensibilities, based ultimately on Leviticus 18:8: "You shall not uncover the nakedness of your father's wife." This background, however, remains implicit.

Even in this disturbing passage, however, the specific directive that Paul gives to the Corinthian church ("Drive out the wicked person from among you" [5:13]) is motivated by a concern for the unitary holiness of the community: "Do you not know that a little yeast leavens the whole batch of dough? Clean out the old yeast so that you [plural] may be a new batch, as you really are unleavened" (5:6b–7a). Thus, concern for the health and purity of the community remains the constant factor in which more specific norms must be grounded. (1996, 43)

It is no accident that Hays introduces 1 Cor 5:1–5 to his discussion of the unity between theology and ethics. This passage marks a major transition in 1 Corinthians (Sellin 1987, 2942), which some regard as so abrupt that it proves the essential discontinuity between Paul's theological (chaps. 1–4) and ethical (5–16) discourses (Conzelmann 1975, 95). Hays seeks to counter this claim in his assessment.

Yet the more Hays says about 1 Cor 5, the less appropriate and adequate the category of morality or ethics seems. The way Hays's language shifts over the course of the quotation above is revealing in this regard. "Behavioral norms," "moral indignation," and "normative judgment" give way to Paul's concern for the "unitary *holiness*" and the "health and *purity*" of the community (emphasis added). What Hays inadvertently shows us is that 1 Cor 5 concerns itself most immediately with holiness and purity, not ethics and morality. If morality plays a role here, it derives from and depends on an orientation that is more at home with categories like holiness and unholiness, purity and pollution. The very language Hays resorts to in describing what Paul is about in 1 Cor 5, therefore, tells against the priority of ethics in this passage.

The trouble with Hays's analysis and the many like his lies not so much in his characterization of Paul in 1 Cor 5—it is quite accurate in some ways—but in the interpretive frame in which he tries to fit it. Here, at a pivotal point in 1 Corinthians, purity and holiness dominate Paul's thinking, so much so that they define community unity and health. Yet prevailing treatments of Paul miss or obscure this orientation by privileging ethics (e.g., Pascuzzi 1997). While this essay cannot reexamine all of Paul, it can review chapter 5 along with the rest of 1 Corinthians and offer a different perspective. This alternative interpretation will find that in chapter 5 and at many other important points in the letter, what preoccupies Paul and thus unites the letter is a concern for purity and holiness.

The great problem at Corinth in Paul's thinking was not immorality per se but its effect. The gravest threat was pollution or contamination because of the threat it posed to the community's purity and holiness (Neyrey 1990, 21–55). In response, Paul, like other inhabitants of the ancient Mediterranean world, turned to ritual as the necessary mechanism for counteracting pollution and restoring holiness, purity, and community health. Read through the filter of theology and ethics, the vital importance of ritual fades from Paul. The alternative interpretation of 1 Corinthians this essay offers, however, restores ritual to its central place in the letter and in Paul's thought.

MORAL PRONOUNCEMENT AND DISCIPLINARY INTERVENTION?

In the verses that open 1 Cor 5, Paul appears to run the gamut: he speaks of individual morality (or immorality), group disciplinary action (its lack), and ceremonial punishment or banishment. Most scholars read the verses through the lens of personal or group ethics and thus minimize what one scholar calls the "highly unusual" scene that actually dominates the passage (Yarbrough 1995, 129 n. 12). By removing the ethical filter, however, one sees that ritual performance dominates.

> (5:1) It is actually reported that there is sexual immorality among you, and of a kind that is not found even among pagans; for a man is living with his father's wife [concubine (so de Vos 1998)]. (2) And you are arrogant! Should you not rather have mourned, so that he who has done this would have been removed from among you? (3) For though absent in body, I am present in spirit; and as if present I have already pronounced judgment (4) in the name of the Lord Jesus on the man who has done such a thing. When you are assembled, and my spirit is present with the power of our Lord Jesus, (5) you are to hand this man over to Satan for the destruction of the flesh, so that his spirit may be saved in the day of the Lord. (NRSV)

The scene evoked by verses 4 and 5—the congregational gathering Paul calls for—has generated numerous characterizations. The verses have undergone analysis as a type of prayer (Wiles 1974, 142–50) and a prophetic judgment (Roetzel 1969). What Paul calls for has been variously described as a "charismatic devotion" (Forkman 1972, 12) and "a judicial act of a sacral and pneumatic kind" (Conzelmann 1975, 97; cf. Doskocil 1958, 59–76). That Paul declares judgment in verse three and that the congregation assembles in verse 4 has led some to see a legal or judicial or even legislative process at work, although the procedure there differs markedly from the application of discipline in other communities of the time (1QS 5:24–6:1; Matt 18:15–17) (Bammel 1997; Wiles 1974, 117). In Ernst Käsemann's view, Paul has pronounced holy law against the man and expects the community to go along with his apostolic injunction (1969, 70–71).

Emphasis in interpretations of this sort, however, is misplaced; it falls on Paul rather than where Paul directs it, namely, to the Corinthians. What he writes are instructions to the Corinthians, which is why scholarly analysis of his words as prophetic pronouncement, holy law, or intercessory prayer has limited value. When Paul talks elsewhere in this letter about the Corinthians assembling—it appears insignificant that he uses *synagō* (gather, assemble) in 5:4 but *synerchomai* (come together, meet) everywhere else—the setting is worship, presumably in a household, not administrative council or courtroom (1 Cor 11:17, 18, 20, 33, 34; 14:23, 26). The numerous references in chapter 11 refer to coming together for the eucharistic meal, participation in which, Paul insists, calls for judgment (11:29, 31–32). Hence, a eucharistic setting for the ceremonial punishment seems very likely (Wiles 1974, 147; Johnson 1998, 175). Alternatively, some scholars posit a baptismal setting, since the expulsion will effectively reverse a baptism (Käsemann 1969, 71; Forkman 1972, 146 n. 169; Bohren 1952, 110 n. 131). That suggestion, however, is not as convincing.

Whatever the case, Paul sets what he expects the Corinthians to do within a cultic ritual setting of some sort, not a deliberative or juridical one.

Confirmation of Paul's ritual orientation in chapter 5 comes in verse 2, which all standard interpretations of that verse miss entirely and many translations obscure. Scholars typically find Paul spelling out his accusation of arrogance against the Corinthians there: their arrogance has led to complacency. They have failed to mourn, that is, to show regret, for the gross misconduct of a community member. Lack of contrition on their part has resulted in a failure to act against that comrade (Rosner 1992). A translation that mirrors this interpretation comes from Jerome Murphy-O'Connor and runs as follows (1979, 41): "Should you not rather have gone into mourning (and shown the sincerity of your sorrow by taking the necessary steps) in order that he who has done this should be removed from among you?" The New International Version puts it more succinctly: "Shouldn't you rather have been filled with grief and have put out of your fellowship the man who did this?" Pitched in this way, verse 2 has everything to do with ethics: a morally outraged Paul is trying to shame the Corinthians into disciplinary action.

This reading makes perfect sense if we assume that ethics is foremost in Paul's mind, but the verse does not fit so readily under that rubric. Paul links mourning with removal, which has puzzled modern interpreters and pushed them to understand mourning figuratively. Yet there is no compelling reason to take the Greek verb for mourning (*pentheō*) as a reference to an inner or psychological disposition—a sense of sadness or regret—rather than ritual practice, that is, the public rite of mourning. While the verb could have an experiential side, it normally meant the mourning connected with a funeral. It clearly has this meaning in the Gospels (Matt 5:4; 9:15; Mark 16:10; Luke 6:25) and in Revelation (18:11, 15, 19). Paul's reference to mourning in 1 Cor 5:2 should be read, therefore, as a reference to the formal actions connected with a state of mourning, not as a psychological expression of sorrow, as appealing as the latter might be to modern Westerners (Thiselton 2000, 388).

A metaphorical or figurative reading of mourning also stumbles over the final clause of the verse. The conjunction that opens the clause, *hina*, cannot easily bear the lengthy explanation that such a reading requires of it—recall Murphy-O'Connor's "(and shown the sincerity of your sorrow by taking the necessary steps)." A *hina* clause may also express command (Campbell 1993, 335 n. 19; Moulton et al. 1906–76, 3:94–95; but see Salom 1958, 138). Accordingly, the New International Version renders the last part of the verse as follows: "Shouldn't you rather have been filled with grief and have put out of your fellowship the man who did this?" But reading the clause as a command is troublesome because it departs so much from the Greek, which has the man as the subject of a verb in the passive voice: "so that *he* who has done this *would have been removed* from among you?" (1 Cor 5:2 NRSV, emphasis added).

A clause beginning with the conjunction *hina* normally has a final sense, expressing the purpose, goal, or aim of the verbal action in the main clause of the sentence. Hence, *hina* is typically translated "in order that" or "so that." Read this way, verse 2 says the expulsion of the deviate is the goal of the Corinthians' mourning. The *hina* clause, as the NRSV translation implies, could even suggest that the expulsion is the result of their mourning (Bauer 1979, 376–78; Smyth 1956, 493, §2193).

The unexpected cause and effect indicated by the likeliest syntax of verse 2 along with the assumption that Paul framed his response in ethical terms lie behind the tendency to read mourning figuratively. Yet from the standpoint of ancient Mediterranean ritual, the linkage of funerary rite to expulsion is not odd at all. A case in point comes from the Babylonian Talmud, which describes the excommunication or execration of Eliezer b. Hyrcanus from the circle of rabbis (*b. Bava Metzi'a* 59b). To report the excommunication to Eliezer, R. Akiba dressed in black—in mourning garb—and once R. Eliezer was informed of his excommunication, he rent his garment, put off his shoes, and sat in the dirt, as Job did when he lost his children. Funerals marked exit from community, so they are functionally like expulsions. Accordingly, funerary ritual could signal execration or excommunication.

More to the point, mourning could enact expulsion, which is what 1 Cor 5:2 indicates. Evidence for this ritual effect comes from the Roman historian Tacitus, who recorded what befell a Roman senator visiting a colony in Italy:

> A senator, Manlius Patruitus, complained that he had been beaten by a mob in the colony of Sena [modern Siena], and that too by order of the local magistrates; moreover, he said that the injury had not stopped there: the mob had surrounded him and before his face had wailed, lamented, and conducted a mock funeral, accompanying it with insults and outrageous expressions directed against the whole senate. (*Ann.* 4.45 [Jackson, LCL])

Along with the expected ways of throwing the senator out of town, the colonists of Sena included a funeral; they mourned as a way of expelling him.

This report from Tacitus portrays what the Greek in 1 Cor 5:2 describes: a funerary exit rite. Such a rite was evidently part of the ritual repertoire of the believers at Corinth, and it represents one of several rites connected with Paul and Pauline communities that show funerary elements or orientation. The Corinthians themselves evidently practiced baptism in a mortuary setting: baptism on behalf of the dead (1 Cor 15:29). And two key Christian rites, the common meal and baptism, had a funerary cast in Paul's thinking. What Paul writes about the Corinthians' dining ritual places the common meal squarely in a mortuary context (11:17–34): "For as often as you eat this bread and drink the cup, you proclaim the Lord's death until he comes" (v. 26). Likewise, he viewed baptism as participating in Jesus' death and burial (Rom 6:3–4). If a rite of entry—baptism—could have a funerary aspect, it is understandable that an exit rite would too.

A look at 1 Cor 5:1–5 attuned to the ritual world of the ancient Mediterranean reveals that Paul spoke not of one rite of expulsion but two. At the center of those verses, therefore, is a ritual crisis: the Corinthians' failure to act ritually and Paul's ritual intervention in response. If Paul already turned to ritual matters in 5:2, how central are ethics or discipline to chapter 5? They appear to be secondary to ritual. Paul may well have been unhappy about Corinthian moral laxity or lack of discipline, but the primary disappointment in 5:2 is over their failure to carry out a rite. In response, Paul intervenes with an alternative rite. Verse 3, therefore, does not broach the subject of ritual but rather continues a ritual discourse, one that controls the opening of the chapter.

POLLUTION AND PURIFICATION: AN ELIMINATORY EXPULSION

The ritual Paul prescribes in verses 4 and 5 was not merely an alternative exit rite, however. The substitute Paul orders comes with a rationale in verses 6 through 8 rooted in pollution and purity concerns. This is not the language of a *collegium* or *thiasos* expelling a delinquent member. Purity was a central concern of the Qumran community, yet the grounds for expulsion from it did not necessarily revolve around the elimination of pollution (e.g., 1QS 7:18–19, 25–27). For Paul they evidently did, at least in this case. To justify his introduction of a new rite, Paul likens the Corinthian situation to a community that must rid itself of a contaminant. It becomes clear in these verses that we no longer have a simple expulsion rite; we have a rite that will purify the community. The NRSV translates verses 6 to 8 as follows:

> (5:6) Your boasting is not a good thing. Do you not know that a little yeast leavens the whole batch of dough? (7) Clean out the old yeast so that you may be a new batch, as you really are unleavened. For our paschal lamb, Christ, has been sacrificed. (8) Therefore, let us celebrate the festival, not with the old yeast, the yeast of malice and evil, but with the unleavened bread of sincerity and truth.

Yeast proved to be a useful metaphor for Paul's articulation of the dangers to the community posed by the presence of the immoral man in it. He began with a common proverb based on the leavening action of yeast. Set in the context of chapter 5, Paul is saying, "even a single individual can affect the whole community." Perhaps it was also common knowledge that yeast was a product of corruption and infected whatever it was in. This, at any rate, is how the ancient Greek writer Plutarch explains why priests of Jupiter cannot touch it (*Quaest. rom.* 109 [289E–F]). But even if Paul's audience did not share Plutarch's view of yeast, Paul's allusion to its infectious or contagious nature would have sufficed to support his point in the passage: removal of the "old yeast," that is, the immoral man, was imperative because even a little impurity tainted the whole community.

The shift from old yeast versus new batch to old yeast versus unleavened bread in verse 7 allows Paul to restate the rationale for acting against the immoral man in the language of purity and impurity. Israelite cultic traditions come into play, as Paul places his readers at Passover time. While it is a novel Passover that has Christ as the paschal lamb, the demand for purification associated with traditional Passover remains in force. Just as Israelite households have to purify themselves by getting rid of all leaven, so too must the Corinthian assembly (Exod 12:8, 15–20). Since one could not celebrate Passover with the old yeast—Paul adds—"of malice and evil," the embodiment of those vices among the Corinthians, the immoral man, has to go. In these verses Paul invokes the requirements of cultic preparation to convince the Corinthian community to cleanse itself.

If Paul called for ritual purification rather than mere expulsion in 1 Cor 5:3–5, the question arises, "who or what would have to undergo purification?" A great many interpreters have answered "the immoral man" and concomitantly understood the action that Paul called for as revocable and remedial (South 1992, 23–88; Joy 1988; Thornton 1972; Cambier 1968–69). Murphy-O'Connor states, "If read carelessly Paul's decision appears brutal, but there is no doubt that he conceived such excommunication, not as a punishment, but as a remedy. The ultimate goal is the salvation of the individual. . . . Paul's hope was that the sinner would change his pattern of behaviour, and conceived excommunication as the stimulus that would produce this effect" (1979, 41–42). This interpretation's emphasis on the individual, however, flies in the face of Paul's consistent emphasis on community purity or holiness throughout chapter 5 (1 Cor 5:7, 9, 11).

So strong is the pull to focus on the individual and his fate that scholars have sought resolution to the situation—often a positive resolution—in various places. The temptation to find an outcome in 2 Corinthians to the crisis of 1 Cor 5 has attracted some. Scholars have found evidence for his expulsion and the aftermath in the second chapter of that later letter (Lampe 1967, 342–55; Hughes 1962, 59–72): "This punishment by the majority is enough for such a person; so now instead you should forgive and console him, so that he may not be overwhelmed by excessive sorrow. So I urge you to reaffirm your love for him. . . . Anyone whom you forgive, I also forgive" (2 Cor 2:6–8, 10a NRSV). Very few scholars go along with this proposal, however, and the reasons for their hesitation are clear. First, the expulsion from the community Paul called for in 1 Cor 5 sounds permanent and irrevocable, quite unlike the limit to punishment Paul calls for here (Thrall 1994, 174). Second, the context of this consolatory language indicates that Paul was recommending reconciliation in an entirely different situation (Furnish 1984, 164–68). The verse that precedes this quotation, 2 Cor 2:5, points to an offense against Paul himself that he hoped would be treated as a community matter: "But if anyone has caused pain, he has caused it not to me, but to some extent—not to exaggerate it—to all of you." If Paul's primary focus in 1 Cor 5 had been on the immoral individual and the disciplining of him, we might expect Paul to have expressed concern for his fate. But Paul's concern lay with the community, not the individual, and with purifying, not remedial or rehabilitating, action.

Relatively few scholars turn to 2 Corinthians to learn the fate of the sexual deviate, but the pronounced individualism of modern Westerners is so powerful that many have found his destiny spelled out in 1 Cor 5:5. Contemporary translations reflect this perspective; over time English translations have made verse 5 explicitly about the immoral individual:

EARLY TRANSLATIONS

> . . . be delivered unto Satan, for the destruction of the flesh, that the spirit may be saved in the day of the Lord Jesus.
>
> Geneva Bible (1560)

> . . . to deliver such an one unto Satan for the destruction of the flesh, that the spirit may be saved in the day of the Lord Jesus.
>
> KJV (1611)

MODERN TRANSLATIONS

> . . . hand this man over to Satan, so that the sinful nature may be destroyed and his spirit saved on the day of the Lord.
>
> NIV (1973)

> . . . you are to hand this man over to Satan for the destruction of the flesh, so that his spirit may be saved in the day of the Lord.
>
> NRSV (1989)

CONTEMPORARY DYNAMIC-EQUIVALENCE TRANSLATIONS

> You must then hand that man over to Satan. His body will be destroyed, but his spirit will be saved when the Lord Jesus returns.
>
> CEV (1991)

> Then you must throw this man out and hand him over to Satan so that his sinful nature will be destroyed and he himself will be saved on the day the Lord returns.
>
> New Living Translation (1996)

In a culture that values individualism, it is almost inevitable that translations made for that culture will reflect a concern for the individual. But this is a modern, western sensibility, one not shared by most of the world and certainly not by ancient Mediterranean culture. Social scientists engaged in cross-cultural research place human cultures on a continuum whose end points are collectivism and individualism. In individualist cultures, values are expressed in personal terms and personal face is foremost. In contrast, collectivist cultures define the self in terms of the group and stress common fate (Triandis 1990, 59–60). Because such cultures recognize that the basic unit of survival is the whole rather than the part, the collectivist psyche focuses on the ramifications of an individual's actions for the group:

> Not only do collectivists believe that the human race is so intricately woven together that one person's misbehavior may harm many, they also feel and experience this interdependence. Hence, in a collectivist culture a person's misbehavior or failure is a disgrace to the family, or even the entire clan. (Hui and Triandis 1986, 231)

As a denizen of a collectivist culture, when Paul expressed his concern about the sexual deviate, we would expect to find him focused more on the Corinthian assembly than any single member of it. Hence, we should be wary of translations and interpretations that direct us to the individual.

When Paul called for purification, we should assume that he had the Corinthian church in mind. Resistance to this understanding has resulted in translations and interpretations of verse 5 that make the immoral man the focal point of the rite: "consign this man to Satan for the destruction of his flesh, so that his spirit may be saved on the day of the Lord" (so Conzelmann 1975, 94; cf. Barrett 1968, 125). Yet this reading does not square with Paul's anthropology: flesh and spirit were not distinct parts of the human being; they were orientations that human beings could embrace, or realms or theaters in which they could operate (Gal 3:3; 5:16–26; Rom 8:1–17) (Collins 1980, 257–58). More important, the Greek at the end of verse 5 does not actually say *his* (the man's) flesh and *his* spirit but *the* flesh and *the* spirit, as reflected in the King James Version. If the group's survival is foremost in Paul's thinking, then we need to consider verse 5 not as a statement about the fate of the offender but about the consequences of the expulsion for the group: their action will purge the community of defilement—the works of flesh embodied in the deviate—and thus preserve the community—God's spirit will continue to dwell there (cf. 1 Cor 3:16–17). As one scholar in tune with Paul's communal orientation concludes, "The more or less explicit reason for expelling the incestuous man in 1 Cor 5 was to guard the holiness of the community and to avoid offense to the presence of the Holy Spirit" (Collins 1980, 263). This community-focused reading of verse 5 is particularly attractive because it resonates with several points in the remainder of chapter 5, where Paul's concern is not individual but corporate purity or holiness (1 Cor 5:7, 9, 11) (Martin 1995, 168–74; Donfried 1976, 150–51; Campbell 1993).

How, then, were the Corinthians to undertake their own purification? Adolf Deissmann suggested almost a century ago that the closest parallel in language to the handing over of someone to a supernatural power came from the magical papyri (1927, 302–3; cf. Preisendanz 1973–74, 1.192–93, pap. V.334–36; fully explored as an act of cultic devotion by Brun 1932, 106–11). He has been joined in recent years by several other scholars exploring magical execrations and curses that deliver a victim to supernatural wrath (Conzelmann 1975, 97; Aune 1980, 1551–53; Collins 1980).

As convincing as the correspondence in language is, however, reference to the magical papyri does not adequately account for the execration's setting. The background in Greco-Roman magic explains the procedural but not the communal aspect of the expulsion, as Adela Yarbro Collins notes (1980, 256). The execration of 5:5 is not a personal vendetta, as is evidently the case with the execrations of the magical papyri. In the instance cited above, an individual was to prepare a *defixio*, a curse tablet, and bury it at the grave of someone whose death had been untimely (Betz 1986, 106). The Corinthian execration, in contrast, was to be neither private nor personal but public and communal. Paul did prescribe it but expected the community to carry it out. Once the community was gathered, presumably for worship, a group leader or leaders would pronounce the curse and thus enact the community execration.[1]

DEALING WITH DISORDER: CHAPTER 5 IN PAUL'S LETTER

The alternative reading of 1 Cor 5 presented above becomes more convincing once one sees how it accords with the logic and flow of the entire letter. Anthropologist Mary Douglas has written extensively on purity and pollution issues and her insights

---

1. In a Mediterranean civic setting, a city magistrate would pronounce a public curse against behavior that threatened public welfare; in a household, the father (Parker 1983, 193–98).

will guide the final portion of this essay, as we try to understand the place of 1 Cor 5 in the whole letter. She has argued that matters of purity, pollution, and purification give voice to a group's or culture's ordering of reality, challenges to that order, and the maintenance or reestablishment of that order (1966). In ancient Mediterranean society, for example, death was polluting, and those affiliated with the deceased, typically family members, had to undergo purification. What such beliefs and practices reflected, Douglas would say, was the disruptive force of death on familial and other social structures. Death left existing family patterns in disarray, but ritual purification enabled and signaled the reorganization of the family and its reintegration in society. Funeral, burial, and mourning rites brought order out of disorder.

In this light we can understand how Paul's attention to purity and purification ritual in chapter 5 served as his answer to the problem he articulated in the opening chapters of 1 Corinthians. As noted at the beginning of this essay, 1 Cor 5 marks a significant transition in the letter, which has prompted much debate about the continuity between chapters 1 to 4 and the rest of the letter. Those opening chapters focused on what Paul identified as the major crisis the community faces, namely, factionalism or divisiveness. Almost all scholars would agree with Margaret Mitchell that 1 Corinthians is an argument for ecclesial unity, introduced at the very start of the letter (1991, 1; cf. Kennedy 1984, 24–25): "Now I appeal to you, brothers and sisters, by the name of our Lord Jesus Christ, that all of you be in agreement and that there be no divisions among you, but that you be united in the same mind and the same purpose" (1:10 NRSV).

If Paul was arguing for group harmony in the letter, how was he doing so in chapter 5? What follows is an interpretation informed by Douglas. When Paul's discussion of divisions concluded at the end of chapter 4, he framed the problem in terms of purity and pollution and prescribed a solution in chapter 5. Paul understood the Corinthian church's disorder as a symptom of pollution or defilement compromising community purity. Accordingly, he insisted on a ritual of community purification: expulsion of the group member who embodied defilement and epitomized disorder in his flagrant departure from cultural norms. So, while Paul changed his vocabulary between chapters 4 and 5, he still had the unity and health of the community in mind.

The linkage Douglas makes among order, purity, and ritual suggests that the disjunction that most scholars note between 1 Cor 1 through 4 and what follows is actually a misperception. That Paul assumed a connection between order and purity is evident in chapter 3, where he moves effortlessly from picturing the Corinthian community as a structure being assembled to the church as a holy temple:

> (3:14) If what has been built on the foundation survives, the builder will receive a
> reward. (15) If the work is burned up, the builder will suffer loss; the builder will
> be saved, but only as through fire. (16) Do you [plural throughout] not know that
> you are God's temple and that God's spirit dwells in you? (17) If anyone destroys
> God's temple, God will destroy that person. For God's temple is holy, and you are
> that temple. (NRSV)

Moreover, the language there about the temple as a holy place, as God's dwelling

place, and about the fate of anyone who threatens to defile the temple fully antici-
pates the discussion of chapter 5, where Paul stresses purity and the purificatory rite
that will achieve it (Rosner 1991): "Clean out the old yeast so that you may be a new
batch, as you really are unleavened" (5:7); "You are to hand this man over to Satan
for the destruction of the flesh" (5:5). Modern readers may perceive a shift from the
theological to the ethical or from the theoretical to the practical as chapter 5 opens,
but the relationship in Paul's mind between order and purity made the transition
seamless.

Douglas can help us in another way to see the coherence of 1 Corinthians and
chapter 5's place in the whole. Her study of purity and pollution led her to real-
ize that human societies typically draw an analogy between society and the individual, between the corporate body and the physical body: "the human body is always
treated as an image of society" (1970, 70). Jerome Neyrey has applied this insight to
1 Corinthians with fruitful results (1990, 102–46). Paul's worry about the integrity
of the body of believers (1 Cor 1–4), Neyrey argues, corresponds to his concern for
bodily matters in the remainder of the letter. Thus, from chapter 5 on, Paul is steadily
occupied with the physical body and bodily actions: illicit sexual union (5:1–8);
fornication (6:12–20); the joining of bodies in marriage (7:1–9, 25–40); the separat-
ing of bodies in divorce (7:10–16); proper eating, be it of idol food (8 and 10) or
during eucharistic dining (11:17–34); proper dressing (11:2–16); proper speaking,
be it in tongues, prophecy, or otherwise (12–14); and the nature of the resurrection
body (15:35–58). Paul's anxiety about bodily disposition and behavior, which begins
in chapter 5, mirrored Paul's fears about the corporate body of believers in Corinth,
which came to expression in the letter's opening chapters. These concerns are two
sides of the same coin, and their interconnection gives the letter its unity.

From the standpoint of purity and bodily matters, it is not coincidental that
the item foremost on Paul's agenda was ritual when he turned to practical matters
in 1 Cor 5. Ritual is the way, after all, human communities achieve and maintain
purity; it is also how they negotiate bodily matters. For his part, Paul counted on
community dining and worship ritual to control bodies: to maintain proper eating,
dressing, and speaking. Likewise, when it came to unifying the splintered corporate
body at Corinth, Paul turned to ritual purification to bring it back to health, order,
and wholeness.

Sins and Forgiveness: Release and Status Reinstatement of the Paralytic in Mark 2:1–12

Dietmar Neufeld

In the story of the paralytic, Jesus is recorded to have uttered, "Son, your sins are forgiven" (Mark 2:5). Traditionally, the meanings attributed to the words *sins* and *forgive* have been driven primarily by the doctrine of original sin and the messianic forgiveness that such sin required. In the words of William L. Lane, the paralytic had "experienced the Messianic forgiveness of the Son of Man" (1974, 98). In such a view, the focus rests chiefly upon the paralytic's release from the liability or penalty entailed by the guilt of personal sin—that "innate depravity common to all human beings in consequence of the fall of the first parents" (Lipinski 2007, 622). Jesus, therefore, released the paralytic from the debt of sin that he inherited from the fall of Adam.[1] Such current theological considerations reveal, however, that something significant has been "lost in translation" (Neyrey 2007b, 2). In order to reduce the "danger for modern readers of meaning being *lost in translation*," a social-scientific approach to this passage casts light upon certain elements of ancient Mediterranean society that help modern readers properly to see the meaning of sin and forgiveness in this pericope (Neyrey 2007b, 1). Setting the notions of sins and forgiveness in the social milieu of honor, shame, and patronage shows that the offer of forgiveness refers to the reinstatement and restoration of the paralytic's status after its loss due to the perception that his affliction was the consequence of sin—after all, he was told to stand up, take up his pallet, and go home. Such considerations lead to a reading of sins and forgiveness in Mark's story of the paralytic that differs from modern English translations but one in keeping with the social world of Mark and Jesus.

Forgiveness and Sins in Mark

The word *forgive* (ἀφίημι) occurs 34 times in Mark. In Mark 2:5, 7, 9, 10; 3:28; 4:12; 11:25, 26 ἀφίημι is rendered as *forgive* and in its other appearances is rendered as *leave, abandon, permit, allow, utter* (Mark 1:18, 20, 31, 34; 4:36; 5:19, 37; 7:8,12,

---

1. Lane states, "Sickness, disease and death are the consequence of the sinful condition of all men" (1974, 94).

27; 8:13; 10:14, 28, 29; 11:16; 12:12, 19, 20, 22; 13:2, 34; 14:6, 50; 15:36, 37). The word *sin* (ἁμαρτίαι) occurs six times in Mark (Mark 1:4, 5; 2:5, 7, 9, 10). A variety of interpretations of the sin for which the paralytic required forgiveness has been offered. One view suggests that *sins* here refers to some spiritual penalty encumbering the man's "nervous organization"—hence, his paralysis, and forgiveness refers to the removal of the physical consequences that impeded his nervous system (Gould 1975, 37). Another view sets the notion of sins and their forgiveness in the context of the OT where sin and disease, forgiveness and healing are frequently interrelated. Sickness, disease, and death are the consequence of humanity's sinful condition. Jesus' pronouncement of the remission of sin came upon recognition that the paralytic could be genuinely whole only after he had been healed through God's forgiveness of sins (Lane 1974, 94). Some take the statement to function formally as a statement of assurance central to healing stories. It was offered as an expression of encouragement, namely, Jesus saying to the paralytic, "take heart" (Theissen 1983, 58–59). Robert A. Guelich, in yet another view, asserts that healing the sick and forgiving the sinner point to the eschatological character of Jesus' work and put him in direct conflict with the religious establishment. Both healing the sick and forgiving the sinner are consistent "with the prophetic hope for the age of salvation" (1989, 86–87).

These readings, however, fail to take into account the social and cultural context within which these words were uttered. As will be shown, a proposed reading of Jesus' statement Τέκνον, ἀφίημί σου αἱ ἁμαρατίαι might be, "Son, you are released from the bondage of your paralysis and free to go home." In support of this reading, our next task will be to contextualize the notions of forgiveness and sin.

CONTEXTUALIZING FORGIVENESS

Depending on context, the verb ἀφίημι could mean to put into motion, let go, cancel, remit, leave, and the noun ἀφεσίς release, pardon, cancellation, and forgiveness. For the most part, since Homer, the word means the voluntary release of a person or thing over which one has legal or actual control (Vorländer 1967, 1:697). The word is used in both a literal and figurative sense—with a personal object, to send forth, to send away, to release, with an impersonal object, to lose a ship at sea or to discharge arrows. In the figurative sense, the verb means to let alone, permit, let pass, neglect, to lose one's life. In the legal sense, to release from legal bond, such as office, shame, a woman from marriage, to acquit, to exempt from shame, obligation, and punishment (Vorländer 1967, 1:698). In the LXX, while the word *forgiveness* was used, it generally was not used to covey the sense of forgiveness. Other words such as *cover, washing,* and *cleansing* in the cultic context were used to express the concept of forgiveness.

In the Old Testament, Israelites were aware that God forgave sins—sins that were the result of the opposition between the will of the divine and human. Again, for the most part, it was God's to forgive the offenses of humans by means of the blood sacrifices during the day of atonement, "the festival whose rites bring forgiveness of sins to every Israelite" (Vorländer 1967, 1:700).

In Qumran, sin was the outcome of human creatureliness that led to the abdication of obeying the laws of God and to the abandonment of communal obligations as required by God. Forgiveness, however, could be obtained through the communal member genuinely seeing the error of her ways and turning from it in humility and right spirit (Vorländer 1967, 1:700). From this assessment, it is evident that sin was not regarded as that innate, corrupting influence in the human that triggered sinful behavior but regarded as that external activity of humans that led to violations both of the laws of God and of the community.

According to the *OED* the root meanings for *forgiveness* are (1) to give, grant, (2) to give up, cease to harbor, (3) to remit a debt; to give up resentment or claim to requital for offense, (4) to give up resentment against, pardon. Thus, the English denotes a private release from some debt incurred by the guilt of personal activity against God, fellow humans, or giving up some personal resentment against someone who has caused offense. Modern sensibilities of forgiveness do not have as part of their meaning range the idea that in the Mediterranean world forgiveness, sin, and sickness belonged together and were culturally defined. They do not take into account the possibility that the paralytic's illness was perceived by his contemporaries to be the result of some personal misfortune—such as the "operation on humans by gods or spirits" that made him paralyzed (Pilch 1991, 201). They do not take into account that forgiveness in the ancient world could denote release from the social stigma of paralysis and the disgrace and loss of status that such a condition brought upon the person.

His paralysis negatively affected his state of being in his household and in public—the shame of his humiliating condition had rendered him an outcast and made him dependent on the care of those compassionately disposed to him. The temptation in the West is to define his illness in terms of the biomedical canons of Western medicine. As a result, we lose sight of the fact that in the ancient world illness was socially defined. Ancients tended to attribute social, not physical, causes to illnesses. Sickness, for example, could have been precipitated by the paralytic's deviance from the cultural norms and values of his kinship or social group. All too often, the blind, lame, or malformed in other ways were considered outcasts and not permitted even to draw near the altar let alone function normally in society (Lev 21:18–20). What is clear is that the paralytic's condition had cut him off from his family and society in general. Jesus the healer, therefore, addressed the paralytic's state of being and restored him to a valued place in that setting (Pilch 2000).

CONTEXTUALIZING SIN

The term *sin* must also be set into its social context in order to deliver a considerate reading of the Markan passage. According to Lipinski, Biblical Hebrew has some twenty different words to denote *sin*. What constituted *sin* was nuanced and reflected the exigencies confronting communities dealing with a variety of human failures that involved both fellow humans and God. Our purpose will be to examine these words in their literary and social contexts in order to get a sense of the incredible diversity of the words denoting *sin*. Lipinski notes that three of the most commonly used terms for sin—*ḥeṭ', pesha'* and *avon* (*'awon*)—are often found together and, while similar in meaning, cannot simply be taken to be synonymous.[2] Lipinski points out that the root *ht'* occurs 459 times in the Hebrew Bible and comes from the verb *hata'* meaning "to miss something" or "to fail" and in a variety of social contexts points to different kinds of failures. For example, the sin denoted in the root *ht'* could be viewed as the failure of carrying out a duty—such as to carry out the obligations inherent in mutual relations among kinship, community, and God (Lipinski 2007, 621). The sin of relational failure in such a context would have been akin to committing an "offense." Jacob asks Laban, "What is my offense that you have so hotly pursued after me" (Gen 31:36). Persons were mutually obligated to uphold the requirements of relationships—one who fulfils the obligations of a mutual relationship was considered righteous (*zaddik*) and one who did not caused offense (*ht'l-*). Furthermore, a lack of obedience towards one's superiors constituted committing an offense—after all, patron-client relations required that subordinates obeyed superiors—otherwise it was a direct challenge to their reputation and a cause of great offense. Both the Egyptian baker and cupbearer were in prison with Joseph because they had failed to obey the Pharaoh (Gen 40:1; 41:9). A deed or an act that contributes to the failure or dissolution of a community is designated a sin. Reuben admits that his brothers have sinned against their brother Joseph (Gen 42:22). They have failed him and their father. Their behavior was a grievous dereliction of duty which, in kinship structures, was understood as having engaged in a sinful act. The sin against their father was, therefore, a colossal failure of relational obligations.

Sin was also the result of the failure to meet one's obligations between one's fellow humans and God. Sin against God was conceived as an offense, that is, the failure to fulfil one's obligations toward God (Lipinski 2007, 622). So, for example, openly defying the requirements of relational decorum as spelled out by covenant, such as committing adultery, unchastity, and bloodshed were seen to be sins against God. While the concept of sin included failures of a moral, juridical, and cultic nature that constituted offenses against fellow humans and God, these offenses were social matters that spoke of a variety of relational ruptures requiring rapprochement.

The root *psh'* occurs in the Hebrew Bible 136 times with the basic meaning of *breach.* It was used to refer to the breach of covenant obligations in terms of international law, in criminal law to wrong doing that resulted in the dissolution of community or the rupture of peaceful relations between two groups, and in human-divine relations to sinful behavior of humans that dishonored God (Lipinski 2007, 622). The verb *'awah* is found 17 times in the Hebrew Bible and expresses the idea of crookedness in the sense of "to wrong" (Lam 3:9) and in the passive form "to become bent" (Ps 38:7). The noun *'awon* occurs 229 times and designates "crookedness" (Lipinski 2007, 622). Metaphorically, the language denotes violations of various kinds, their consequences, and the shame they incur. Human sins were misdeeds labeled as *failure, breach,* and *crooked* and often found their focus in human failure to keep the requirements of covenantal law as stipulated by God. These breaches resulted in the collapse of relationship between humans and God. The breaches, crookedness, and

---

2. Exod 34:7; Lev 16:21; Num 14:18; Isa 59:12; Jer 33:8; Ezek 21:29; Mic 7:18–19; Pss 32:1, 5; 51:3–7; 59:4–5; Job 7:20–21; 13:23; Dan 9:24.

failure were not regarded as indications of original sin and the innate depravity of all humans the result of the fall. Rather, they were the result of the human propensity in differing social contexts to perpetrate sins against fellow humans and God. Sinful behavior might be involuntary, proceed from ignorance, and be inadvertent. Humans, however, were called to be responsible for their actions. Given this sense of duty to one's actions, sick persons could potentially conclude that their illnesses were punishment for having offended God in some way (Lipinski 2007, 622).[3]

In the LXX, conceptions of sin are found within an extremely rich linguistic environment which, in modern translations, is all too often not expressed. Our translations miss both the richness of the original and do not catch the decisive point in many cases (*TDNT* 1:268). In the discussion of sin, prominence is given to the presumptuous or arrogant person. Arrogance is considered as the sin par excellence and one who exhibits such presumption before God deserves the label sinner. Rich and powerful persons are regarded as sinners on occasion (Prov 23:17). Sin is also seen as sickness (Isa 53:4). In Deut 30:3 the equation of sickness and sin leads to the notion that sickness can therefore be healed. Those who apostatize are regarded as sinners, and the expectation is that they will be delivered from and healed of this sin (Jer 14:7). The folly of the foolish and the idolatrous is regarded as sin (*TDNT* 1:268).

In Greek and Roman culture, sin was the outcome of missing a definite goal, whether by mistake or intentionally, and covered everything from crime, intellectual and artistic failings, cultic neglect, perjury and violation of the law of hospitality, dishonoring parents, divorce, oppression of orphans and other marginalized people, and other forms of social injustice. It also included errors on the part of legislators or judges and political blunders. The conception of sin in Phrygian and Lydian inscriptions from Asia Minor consisted of ingratitude, insulting speech, violation of the regulation for cleanness, violation of sanctuary, non-observance of required cultic chastity, cultic misdemeanor, and perjury (*TDNT* 1:300). Important for this essay was the perception that sickness was especially regarded as punishment for sin. Sin was perceived to be a substance that brought illness of a sort that profoundly acted upon the social well-being of the person (*TDNT* 1:302). So, generally, sin was not regarded to connote the inner disposition of the human but to indicate an outer habitus that was conditioned and driven by a specific social context.

My thesis then argues that the terms *forgiveness* and *sin* must be interpreted in terms of the appropriate cultural scenario of the ancient world. A considerate reading must involve becoming familiar with the social system of Mark. What was his social system like? What perceptions did he have of the way his world worked as regards sins and forgiveness that modern readers must know in order for them to be considerate readers? Our next task will be to contextualize ἀφίημι and ἁμαρτίαι in the foundational models of honor/ shame and patron-client relations, the basic building blocks of institutionalized hierarchies in antiquity.

---

3. Pss 38:4, 19; 41:5.

THE GRAMMAR OF HONOR AND SHAME

While what counted as honorable and shameful in the ancient Mediterranean world was not defined the same everywhere (Swartz 1988, 21), anthropologists have nevertheless shown that Greeks, Romans, and Judeans regarded honor and shame as pivotal values in their social milieu. Xenophon acknowledged that love of honor distinguished human from animal (*Hier.* 7.3), and Aristotle thought honor to be the "greatest of all external goods," identifying it with "happiness" akin to "being loved" (*Eth. Nic.* I). Philo avers that "wealth, fame, official posts, honors and everything of that sort" are a human's constant preoccupation (*Det.* 122). Indeed, he complains that "fame and honor are a most precarious possession, tossed about the reckless tempers and flighty words of careless men" (*Abr.* 264). As testament to this precarious preoccupation, Philo often mentions honor, glory, fame, high reputations, being adorned with honors and public offices, noble birth, the desire for glory, honor in the present, and a good name in the future (*Migr.* 172; *Leg.* 3.87; *Det.* 33, 157; *Post.* 112; *Abr.* 185, 263). Similarly, Josephus speaks of Caesars, Vespasian, David, Saul, Jonathan, Augustus as men of honor who confer honors upon others (*B.J.* 1.194; 1.199; 1.358; 1.396; 1.607; 3.408; *Vita* 423; *Ant.* 7.117; 6.168, 6.251, 13.102). In addition, he mentions the dignity and distinction held by judges, consuls, village priests, governors, and prophets (*B.J.* 4.149, 7.82; *Ant.* 4.215, 10.92, 11.309, 15.217).

This concern for honor and the avoidance of shame pervaded ancient Mediterranean societies. Thus it is not surprising that the Markan narratives play themselves out in the keys of honor and shame (Rohrbaugh 2007, 32; Neyrey 1998, 1–12). Honor and shame are values characteristic of face-to-face societies in which public evaluation of a person's standing provides a basis of social control (Peristiany 1966; Adkins 1960; Gilmore 1987; Malina 1993; Rohrbaugh 2007). Honor is an abstract term that anthropologists use to designate a person's worth, reputation, status, value, and fame. Moreover, honor is at the center of a social system of interconnected values in which power, personal loyalty, wealth, high-mindedness, relative importance in rank and status, sense of shame, courage, and excellence of character are operative (Friedrich 1977, 290). Claims of superiority over others and demands of one's rights commensurate with one's position in society are common in honor-based societies. Honor is, however, also a limited good related to the scarcity of all resources including land, live stock, crops, reputation, and political influence. Therefore, honor gained came at the expense of honor lost by another.

Honor refers to two social actions: (1) a person's claim of respect for the importance and value of her character, life, efforts, and achievements and (2) the public acknowledgment of that claim (Malina 1993, 30). The claim may be accepted or rejected. A person attains honor in several ways: she may be ascribed it by another or achieve it on her own merits. Ascribed honor refers to bestowed or inherited worth: born into a distinguished family, studying under an esteemed teacher and the requisite academic pedigree that follows, and receiving an important posting. Achieved honor is earned through merit and hard work, such as athletic talents, military prowess, accumulation of wealth, benefactions, artistic accomplishments, and through the practice of challenging another and taking her honor as one's own. Honor, therefore, describes a social dynamic whereby persons compete for the purpose of winning respect, praise, status, and reputation.

Gains and losses of honor are the consequence of the face-to-face game of challenge and response in which virtually every public encounter is construed as a challenge to one's honor. Challenges must be met with something said or done quickly and effectively in response or honor is lost. All such claims, challenges, and responses whether in kind, by a greater challenge, or deeper insult, take place in the public domain, and the verdict of success or failure determines the outcome in the game of challenge and riposte (Malina 1993; Neyrey 1991; Rohrbaugh 2007). The game of challenge and riposte is frequently an engagement of wit—the wittier the response the greater the honor. In the healing of the paralytic, Jesus and his opponents became involved in a witty display of verbal virtuosity not uncommon when significant issues were being publicly debated.

Honor is to be found in one's inherited name where sons enjoy the honor of the father and membership in his clan. Fathers, in turn, enjoy great honor in their households. Fathers protect the honor of the household at all expense. He is enjoined with the task of managing the household equitably so that it is well represented to the outside world. Sons and daughters are obligated to behave in such a way that the honor of the family is not compromised and the father publicly humiliated. One of the characteristics of the household is the willingness to extend reconciliation and forgiveness to members of the kinship group. Not to extend patience and tolerance when a breach had occurred would eventually stain the reputation of the whole family (DeSilva 2000, 172). Plutarch advises that among family members, gentleness and forbearance ought to be the normal mode of relating when egregious errors have been committed:

> We should make the utmost of these virtues in our relations with our families and relatives. And our asking and receiving forgiveness for our own errors reveals goodwill and affection quite as much as granting it to others when they err. For this reason we should neither overlook the anger of others, nor be stubborn with them when they ask for forgiveness, but on the contrary, should try to forestall their anger, when we ourselves are time and again at fault, by begging forgiveness, and again, when we have been wronged, in our turn should forestall their request for forgiveness by granting it before being asked. ("On Fraternal Affection" [*Mor.* 489 C–D], LCL)

In an ideal world, being patient, tolerant, and extending forgiveness to recalcitrant family members was one thing, in the real world quite another. If a gentle approach did not work, sons and daughters who caused shame to the family were often severely dealt with. Family disagreements in the sight of outsiders were damaging to the status and reputation of the family and had to be repaired quickly (DeSilva 2000, 173). Because parents had given their children the gift of life, they had great, legitimate authority over them during the course of their lives. Philo, for example, states that "parents are . . . seniors and instructors and benefactors and rulers and master; sons, and daughters are . . . juniors and learners and recipients of benefits and subjects and servants" (*Spec. Laws* 2.226–27, LCL). Children were thus obligated to honor and respect their parents in word and deed.

Parents were providers of benefactions for their children that left them indebted to their parents for life, and children in turn returned the favors once parents were old and could no longer provide for themselves. Seneca discusses father-son relationships and reinforces the patron-benefactor relationship between them when he says, "Can there be any greater benefits than those that a father bestows upon his children?" (*Ben.* 2.11.5). As benefactor, the head of the household held authority over his adult, married sons until his death (DeSilva 2000, 186). Fathers bestowed inducement (food, clothing, support), power (protection), and commitment (fidelity, loyalty) to them (Neyrey 2007a, 274). Fathers also provided strict social upbringing and education for their children:

> Do you see how parents force their children in the stage of tender infancy to submit to wholesome measures? The infants struggle and cry, they tend their bodies with loving care, and fearing that their limbs may become crooked from too early liberty, they swathe them in order that they may grow to be straight. . . . And so the greatest benefits are those that while we are either unaware or unwilling, we receive from our parents. (Seneca *Ben.* 6.24.1–2)

Sons were therefore under the obligation of living up to the standards of the family ancestors, of showing loyalty to their fathers, and of honoring and obeying their fathers. If sons or daughters erred so that they brought contempt, loss of face, defeat, or ridicule upon the father he was in the position to declare sons and daughters honorless and worthy of contempt. Sons might achieve shame on account of their own folly, by cowardice, and failure to respond appropriately to their fathers. They might also become unproductive members of the household through their own foolishness and cause the fathers great humiliation before their peers (Luke 15:11–32). Sons must also give proof of their courage and their ability to defend the honor of the family—to demonstrate that they are worthy of the family's name. When they are older, they must show the capacity to lead their familial group with the same sagacity and reputation of their father (Di Bella 1992, 153). This left them in a delicate position "for they are constantly pressed into intrepid actions by other members of the family who urge them to add to their collective reputation by a gesture of panache or a demonstration of generous intelligence and fine judgement" (Di Bella 1992, 154). This rise in expectation could incite them to transcend the deeds of their ancestors and risk making mistakes damaging the honor of their families.

In the case of Mark's story, the paralytic might have become a source of dishonor to his father. Perhaps, on account of his paralysis, either through accident or birth, he had become an unproductive member of the family unit. His infirmity had rendered him useless to the family system. Ideal ancient households were both producing and consuming units. Members of a household worked together in some trade or craft for purposes of generating income (Osiek and Balch 1997). Unproductive sons and daughters were a strain upon family resources and therefore a potential source of shame to the family. Had his father on account of his paralysis shoved him out of the domicile or had the son voluntarily withdrawn knowing that his infirmity was a source of shame to his father?

Honor also resided in holding certain public offices, performing fixed roles, and achieving publicly recognized statuses. So, for example, kings, high priests, rabbis, scribes, governors, and other imperial and civic officials enjoyed high honor. The scribes mentioned in Mark's story would have been esteemed members of their communities. Their valuations and words would have held considerable clout. Keenly aware of this status, they would have protected it with great vigor. While among the aristocrats the hierarchical ranking of honor was clearly known it was not so the case among peasants and artisans where significant debate and controversy took place over issues of honor. It was therefore not uncommon to squabble about seating arrangements at banquets (Luke 14:7–11; Jas 2:1–3; Plutarch, *Quaes. conv.* 3). Honor also had a strong material orientation measured by one's possessions and ostentatious display of them. The consumption of wealth and not its accumulation or amount symbolized honor (Jas 2:1–3). Fine apparel, banquets, villas, and other precious gifts in their public display and benefaction denoted a person of substantial honor.

While honor was to be protected shame was equally to be avoided. As much as honor played itself out in the social context, so also did shame. Shame was basically the reverse of honor wherein one lost respect, status, and reputation because of contempt, defeat, and ridicule. Shame, however, functioned as form of social control because a person with a sense of shame would have been acutely aware of the opinions of others and fearful of public disapproval or condemnation.[4] The court of public opinion counted and served to maintain a certain level of performance commensurate with a group's norms. Shameless persons, in contrast, did not care about what others thought of them and, therefore, would engage in behavior not in accord with the codes of expected behavior. Shame had a decidedly negative meaning when it referred to a tarnished reputation. Synonyms of shame in a negative sense would be loss of face, disgrace, and humiliation; a person who was shamed would be scorned, despised, reviled, rebuked, insulted, and the like (Malina 1993, 59). Shame essentially related to an unfavorable public reputation and the indignation that it aroused in the one shamed.

MODEL OF PATRON-CLIENT RELATIONS

I mentioned earlier in the essay that the father of the household was its manager as well as its patron. Sons were recipients of his benefactions that in turn obligated them to give honor to the father. Patronage was understood as a social relationship between persons of unequal status, father-son, God-humans, lord-vassal, priest-laity.[5] In the words of Elliott, "The institution involves issues of unequal power

---

4. "From the perspective of community life, shame's most significant attribute is its role in promoting socially desirable or, at least, acceptable modes of behaviour and general qualities of being" (Swartz 1988, 21)

5. Status is the main instrument "whereby culture is distributed among actors and across situations . . . and refers to a set of shared understandings that categorize actors and indicate their appropriate behaviour, qualities, contexts, and situations" (Swartz 1988, 22).

relations, pyramids of power, power brokers, protection, privilege, prestige, payoffs and tradeoffs, influence, *juice, clout, connections, Beziehungen, reccomendazioni*, networks, reciprocal grants and obligations, values associated with friendship, loyalty, and generosity, and the various strands that link this institution to the social system at large" (Elliott 1996, 148; Eisenstadt 1984). The structure had several typical features: (1) *asymmetrical relations* between persons of unequal status; (2) *interpersonal obligation*, with a focus on loyalty; (3) *favoritism*, giving preferential treatment to those closest to you; (4) *reciprocity*—the exchange of goods and services that burdened the client with debt and obligation to the patron; (5) *kinship glaze*—this reduced the crassness of the relationship; (6) *honor*. These characteristics determined the human patron-client relationship but also of divine patrons and mortal clients (Neyrey 2007, 273–74; Elliot 1996; Saller 1982).

The patron-client relationship worked itself out in the realm of mortals between superiors who had something to give and their clients who desired to receive it and in the realm of the deities who had something to give and their human clients who desired to receive their material benefaction. The portrayal of Jesus as benefactor in Mark is modeled on the generally positive Greek and Roman image of the emperor as ideal patron. Both Greeks and Romans shared a general model of what the ideal benefactor-beneficiary relationship should be (Stevenson 1992, 423). This was based on an understanding of how citizens related to the Roman emperor as the ideal benefactor. The model arose as the outcome of strong responses to power, or of reactions to the elevation of prominent individuals above their peers (Stevenson 1992, 423). The act of raising distinguished persons to new heights was justified in a number of ways: "by force as its own justification, by divine right, by right of law, or by the moral superiority of the person concerned" (Stevenson 1992, 423). Personal preeminence was most often justified on the basis of the moral superiority of the individual in terms of either *pietas* or *fides*. Moreover, the power of a potential benefactor was framed in the role of being a guardian or broker, namely, in terms of the power to give, sustain, and protect life (Stevenson 1992, 424). Indeed, this power could be extended to parents, rulers, the state, and to charismatic figures. Mark's Jesus was a distinguished teacher and healer, was raised to extraordinary heights by God, and was a broker with the power to dispense the good gifts from God's world to his human patrons. He did so without an expectation of the mutual exchange of goods, services, or obligations.

The ideal model of the benefactor-beneficiary relationship stood at odds with real-world relationships that were exploitative and self-interested. The ideal model promoted selflessness even when powers were extended to give and sustain life. There was no expectation of reciprocity as was the case in real-world asymmetrical relationships of this type. In this relationship, the ideal beneficiary was willing to commit totally to the cause of the ideal benefactor. Of course in the agonistic give-and-take of conferring or showing honor, the ideal and real worlds did not coincide. Yet, even when they did not coincide, the ideal model was of value during times when mortals were elevated above their peers either on account of public acclamation, on account of personal claims to greatness, or during times of great upheaval and social distress (Stevenson 1992, 436).

Mark considered Jesus to be more than merely a mortal. He had been elevated to a broker of God's riches in a position to be of great benefit to humans. He was presented as a person trusted by both patron and client. As son of God he had direct access to God's world from whose beneficence he was able to draw and dispense to humans for their benefit. He thus had a foot in both the world of mortals and God, so that he appreciated the interests of both parties and strove to bridge them effectively (Neyrey 2005, 476). He was in the position to bestow such potential benefactions as food and drink, righteousness and justice, deliverance from enemies, demon-riddance through exorcisms, and health and healing. As broker of God's wealth, he offered to release the paralytic from the affliction that held him prisoner, to liberate him from the shame of his affliction, and to reinstate his lost honor by sending him back to the house of his father.

A READING OF MARK 2:1–12

It is clear from the way that Mark begins the story of the healing of the paralytic that Jesus' reputation had skyrocketed. The gossip network had been busy circulating information of the success of this powerful and effective healer (Rohrbaugh 2007, 145). Consequently, upon return to his home in Capernaum, news quickly spread of Jesus' arrival; people gathered and crowded about the house to such an extent that the door to the house was blocked. Jesus was preaching the word to them (2:2). The stage was set for the arrival of the four bearing a paralytic (2:3).

Unable to get the paralytic close to Jesus because of the crowds, they dug out the roof above Jesus and lowered the paralytic down to him (2:4). Upon seeing the extraordinary effort that the four had expended to get the paralytic close to him, Jesus commended their faith (τὴν πίστιν αὐτῶν—2:5). The plural, "their faith," causes some to suggest that it was the faith of the five that was the focus (Gould 1975, 36). But it was not the faith of the paralytic that was the focus of Jesus' commendation but the faith of the four bearers of his bed (Malina and Rohrbaugh 2003, 153). What to make of the word "faith" has led to a number of different contemporary amplifications and translations:

Impressed by their bold belief, Jesus said to the paraplegic, "Son, I forgive your sins."

Message (1993)

When Jesus saw how much faith they had, he said to the crippled man, "My friend, your sins are forgiven."

CEV (1991)

And when Jesus saw their faith [their confidence in God through Him], He said to the paralyzed man, Son, your sins are forgiven [you] and put away [that is, the penalty is remitted, the sense of guilt removed, and you are made upright and in right standing with God].

AMP (1954)

And when Jesus had seen the faith of them, he said to the sick man in palsy [Soothly

when Jesus saw the faith of them, he saith to the sick man in palsy], Son, thy sins
be forgiven to thee.

WYC (2001)

Some define faith "Christologically as being paradigmatic for true faith in the
proclamation about Jesus," others limit faith to the confident trust of the four in
Jesus' healing power, and still others to faith as a trust that was exemplified by intentional effort to gain the help of Jesus (Guelich 1989, 85). While there is very little
doubt that their extraordinary efforts displayed trust in this healer to bring about a
change in the condition of the paralytic, the commendation had more to do with
the loyalty that they exhibited to someone who obviously required their help and the
great lengths to which they had gone to make certain that he received it. Jesus praised
them for the devoted support they had given to the paralytic. They had gone beyond
the second mile and were commended for doing so.

The extravagant compassion of the paralytic's four bearers sets the stage for the
showdown that was about to take place between Jesus and the detractors in the
crowd. Jesus instigated the showdown with the words, "Son, your sins are forgiven"
(2:5). Startling words, in some ways irrelevant words, but words that were certain to
inspire a reaction from those sitting nearby. Sitting off to the side were some scribes
dissecting his every word. The shocking declaration to the paralytic that his sins had
been forgiven did not pass by them unnoticed. The social dynamic began with a
challenge—the offer of forgiveness—which was understood by the scribes as Jesus
entering their social space with a challenge to which they must respond. In their
hearts they thought out carefully this declaration and then concluded that not only
had Jesus had uttered blasphemy before God but also called into question their status
as figures of authority on religious matters. They were of the opinion that it was in
the purview of God only to forgive sins and in the purview of scribes to adjudicate
on religious matters—but not only that, without an appropriate response they stood
to be shamed before the crowd. Yet here this teacher arrogantly assumed that he was
in the position to offer this man forgiveness of sins—he usurped an authority that
was God's and the scribe's prerogative only. On an issue as integral to the religious
sensibilities of the scribes as this one, one can imagine a quiet but heated conferral
taking place. The heated whispering would not have escaped the notice of the crowd
or Jesus. The stakes were high.

As we pointed out, challenge and riposte were a game of wits—of trading questions, insults, and witty comebacks. A pointed question or negative response to an
issue must not be ignored. Every honor challenge must be met by a greater challenge
in a game of one-upsmanship. On this social occasion, Jesus and the scribes were
given the opportunity to enhance their respective honor standings at the expense of
the other. Thus, for either Jesus or the scribes to run from this challenge was out of
the question because they would have experienced the ultimate loss of face before a
public audience scrutinizing their every word. The pressing crowd, no doubt, had
heard the animated exchanges of thought taking place among the scribes and were
waiting for some verbal repartee to begin. True to form, Jesus, immediately perceiv-
ing the scribes' question and negative evaluation of him, countered with a preemptive

question designed to gain a strategic advantage in the impending verbal duel, "Why do you thus question in your hearts?" (2:8). With this question, he exposed them to the same public scrutiny under which he found himself. They could not hide their real thoughts behind the inner dispositions of secret thoughts, criticisms, and hushed deliberations. The question exposed them to public evaluation and forced them to defend and protect their honor or else face the public scorn that would inevitably ensue. As men of honor, they had a finely tuned sense of shame. They were sensitive to their honor standing in the community and were keenly aware of when that honor standing was being challenged.

Indeed, Mark's Jesus quickly upped the verbal stakes with another question, "Which is easier to say, 'Your sins are forgiven,' or to say, 'Rise, take up your pallet and walk?'" (2:9). The challenge had been put to them in no uncertain terms. The cleverly worded question, however, put them on the defensive and rendered them mute. Limited in their thinking, they were at a loss about how to respond to the logic of the question. The word of healing would have been verified through observation whereas the word of forgiveness would not have been empirically verifiable—so which one was easier to expedite? In their minds, the logic of the question was that because the word of healing could potentially fail publicly, it would have been harder for Jesus to pull off, and that because the word of forgiveness could not be publicly verified, it would have been easier for Jesus to claim success. The crux for them was, were he to succeed in the harder word, their reputation would plummet and Jesus' rise and were he to persist in his offer of forgiveness, their accusation of blasphemy would stand and Jesus' reputation would plummet and theirs' rise. So, there they sat mute pondering the right response. Jesus deliberately played into their hands while all along, however, he was redefining what counted for sin and what counted for true forgiveness. In a word, granting forgiveness was as hard or harder as bringing about a successful healing. Moreover, forgiveness and healing were integral to the other; the paralytic was to be released from the paralysis that rendered him an outcast in society, and, to make the release publicly verifiable, he was instructed to stand up and go home—he had been released from the social stigma of his affliction.

Deliberately applying verbal pressure in successive and irreversible stages, Jesus said, "'but that you may know that the Son of Man has authority on earth to forgive sins'—he said to the paralytic—'I say to you, rise, take up your pallet and go home'" (2:9–11).[6] Jesus claimed the right to forgive sins, which in the case of the paralytic was publicly and wrongly perceived to be at the root of his paralysis. Jesus as God's

---

6. The Son of Man (ὁ υἱὸς τοῦ ἀνθρώπου) designation in 2:10 has three major interpretations: (1) an Aramaic expression for humanity in general; (2) an Aramaic circumlocution for "I"; (3) a Christological title, "the Son of man" (Guelich 1989, 89). I take the "Son of Man" to function as a circumlocution for "I." Essentially, it justified the claim of Jesus that he had the right to forgive sins as did any other human. Verse 10 also constitutes a well-known interpretive crux. There is an awkward transition of addressee—from the scribes to the paralytic—commonly resolved by treating verses 5b–10 as an interpolation. Verse 11 would originally have followed 5a: "And when Jesus saw their faith he said to the paralytic, 'I say to you, Arise, take up your mattress and go home.'" The solution, however, is unwarranted for, in the give-and-take of heated honor challenges, such statements functioned strategically to throw the challengers off-balance.

broker offered to the paralytic a forgiveness that entailed release from his affliction and the social stigma attached to it. This offer of liberation from the burdensome and oppressive paralysis of his limbs, however, was misinterpreted by the religious authorities. They understood Jesus to be taking it upon himself to offer the man forgiveness for some offense that he had committed before God that he was not in the position to pardon. Jesus, however, was not claiming power to forgive sins—rather, acting as a go-between for God, he was offering the man release from his immobility, offering him reinstatement of status lost because of his ailment, and offering him renewed access to his domestic space—"son, you are released from the bondage of your paralysis and free to go home."

In the case of the paralytic, his body of dishonor appeared to have triggered a shameful episode in his father's house that had either led to his expulsion or to his voluntary withdrawal from it. Thus, Jesus instructed the paralytic to go home and, in the process, he reinforced the ethos of mutual forgiveness enjoined by ancient moralists. Jesus thereby supported the process that would have permitted the son to gain full access to his domestic space so that he might once more assume his position of honor in the family system. All in all, the result of this verbal contest led to exclamations of amazement from the crowds. Never had they seen such a thing.

CONCLUSION

Cross-cultural reading of the Bible is not a matter of choice (Rohrbaugh 1996, 1). The meanings that the writer of Mark exchanged with his contemporary audience were rooted in the social systems that enveloped them. As I have argued, the notions of forgiveness and sin were embedded in these social systems, and, unless modern exegetes engage that social context, meaning will become lost in translation. In particular, the ubiquitous Mediterranean values of honor and shame and the institution of patron-client relations were at the heart of the paralytic's world. Mark is at pains to present Jesus as patron and benefactor, a broker of the benefices of God's world, to his earthly clients. Moreover, the paralytic's bodily condition had bankrupted his honorable status in the home of his father and left him a shamed man. The social stigma of his illness, perhaps perceived by his kin and home villagers as the result of sinning against God, required redressing. In his encounter with Jesus, he was released from the stigma of his illness and the erroneous public perception that sin was at the root of it, commanded to stand up and go home—"Son, you are released from the bondage of your paralysis and free to go home." These words were symbolic of an extraordinary reversal of his status that permitted his return to the *familia*.

THE DEGRADED POOR AND THE GREEDY RICH: EXPLORING THE LANGUAGE OF POVERTY AND WEALTH IN JAMES

Alicia Batten

Many people today disagree about what should be done concerning the gap between rich and poor both within and between countries, but no one can deny that such a rift exists, or that it is not expanding. In the Pacific Northwest, where I live, the Northwest Environment Watch has observed that the richest families in the region saw their incomes grow on average by $38,000 between the late 1970s and the late 1990s while the middle class saw an increase of less than $3,800 and the poorest families' income actually declined (2002, 14). Despite the profits that some enjoyed from the economic boom of the 1990s, the number of people living below the poverty line expanded throughout the area. Individuals and families had continued to manage their resources as thriftily as possible, but economic forces beyond their control contributed to growing rates of bankruptcy or to worse disasters.

How to address these economic problems throughout the region and world is complex, controversial, and obviously not the focus here. As one of the purposes of this volume, however, is to highlight the central significance of social contexts when interpreting and translating ancient texts, it is important to acknowledge some aspects of the modern economic situation before attempting to understand such issues in antiquity. As historians and biblical scholars have duly observed (Holman 2001, 6–12; Friesen 2004, 324–37), analysis of ancient economic social relations is influenced by the ideological orientation of the interpretive community, whether that be Marxist, capitalist, or other views, and thus, at minimum, recognizing the tremendously powerful role of the market-driven economy in the current day is important. Moreover, some discussion of the objectification of the economy is requisite because although the ancient world had an economy, it did not perceive it as an independent phenomenon that one could observe and analyze using numerical formulae.

Therefore, after briefly noting some aspects of the development of the contemporary and primarily Western approaches to economics, this essay will turn to those of the first-century Mediterranean basin to examine some of the views people held toward the distribution of resources and economic practices. The essay will not provide a structural macroeconomic perspective, but focus on attitudes and mores. It is important that we try to understand what ancient peoples' perceptions were before attempting to interpret the texts that they produced.

The text in question here is the letter of James, a correspondence that bears sharp words for the rich and considerable concern for the poor. Much labor has gone into studying James's ideas about poverty and wealth (Maynard-Reid 1987), but less energy has been spent upon elaborating what the terms *rich* (πλούσιος) and *poor* (πτωχός), both of which appear in James, mean within the author's general social context. This essay thus centers on these meanings and will argue that when we encounter these terms in James, they certainly include what we think of as an economic dimension, but that they also reflect moral and social characteristics.[1]

THE RISE OF ECONOMICS

The perception of an economy as separate from other facets of life, and as the subject of the social science of economics, is a relatively recent development that did not occur naturally but in relation to specific social, cultural, and religious changes. It is not the task here to trace this history, but to identify a few aspects of it that will enable us to see that the concept of economics has clearly shifted over time.

The eighteenth-century Scottish philosopher Adam Smith is sometimes credited as the founder of modern economics,[2] and it goes without saying that his ideas of free trade and *laissez-faire* have played central roles within the development of modern capitalism.[3] Smith's ideas emerged within the particular context of a post-Reformation and industrializing British Empire, and some significant developments had occurred prior to his lifetime that made the emergence of his ideas possible. For example, the Reformation had raised everyday life—a life of marriage, family, and work—to the level of religious vocation in the sense that such ordinary living was understood to be no less Christian or holy than that of a religious life.[4] This "sanctification of ordinary life," as Charles Taylor puts it, is part of the background of the growing place of the economic as a focus in people's lives (Taylor 2004, 74). Moreover, leaders in seventeenth-century Europe had observed that more production and profitable trade strengthened individual states, which, in turn, forced other countries to follow suit. A flourishing economy was understood to contribute to political power, and in fact the person attributed with first using the term *political economy*, de Montchrétien (1615), developed a theory of the state that serves the interests of the economy and not vice versa (Taylor 2004, 72).

---

1. Indeed, references to poverty and wealth throughout the Bible and the ancient world generally encompass not only economic characteristics, but those of a social and political nature. This is why, states Hoppe, the "biblical response to poverty is not merely charity but justice" (2004, 15). Edgar Hutchinson does explain that in James the πτωχός is a person of devalued social status (2001, 106–7).

2. Dalton makes the comment, however, that "[w]ith Adam Smith, political economy ended; with David Ricardo, economics began" (1965, 9).

3. Smith thought that the "invisible hand" operating in a freer market would translate self-interest into public good. For Smith, the greed of the wealthy would be kept in check by their desire to manifest local civic pride and serve the common good (Whybrow 2005, 252).

4. In addition, a life of industry and family was understood to be an even better way to be Christian because it was not "based on the vain and prideful claim to have found a higher way" (Taylor 2004, 74).

During Smith's day, *political economy* was the term used for the world of markets, and thinkers such as Smith thought that despite the fact that people would promote their own self-interests first, "[I]t is the great multiplication of the productions of all the different arts, in consequence of their division of labour, which occasions, in a well-governed society, that universal opulence which extends itself to the lower ranks of the people" (Adam Smith 1776, 12). A century after *The Wealth of Nations* was published, however, *political economy* had shed *political* and the notion of *economics* emerged, the name change effectively cleansing "the discipline of its original involvement with 'politics'—that is, with moral philosophy and social theory—and [restricting] it to the positive description of market behaviors alone" (Bigelow 2003, 3). In Britain, a motivating factor in the development of economics as a social science was the nineteenth-century romantic critique of political economy as beneath those activities that embodied the search for truth, such as poetry, philosophy, and religion. Economic activity was viewed as separate from and lesser than culture and, as such, it retreated "into the laboratory" to be studied as a science that operated according to its own mathematical laws (Bigelow 2003, 3). In reality, however, it never was isolated from social, political, and religious influences, and Gordon Bigelow shows how particular economic policies and attitudes, such as the Poor Law Amendment of 1834 that dismantled the system of care for the poor and aged in parishes throughout Britain, as well as the Irish potato famine, among other catastrophes, were influenced by Protestant evangelical thinking that poverty and suffering would provoke the consciences of sinful people. As Bigelow puts it, some of these evangelicals thought that "poor people were poor for a reason, and helping them out of poverty would endanger their mortal souls" (2005, 35).[5] Thus, for Bigelow, examination of the history of economics illustrates that "what is entirely missing from the economic view of modern life is an understanding of the social world" (2005, 33).

THE ECONOMY IN ANTIQUITY

The ancient world does not exhibit consciousness of economics in the same way that the modern world does, even though an economy certainly existed. The pioneering work of Karl Polanyi (1944; 1957)[6] has argued that the economy was "embedded" throughout the ancient world, meaning that it was subordinate to and a by-product of other social institutions such as those of kinship, religion, and politics. Moses Finley's influential book on the ancient economy, first published in 1973,[7] did not adopt the language of "embedded economy" but did stress, like Polanyi, that the ancient economy could not be understood as separate from social relations and that the application of contemporary market analysis to such an economy would be anachronistic (1985, 26). Polanyi's emphasis upon the importance of distinguish-

---

5. Bigelow (2005, 36) also comments that "looking back two centuries at these early debates, it is clear that a pure free-market ideology can be logically sustained only if it is based in a fiery religious conviction. The contradictions involved are otherwise simply too powerful."

6. On Polanyi's contributions to the history of economics, as well as the criticisms of and opposition to his views, see the very informative essay by Humphreys (1969).

7. The second edition was produced in 1985 and an expanded one in 1999.

ing between embedded and disembedded has been adopted by many, including by those who study biblical literature (Malina 1986; Oakman 1991a, b). The issue of how to describe the ancient economy, however, remains far from resolved, with some scholars contending that the terms *embedded* and *disembedded* are not useful. For example, Scott Meikle argues that a better distinction between contemporary market societies and non-market societies of the past is that today's economy focuses on exchange value whereby the strongest controls are those that arise from "the social system of exchange value in itself rather than from natural causes," versus the ancient economy's emphasis upon use value in which the constraints are "natural necessities and social mores" (2002, 246). Meikle does not reject outright the application of modern economic theory to aspects of "primitive" economic life, for there were some forms of exchange value. But he cautions that things such as inflation, for example, did not play the central role that it does in economies today, that "the institutions and relations of exchange value were peripheral to ancient society, not central and dominating, as they have become in modernity" (2002, 247).

The questions of how interconnected and sophisticated markets were in the Greco-Roman world will probably remain unresolved for some time,[8] as will the issue of whether and, if so, to what extent, there was significant "growth" in productivity.[9] It is fair to say, however, that in no way did the economy figure so centrally in the lives of people as it does for so many today, nor was the economy understood to function completely autonomously according to its own set of intricate principles. And although ancient writers reflected considerably on household management (οἰκονομία), nothing equivalent to the modern social science of economics existed.

Limited Good

Another significant conceptual difference between antiquity and modern Western societies is that ancient texts evidence a notion of limited good, a concept first articulated in anthropology by George M. Foster (1965, 1972). People who live in limited-good societies (1) perceive their environment to be closed; (2) understand that all goods are finite and usually insufficient; (3) think that one person's gain is another's loss; and (4) try to avoid being the loser by opting "for a shared-poverty equilibrium" that maintains the status quo (Foster 1972b, 58). In such societies, which tend to be pre-industrial, peoples' perception that they have a right to subsistence then becomes "an active moral principle" (Malina 1978, 168) that shapes behavior such that the

---

8. In his study of the role of *amicitia* and patronage in Roman economics, Verboven (2001, 349) argues that the Roman economy was, to some extent, a market economy. He concludes that "[w]e should beware of concluding that the Roman economy was at heart a non-market economy. Although conceptually reciprocity and market exchange may be opposed they not only coexist in reality but interact continuously. While the market economy profoundly influenced the operation of reciprocity relations and networks, the latter in turn influenced the market system."

9. On the issues of the integration of markets and growth in the Greco-Roman world, see Saller (2002).

aim of life is not to accumulate riches, but to survive.[10] Moreover, if one family unit within the community is wealthier than others, that family is under pressure to provide more for the group. As James C. Scott explains in his study of modern "moral economies," "[R]ich peasants [are] expected to be charitable, to sponsor more lavish celebrations, to help out temporarily indigent kin and neighbors, [and] to give generously . . ." (1976, 5).

Jerome H. Neyrey and Richard L. Rohrbaugh have provided numerous examples from first-century Greek texts as evidence that inhabitants of the Greco-Roman world shared this perception of limited good (2001, 468–76), and they also show that consistent with the limited-good model, envy is often the result of some person or persons in the community acquiring more, whether it is money, land, or intangible things such as honor (2001, 476–81).[11] Christopher Gill comes to a similar conclusion, indicating that where "goods are conceived as both finite and as (at best) only partly dependent on the agent herself, this is a situation that naturally gives rise to competitive rivalry and emotions such as envy and spite" (2003, 32). Envy (φθόνος) was a vice within the ancient world, with numerous Greek authors devoting considerable attention to it (see Konstan and Rutter 2003; Konstan 2006). Aristotle says envy is a pain one feels when an equal possesses or acquires things that one does not have (*Rhet.* 2.9.3). Neyrey and Rohrbaugh point out that, centuries later, Cicero echoes this view (*Tusc.* 4.8.17), as does Plutarch (*Curios.* 6C). Another example they cite is from Fronto's letter to Marcus Aurelius, when Fronto tells the emperor to destroy the mutual envy among his friends so that when the emperor does something for one of them, the others will not think that they have lost something (2001, 471).[12] But perhaps Dio Chrysostom's discourse, Περὶ φθόνου, presents even clearer evidence for the connection between limited good and envy when he says that persons are envious (φθονερούς) toward one another when someone of the same occupation moves to the town or village (*Or.* 77/78 3). Clearly there is only so much business to be had in town, and thus, if a second sandal-maker moves in, the sandals might start to fly.

THE ECONOMY, MORALITY, AND STATUS

For many ancient writers, economic activities, including practices which many moderns might consider benign or natural, were not disconnected from philosophical questions. Some authors reveal ambivalence if not disapproval for commercial ventures and clear distaste for those who seek wealth excessively as a good in and of itself. Aristotle rejects wealth-getting through exchange and charging interest because it does not serve a higher aim, other than to increase money and acquire commercial goods. This manner of seeking wealth is unnatural; its end is only to acquire more riches—an end which has no limit (*Pol.* 1.3.17). The gain of wealth through agriculture for the purpose of maintaining the household, however, is natural, for food

10. As Malina states, "[A]ny apparent relative improvement in someone's position with respect to any good in life is viewed as a threat to the entire community" (1981, 75–76).
11. Foster had detailed this phenomenon of envy as a common result in limited-good societies in an article from the early 1970s (1972a).
12. *Correspondence of Marcus Cornelius Fronto* 4.1.

nourishes people (*Pol.* 1.3.21–35). Moreover, householding is trade-less, and its aim is to support an ordered household that is self-sufficient and limited. Such self-sufficiency is necessary for a good life and not a life that constantly seeks more gain.[13] This stress on self-sufficiency is maintained by later philosophers, notably Philodemus of Gadara. For him, moderate wealth is important, but problematic is a person who is preoccupied with seeking more wealth and not engaging in philosophy (Balch 2004, 184).[14] Like most Epicureans, however, Philodemus scorns the poverty (πτωχεία) of people such as the Cynics, who lived as mendicants (Balch 2004, 184). Living in poverty is just as problematic as an obsession with wealth, for one can be as equally distracted by the struggle for survival as by the scramble for more possessions.

Notions of poverty and wealth were also connected to status and morality. Perhaps de Ste. Croix sums up the situation best when he states:

> The Greeks, from archaic times through the Classical and Hellenistic periods and on into the Roman age, habitually expressed political complexion and social status in a fascinating vocabulary which is an inextricable mixture of socio-economic and moral terminology, with two sets of terms applied more or less indiscriminately to the propertied and the non-propertied classes . . . we have not only words which mean property-owning, rich, fortunate, distinguished, well-born, influential, but also, as alternatives for virtually the same set of people, words having a basically moral connotation and meaning, literally the good, the best, the upright, the fair-minded. . . . And on the other hand, we find applied to the lower classes, the poor, who are also the Many, the mob, the populace, words with an inescapably moral quality, meaning essentially bad. (1983, 425–26)

There are some examples of poor people portrayed as moral and virtuous (Dover 1974, 110), but generally, as de Ste. Croix indicates, the poor are associated with negative characteristics, and, indeed, Origen says that they have bad characters (*Cels.* 6.16).[15] The two words that refer to a poor person, πένης and πτωχός, often reflect a distinction between a πένης as someone with minimal resources, or member of the "working poor," and a πτωχός as an absolute poor person, or mendicant (Holman 2001, 5). The working poor had to toil with their hands and hire themselves out as laborers for others, all activities associated with dishonor and disgust by aristocratic standards (Stambaugh and Balch 1986, 66). The rich, on the other hand, are positively regarded in many literary sources (which generally represent the interests of the elites) provided they do not seek wealth to excess or love it too much[16] and that

---

13. Booth thinks that this rejection of "the market" in favor of household economics may well reflect classical philosophers' fear "for material sustenance . . . arising from the absence of material self-sufficiency, and from the vulnerability of market-provided food supplies, but more than that a fear of the denial of the possibility of the good life" (1994, 216).

14. For the Greek text and English translation of Philodemus's fragmentary "On Wealth," see Balch (2004, 177–96).

15. Cited by de Ste. Croix (1983, 425).

16. Plutarch devotes an essay, Περὶ Φιλοπλουτίας, to criticizing those who love wealth, although he lived quite comfortably himself.

they are generous toward others—generosity being a central virtue in the ancient world.[17]

Moreover, some authors understand πένης to refer to those who are consistently poor—they are born poor and will die that way—while a πτωχός is a person who has been lowered in status. He or she perhaps had wealth but lost it, as well as the honor that was inextricably bound up with it. Susan R. Holman points out that Origen, for example, holds this view, as do the Cappadocians (2001, 6).[18] Bruce J. Malina particularly emphasizes that the poor must be understood as those who "cannot maintain their inherited status" (1986, 356), and Paul Hollenbach supports this focus on status, but he thinks, as I do, that there is also sometimes an economic dimension "that should be retained" (1987, 57).[19] Being poor in the ancient world often involved a loss of status, which may not primarily be an economic loss, but a loss of honor or family. But it also usually had an economic dimension that forced one to survive through manual labor or, worse, begging.

People also took out loans in order to survive, and many affluent Greeks and Romans regularly charged interest on these loans although discussing money-lending was considered vulgar by the educated and elite classes (Holman 2001, 115–16). The granting of loans was at the discretion of the wealthy, and, according to Holman even those who received loans viewed such arrangements as part of "quasi-legal system of extortion" (2001, 118). The non-elites likely perceived their experience in becoming indebted to others as an injustice (Holman 2001, 118), especially if they had to repay the loan through forced labor or their family's forced labor (Finley 1985, 40). During urgent situations such as drought or war, there was no guarantee of the provision of grain, and outside of Athens and Rome there was little regulation of trade and merchant activity. These features of the ancient economy made many poor people dependent upon acts of *euergetism* or benefaction by the elites, especially at crisis moments (Garnsey 1988, 272). Although there were gradations of economic and social status in the first century, there was no middle class, most people were poor, and the elites were small in number, thus concentrating property ownership and other resources in the hands of the few (Friesen 2004, 337–47). Local economies were further undermined when emperors and aristocrats expropriated natural resources, such as land, that had previously been the lifeblood of the community (Garnsey 1988, 276). Thus, we see why often those who sought wealth were considered to be greedy, even by well-off writers such as Plutarch, who says that the greed (πλεονεξία) for more never stops from acquiring more (*Cupid. divit.* 523E). In a limited-good society, if one gained more and more without giving to others, one would be perceived as avaricious. Although self-sufficiency was frequently advocated, hoarding and lack of generosity were not admired, thus leading some to think of the rich as "demented, vicious [and] evil" (Malina 1986, 363).

---

17. Cicero (Off. 2.52–64) says wealth is justified because then one is able to be generous toward others.

18. See Origen, *Fr. Ps.* 11.6.

19. In Pauline studies, Friesen (2004) attempts to return to an economic, or resource-based, analysis of the Pauline groups, while Oakes (2004), in his response to Friesen, grants the importance of economics but also wants to include sociological analysis, which attention to status would entail.

THE LETTER OF JAMES

In light of the above discussion, I propose that the references to the poor in James should be translated as "degraded poor" or something equivalent, for such a translation not only retains the aspect of economic marginality, but also points to the loss—of honor, of status—that was part of what it meant to be a πτωχός especially.[20] The letter, as we shall see, explicitly refers to this loss. Moreover, awareness of the attitudes toward ancient economic practices supports the argument that when the letter refers to a rich person (ὁ πλούσιος) or "the rich" (οἱ πλούσιοι), it is including a reference to economic wealth but also a morally negative feature, namely greediness. Therefore, *degraded poor* and *greedy rich* would provide a better sense of the social and moral meanings that the author had in mind. The terms would not automatically occur to a modern reader given the shifts in the understandings of the economy described earlier.

JAMES 1:9–11

James 1:9–11 is the first example of James's engagement with the themes of rich and poor. Here πτωχός does not appear, although ὁ πλούσιος refers to the rich man twice. The author employs ὁ ἀδελφὸς ὁ ταπεινός (1:9), often translated as "the lowly brother" or the "humble brother," for the poor man and exhorts him to boast in his exaltation while the rich one (ὁ πλούσιος) is exhorted to boast in his lowliness (ἐν τῇ ταπεινώσει αὐτοῦ) (1:10), indicating a complete reversal between the lowly and the rich. I concur with most scholars (Hartin 2003, 61–62) in understanding ὁ ἀδελφὸς ὁ ταπεινός to include the notion that the lowly person is materially poor, for he is contrasted so explicitly with a rich person. The pericope subsequently focuses upon the demise of the rich person, invoking the prophetic language of LXX Isa 40:6–8 to describe how the wealthy man will fade away in the midst of his activities (πορείας). The rich person is given no second chance—no chance to repent and share—but simply declared to be doomed to destruction. The latter point is the reason some scholars think it likely that James does not imagine this representative of affluence to be part of his audience.[21]

Rather than the issue of inclusion or exclusion, the interest here is simply in the depictions of the rich and poor and how they can be understood within the general social context. First, the letter uses the word ταπεινός to describe the poor person. As interpreters agree, this word is polyvalent (Johnson 1995, 184–85), but a key feature of it is the notion of being low, especially of low status (Grundmann 1972, 2–3). James uses this word again in 4:6 when he cites LXX Prov 3:34, a text that reverses the proud and the humble. Ταπεινός can certainly include the notion of material pov-

---

20. James never uses πένης; in fact, this word only appears once in the Second Testament (in 2 Cor 9:9, where it is part of a citation of LXX Ps 111) while there are thirty-four instances of πτωχός, with four of them in James (twenty-four times in the Gospels, twice in Revelation, and four times in the undisputed Paulines).

21. Laws (1980, 63), for example, takes this view. Hartin (2003, 69) thinks that ἀδελφός should be supplied in verse 10, concluding that the rich are within the audience and will "boast in the humiliation that has brought them into a relationship with God and the community."

erty, but the idea that this is a person of low social status is central. Moreover, given that the rich person is called to boast ἐν τῇ ταπεινώσει αὐτου, we have here not only the notion that the wealth of the man will disappear, but that he will be socially disgraced as well. He will suffer the public humiliation that such debasement entails. This reversal would also preserve the balance of status and honor available in a society in which everything was understood to be in limited supply.

Second, verse 11 states that the rich man will fade away ἐν ταῖς πορείαις αὐτοῦ. Πορεία literally means a journey, passage, or way (Luke 13:22) but in some contexts can refer to a way of life, conduct, or activities (see LXX Prov 2:7). Many commentators have argued for a literal meaning, thus connecting the verse to the business trips of the merchants in Jas 4:13 (Mayor 1892, 44). Hort, in particular, makes the point that "the rich man perishes while he is still *on the move*, before he has attained the state of restful enjoyment which is always expected and never arrives" (1909, 18). Such a reading maintains the parallel with the grass, which is in the midst of flowering when it perishes. Other interpreters prefer to understand πορεία in the figurative sense as a means of living (Hartin 2003, 63), but this would lose the "prematurity" (Hort 1909, 18) that parallels that of the grass. I lean toward the literal interpretation and think it likely that there is a deliberate link with Jas 4:13 that clearly refers to merchant ventures. If we read this verse while keeping in mind the suspicion if not hostility toward seeking wealth through market dealings outlined earlier, we see that James is consistent with this critique. It is not simply the wealth that is the problem, but how the wealth is procured. The rich man here is a greedy man, for he seeks gain for the sake of gain through his business enterprises.

James 1:9–11 does not provide tremendous detail about the poor and the rich, but it contributes initial evidence for the argument that it is not only material poverty and wealth that are at issue, but questions of status and morality. The poor are the lowly who will be raised up, while the rich, in the middle of their money-making ventures, will be humiliated and, like the grass, will fade away.

JAMES 2:1–7

This section of the letter provides more detail, for here we get a description of a wealthy person (although he is not explicitly called ὁ πλούσιος) and a corresponding image of a πτωχός (2:2). The attire of each figure is contrasted the affluent man wears gold rings and fine clothes while the beggar enters the assembly in rags. By focusing on their respective garments, James is obviously underlining the difference in material means between the two men. The author then uses the scenario to dissuade his audience from showing partiality (2:1). By giving the good seat to the man in fine clothing and ordering the destitute man around, the audience has made distinctions (2:4) and dishonored (ἀτιμάζω) the poor man (τὸν πτωχόν) (2:6). This violates the fact that God has chosen "those who are poor in the world" to be "rich in faith" and to be recipients of the kingdom promised to those who love God (2:5). The letter subsequently reminds the audience that it is the rich (οἱ πλούσιοι) who oppress (καταδυναστεύω) them, drag (ἕλκω) them into court, and blaspheme the good name invoked over them (2:6–7).

The well-dressed man does not receive any direct castigation by the author; rather, the focus is on the audience's behavior and the meaning of their display of partiality (Wachob 2000). I do not think, however, that the wealthy character is a neutral figure. This image of a man decked out in gold rings[22] and luxurious clothes may recall a stock character from satire, such as in Lucian's *Nigrinus*, in which rich men flash their rings expecting praise and bows from others (*Nigr.* 21; see Kloppenborg 1999, 765). These inappropriate displays of wealth by the affluent were understood to be distasteful, even in Rome, for they indicated that the person attached an inordinate significance to his or her riches (Berg 2002, 24–25). Some early Christian texts explicitly warn against such decoration, especially for women (1 Tim 2:9; 1 Pet 3:3). Because the letter writer imagines that the rich man would get a good seat, he must be presuming that the fellow had made his wealth obvious. James could have simply indicated that the person was rich, but he makes the effort to describe him as exhibiting *luxuria* in contrast to the pauper.

The status implications of poverty and wealth are clear in this section. As is well documented, where one sat at a dinner party or gathering was a reflection of one's status (Plutarch, *Quaes. conv.* 3). In a culture in which the values of honor and shame were paramount (Hartin 2003, 146–48), the expectation would be to give a fine seat to the wealthy person and to order the poor man around. James goes even further in describing such a scene, noting that the poor person is commanded to stand or, worse, to sit below a footrest (ὑπὸ τὸ ὑποπόδιόν) or to "sit on the floor," which "is even more humbling than being made to stand at a distance; it is a form of mockery" (Johnson 1995, 223). While the rich man is silently flattered with the offer of a comfortable chair (Plutarch, *Adul. amic.* 58B–C), the poor person receives the corresponding humiliation and dishonor with which poor people lived on a daily basis. James makes this explicitly clear in 2:6 when he accuses the audience of dishonoring the raggedy man.

Finally, the rich (οἱ πλούσιοι) face James's criticism in 2:6–8 when he uses rhetorical questions to point out how the rich treat the audience. Here James uses the verb καταδυναστεύω, a common word used by the prophets in the LXX to describe the "oppression" of the poor by the rich (Amos 4:1). They also drag people into court, the verb ἕλκω suggesting violence, as it does in other contexts such as in Acts 21:30. There is not sufficient evidence to conclude that the audience is being persecuted here; rather, James is referring to the common occurrence of rich people taking the more vulnerable to court to force payment of debts, rent, or other types of compensation. Steven J. Friesen (2005, 245) makes the point that James is underlining the injustice of a judicial system that the rich could manipulate to their own advantage. This view is supported by de Ste. Croix's discussion of the ways in which the courts catered to those of higher social status (1981, 455–65) and the number of times the Roman senate had to renew and reinforce laws prohibiting large gifts to be given to "court-*patroni* . . . in exchange for their services" to litigating parties (Verboven 2002, 76). By reminding the audience members of how the rich abuse them in these ways, the letter is again taking a swipe at the wealthy for their immorality and greed.

---

22. The word χρυσοδακτύλιος is unique to James and may be his invention.

JAMES 5:1–6

James saves his big blast for last when he rips into the rich (οἱ πλούσιοι) in 5:1–6. This section directly follows James's criticism of those who behave arrogantly in a variety of ways, including slandering and judging others (4:11–12), doing business (ἐμπορεύομαι), and making a profit (κερδαίνω) (4:13). Johnson thinks Jas 4:11–5:6 is a single unit on the topic of arrogance (1995, 292) and certainly the pattern of slandering, judging, engaging in commercial ventures, storing up treasures (5:3), exploiting workers (5:4), living in luxury (5:5), and killing the righteous one (τὸν δίκαιον) (5:6) are all actions that can connote arrogance in the ancient world. The death of the "righteous one" is likely from Jewish tradition, in which τὸν δίκαιον is a poor righteous person whom the rich put to death (LXX Wis 2:12).[23] Although the first part of the section, 4:11–17, does not focus on treatment of the poor specifically, 5:1–6 makes it clear that the vulnerable, including day laborers (5:4), are the victims of rich peoples' arrogance and greed.

If Johnson is correct that 4:11–5:6 is a unified section, it is also interesting to observe that just prior to 4:11 is a unit that conforms to an elaboration of a theme exercise in 3:13–4:10 (Batten 2000, 167–201)[24] in which the theme of envy is central (Johnson 1995, 286–89). As discussed earlier, in a limited-good society envy (φθόνος) is often the result of one or more persons gaining more and upsetting the equilibrium in the community. Φθόνος does not actually appear until 4:5, but ζῆλος, often translated as jealousy, is named in 3:14 and 3:16, where it is accompanied by ἐριθεία (bitterness), while a verbal form emerges in 4:2. Although Aristotle understood ζῆλος in the positive sense of emulation—for good people should want to possess worthy goods (Rhet. 2.11)—by the first century C.E. it had become a negative characteristic and was grouped as a vice along with envy (Viano 2003, 203–17).[25] Many ancient writers condemned this vice, which suggests that it raised its ugly head quite often. Plutarch, for example, objects to envy (φθόνος) and criticizes those who fall into emulation (ζῆλος) because such things threaten friendship (Adul. amic. 54C). James 3:13–4:10 is clearly a call to avoid envy and jealousy, both of which appear to be characteristics "of the world," and to submit to God (4:7). The audience is exhorted to be humble and assured that God gives benefits to the humble (ταπεινοῖς) but opposes (ἀντιτάσσεται) the proud (4:6). James 4:11–5:6 then picks up the opposite of being humble—that is, being proud—with various examples of such arrogance including how it can manifest itself in the exploitation of the weak in Jas 5:1–6. James 4:11–5:6 is then further connected to the prior unit by the final rhetorical question of 5:6, in which ἀντιτάσσεται appears in identical form to that

---

23. See also 1 En. 96:7–8.

24. Hartin (2003, 203–17) also understands Jas 3:13–4:10 to conform to an elaboration of a theme exercise but structures the unit somewhat differently than Batten.

25. Gill (2003, 49) argues that this shift is in part due to changes in the notion of the human good or happiness: "When human happiness is identified with 'external goods' (or a combination of 'internal' and 'external' goods), competition for these—inevitably limited—goods is assumed to be the normal human state and the correlated rivalrous emotions are regarded as, in principle, normal, though they take virtuous or defective forms. Where happiness is located solely in 'internal goods,' which are sometimes seen as universally available, competition and the rivalrous emotions are presented as necessarily misguided."

found in 4:6. For James, both envying the gains of others or seeking more benefits for oneself at the expense of other people are contrary to the way in which God wants humans to live. Such behavior manifests friendship with the world and makes one an enemy of God (4:4).

As indicated above, "the rich" (5:1) are clearly identified within the section on arrogance. Although no LXX texts are directly cited, some prophetic imagery[26] appears in 5:1–6 creating what Penner calls a "prophetic funeral dirge and mourning cry" (Penner 1996, 175) such that the demise of the rich, with their rotting clothes and rusting gold and silver, is envisioned. James 5:3 might be a recollection of the man with the gold rings in 2:2, especially if 5:3 is a reference to gold jewelry that will wear into human flesh and eat it (ἐσθίω), but it is also consistent with other texts that condemn the hoarding of wealth, such as in *1 En.* 97. In the final moments, this wealth will not save the rich; rather, its rustiness will be evidence against them (5:3). Moreover, the money that the rich have kept back by fraud from their workers will "cry out." Storing up these treasures will be no insurance against eschatological disaster.

James 5:1–6 particularly stresses the greed of the rich. Not only did they stockpile wealth and cheat their workers (5:4), they have lived in luxury and pleasure (5:5). Τρυφάω is used in a negative sense here for someone who has lived a soft life and feasted sumptuously. This image of a lounging and likely overfed rich person is probably best described by Aristophanes when he describes "wealth's people" as "fat rogues with big bellies and dropsical legs, whose toes by the gout are tormented" (*Plut.* 559, Rogers). James does not intend the humor of Aristophanes, but the references to pleasurable living coupled with image of the rich feeding (τρέφω) or fattening their hearts in preparation for the day of slaughter (Hartin 2003, 229–30) are consistent with the well-established Greek tradition of disapproval and even mockery of those who succumb to greed and become flabby. Such characteristics were also considered "unmanly," for softness "made for poor endurance on campaigns and cowardice in battle" (Dover 1974, 111). These rich have also condemned the righteous one, which recalls the dragging into courts from Jas 2:6, as the verb καταδικάζω commonly appeared in forensic contexts (Johnson 1995, 304)—and they have killed (φονεύω) him. Like the envious people who "desire and do not have" and subsequently "kill" (φονεύω) in 4:2, the greed and gains of the rich have led to the destruction of others, especially the poor.

CONCLUSION

This essay has argued that, for James, "the rich" are by definition avaricious, and the poor are dishonored and lowered. Translating πλούσιος as "greedy rich person" and πτωχός as "degraded poor person" would better reflect the moral and social connotations of these words. It would also point readers to the interrelationship between rich and poor in James. In other words, the behavior of the rich, especially their greed, is shown to have direct and negative consequences for the poor. Such consequences would be expected but not appreciated by most people within a limited-good society.

---

26. For example, Jas 5:5 is probably a recollection of the "day of slaughter" in Jer 12:3.

The letter reflects traditions from the Jewish prophetic tradition in its concern for how the poor are treated, as well as various streams from Hellenistic moral teaching that were suspicious of commercial dealings, of usury, and of loving wealth. Unlike Jesus (Oakman 2002), James does not attack money directly, although as many authors have explored, Jesus' teachings likely served as sources for James's instructions on a variety of issues, especially those that relate to the rich and the poor (Hartin 1991; Bauckham 1999; Wachob 2000; Kloppenborg 2007). The reasons for this shift are undoubtedly complex, but one may be the fact of Christianity's spread through largely urban environments, in which an attack upon money per se would have been less feasible.[27]

James remains different, however, from some other early Christian texts that address poverty and wealth. Although he does advocate caring for widows and orphans (1:27), there is no impression that it is acceptable to be rich provided one is generous, which is how some would characterize the view of Acts (Friesen 2005, 259). James does not even indicate that the rich may be saved if they repent and share, or give up their riches altogether. The letter, which in many ways can be understood as part of the Jewish wisdom tradition, does not reflect the elite perspective that some of the other texts in this tradition that show concern for the poor, such as sections from Proverbs, do (Pleins 1987, 61–78).[28] As we saw in 1:9–11, the rich and their wealth are on the way out, while the poor will be lifted up. For James, the true benefactor is God (Batten 2004) and not a wealthy person. Whether we understand the rich to be inside or outside of the audience to which James is directed, they are never a positive or even neutral group, but by definition "greedy." Perhaps the author presupposes "a situation in which neither members of the social elite nor absolutely poor people are to be found" (Stegemann and Stegemann 1995, 306), although, as has been argued elsewhere, the letter does seek to establish the identity of the audience members as the honorable poor who assist the needier people among them (Wachob 2000, 178–85; Batten 2007, 24–26).

Commenting on Jas 4:13–17, Friesen says that "with the rise of capitalism, of course, what Jacob called arrogant and evil became codified as standard economic practice" (2005, 246). Earlier, this essay referred to Bigelow's observation that an economic view of modern life would do well to have an understanding of the social. Perhaps if references to rich and poor in ancient writings were translated in ways that reflected the social and moral dimensions with which their authors and readers invested them, it would aid contemporaries to think about the economy within broader frameworks? As a result, maybe "standard economic practice" would no longer be business as usual?[29]

---

27. Although the provenance and audience of James remain unknown, the letter reflects an awareness of urban features such as courts, men with fine clothes and gold rings, and crowns.

28. Wittenberg (1987, 1–23) has observed, however, that one can trace a shift in some of the proverbs regarding the understanding of the rich. Proverbs 22:2 identifies the rich as neutral, while an almost identical proverb (Prov 29:13) refers to "oppressors." Wittenberg accounts for the pejorative reinterpretation of the rich as the result of socioeconomic shifts whereby the Israelites encountered Canaanite commercial activities that had disastrous results for Israelite peasants. The negative view of the rich in some of the proverbs is part of an overall critique of gaining wealth through commerce and trade as opposed to farming.

29. Thanks to Douglas Oakman and Terry Rothwell for reading earlier versions of this essay and for providing helpful questions and comments.

GOD—ZEALOUS OR JEALOUS BUT NEVER ENVIOUS:
THE THEOLOGICAL CONSEQUENCES
OF LINGUISTIC AND SOCIAL DISTINCTIONS

John H. Elliott

The renowned Spanish author and former rector of the University of Salamanca, Miguel de Unamuno, on more than one occasion declared envy to be a "deadly cancer" of the human spirit, but a vice characteristic of Spain in particular. "The national Spanish leprosy,"[1] he called it, "the ferment of Spanish social life."[2] The lament is a remarkable confession, given the malignancy and repugnance that has always been associated with the vice of envy. In a land where envy has had such a history, it seems appropriate to consider the topic of envy in the Bible and whether God, too, shares the Spanish vice.[3]

There are similarities and differences involving the dispositions of zeal, jealousy, and envy, including the social relations and social dynamics implied by each that must be clarified. In order to gain clarity, attention turns to the Hebrew and Greek biblical terms and passages for a critical evaluation of where zeal, jealousy, and envy are used to translate the less differentiated terms קנא and ζῆλος and their respective word families. God, it will be shown, is said in the biblical writings to be zealous or jealous but never envious. An explanation for this fact, which differentiates YHWH from the Greek gods and the φθόνος Θεῶν, is presented.[4]

The issue is more complex than one might first expect. Part of this complexity is linguistic. In the Hebrew Bible there is one family of terms of the קנא root that can denote not only envy but also jealousy or zeal, all dependent on context. In the Greek Bible, the standard term for envy, φθόνος, occurs only rarely and then only in the apocryphal writings. The Greek word that virtually always translates the Hebrew קנא and its paronyms is ζῆλος and its family of terms. Ζῆλος, however, resembles קנא in

---

1. Miguel de Unamuno (1942). Cited by de la Mora (1987, 55).

2. Miguel de Unamuno (1980). Cited by de la Mora (1987, 55). On Spain and envy see also Salillas (1905).

3. This paper was presented at the International Meeting of the Context Group on *Early Christian Writings in Context* held at the Universidad Pontificia de Salamanca, Salamanca, Spain, June 28–July 2, 2006.

4. An abridged version of this essay is found in Gottwald and Coote (2007).

its semantic breadth so that here, too, context and social relations determine whether the term means zeal, jealousy, or envy. Adding to the complexity is that in common modern parlance, *jealousy* regularly is used as a synonym for *envy* as though the terms denoted the same things. This laxity of usage creates problems in understanding since *envy* and *jealousy*, while related, denote different emotions involving different social relations, different social consequences, and different moral implications. When zeal as a further possible meaning of קנא is considered, the semantic dilemma becomes even more problematic. So how do we determine when in the Bible the topic of envy is in view? And how shall we explore the question of whether or not God is ever thought of as envious?

I shall undertake an examination along social-semantic lines. First, I shall define and delineate the concepts of envy, jealousy, and zeal, with attention to their similarities and differences as affected by the different types of social situations, social relations, and social dynamics involved. Then, after reviewing all the occurrences of the קנא, ζῆλος, and φθόνος word families in Old and New Testaments, I shall classify these passages as to their meanings of either zeal, jealousy, or envy. I shall make this decision on the basis of the content of the verses, their literary contexts, and the social relations that they involve. On the basis of this total biblical inventory, I shall then summarize salient aspects of zeal, jealousy, and envy as presented in Old and New Testaments. Finally, I shall return to the opening question concerning God and envy.

ZEAL, JEALOUSY, AND ENVY DEFINED

The emotions of zeal, jealousy, and envy are related but also distinct. One representative set of dictionary definitions is that provided by *Webster's New Collegiate Dictionary* (1977).

Zeal is defined as "eagerness and ardent interest in pursuit of something; fervor." *Zealotry* is "fanatical devotion."

The adjective *jealous* is defined as being (1a) "intolerant of rivalry or unfaithfulness"; (1b) "disposed to suspect rivalry or unfaithfulness"; "apprehensive of the loss of another's exclusive devotion"; (2) "hostile toward a rival or one believed to enjoy an advantage"; (3) "vigilant in guarding a possession." The noun *jealousy* is defined as (1) "a jealous disposition, attitude, or feeling"; (2) "zealous vigilance."

Envy, deriving from the Latin *invidia* and its verb *invidere*, meaning "to look askance at, envy," is defined as (1) "malice" (obs.); (2) "painful or resentful awareness of an advantage enjoyed by another joined with a desire to possess the same advantage"; (3) "an object of envious notice or feeling."

The dictionary's entry on *envious* adds the important comment that *jealousy* and *envy*, while having something in common, "are not close synonyms and can rarely be interchanged without loss of precision or alteration of emphasis" (1977, 382). The dictionary violates, however, its own observation when in its definition of *jealous* it lists *envious* as a synonym. This illustrates the ease as well as regularity with which envy and jealousy are confused in modern parlance as well as dictionaries. It is thus imperative that we be clear from the outset on their relation and peculiar features.

That which relates the emotions of zeal, jealousy, and envy is the intensity or high degree of feeling pervading all three. The English terms *zeal* and *jealousy* are also related linguistically since *jealous, jealousy,* as well as *zealous, zeal,* are both cognates of the Latin *zelus, zelotypia,* which in turn are cognates of the Greek ζῆλος, ζηλοτυπία. This is the case not only for English but also for Italian, French, and Spanish. From a sociolinguistic point of view, however, zeal, jealousy, and envy entail different social relations and dynamics.

The key quality of *zeal* is the intensity of feeling a person or group has toward another person, group, object, or cause. It can have both positive or negative promptings and consequences, expressing a high degree of laudable devotion and loyalty, on the one hand, or deplorable fanaticism or zealotry, on the other. It can also shade into feelings of ardor and positive affection, or negative anger, fury, or wrath. Being zealous is being enthusiastic or intensely serious about something; showing earnest concern; or setting one's heart on something. Zeal is not about possessing; jealousy and envy are.

Jealousy is intense feeling concerning one's assumed possessions and rivalry with others. Jealousy arises in a social situation of perceived rivalry between two persons or groups, with the jealous person or group fearing the loss of something possessed due to the machinations of a rival. Jealousy is intense concern for protecting one's possessions from the encroachments of perceived rivals. One biblical dictionary correctly defines it as "the intense emotion aroused by the infringement of one's right (or presumed right) to exclusive possession or loyalty" (Opperwall and Wyatt 1982, 972).[5] In regard to the interpersonal relations involved, jealousy involves threesomes or triads—the jealous agent, the object presumed to be possessed, and a rival third party (Schoeck 1987, 88). Envy, by contrast, involves an interaction of only two parties, the envier and the envied.

Jealousy, like zeal, can be either positive or negative, depending on circumstances and social-cultural context. On the one hand, it can be a feeling of insecurity and vulnerability to attack and loss. In our contemporary individualistic culture, it can be viewed as self-centered, obsessive possessiveness. In biblical times it also could be regarded positively and seen as an expression of emotional attachment and of faithful responsibility toward those under one's control, assuring their well-being and protection. In this sense, husbands are laudably jealous concerning their wives, as parents and patrons are appropriately jealous concerning their children and clients.

A feeling often confused with jealousy but better categorized as *competitiveness* or *friendly rivalry* is a craving to possess what perceived rivals and neighbors also possess, but with no interest in harm to the rivals. Aristotle and others mention this as one aspect of Greek ζῆλος.

Envy is an intense feeling like zeal and jealousy, and, like jealousy, concerns possessing someone or something. Envy, however, has no positive quality. While zeal and jealousy can be either positive or negative depending on the situation, envy is always evil and never virtuous. Envy is the grief or pain of a person or group at the sight of

---

5. Unfortunately, despite the apt definition of jealousy, the entry often treats jealousy and envy as synonyms.

valued goods possessed and enjoyed by a perceived rival, accompanied by the wish that the rival be dispossessed of the things causing happiness. The jealous person is anxious about some valued good that he or she possesses and wants to keep. The envious person is grieved at the valued good that someone else has, with the desire that the rival lose it. Jealousy fears damage to self, envy intends damage to others.

Envy arises in a social situation where one person or group sees another person or group possessing something of value and feels distress over the possession of the valued item and the happiness it brings its owner. Prompted by a sense of inferiority deriving from a comparison of self with others—hence the origin of the expression *invidious comparison*—envy wishes the deprivation of the fortunate. This sense of inferiority and deprivation generally is coupled with a notion of limited good, a belief that in this *zero-sum game of life* all the good things of life are in limited and scarce supply. Thus, whenever anyone gains, another loses. Your rise in status and honor is at the expense of my demotion and shame. Even if an envier gives food or alms to others—an ostensibly positive act—the envier can begrudge the gift out of fear that this gift could result in his own loss. Accordingly, envy and the Evil Eye (by which envy is directed at targets) can entail or imply miserliness, stinginess, tight-fistedness, and begrudging.

Achievement and ambition are no threats to the zealous and the jealous, but they are noxious to the envious. If you improve your situation in life and rise above me and the pack, you will make us look bad and inferior. So our interest is in keeping you and all ambitious persons in their place. The peg that sticks up will be struck down. Since envy entails malice and destructive intent toward others, it is considered inimical to social harmony and cohesion and is often condemned together with the vices of strife and dissension. On the other hand, to be envied, while dangerous, can also be a feather in one's cap since this shows that the envied person is deemed to possess something of high value. Finally, envy is linked with the Evil Eye; zeal and jealousy are not (Schoeck 1970; Foster 1972; Fernández 1987).[6] In the language of Shakespearean drama, Othello is the tragic exemplar of jealousy, and Iago, the despicable agent of envy.

GREEK AND ROMAN NOTIONS

The proximity of all three emotions was apparent to both the Greeks and the Romans (Hagedorn and Neyrey 1998; Malina 2001, 108–33; Elliott 2007). The standard Greek term for envy was φθόνος and paronyms. Ζῆλος and its family of terms[7] also denoted envy as well as zeal and jealousy.[8] This overlap in usage led to

---

6. On envy and the notion of limited good see Foster (1967, 293–315; 1972, 165–202); Pilch and Malina (1998, 59–63); Rohrbaugh (2001, 464–83). On Evil Eye, envy, and limited good see Elliott (1990, 262–73; 1992, 52–65; 1994, 51–84; 2005b, 157–68); Malina (2001, 81–107; 108–33); Parrott and Smith (1993, 906–20).

7. The terms include ζηλεύω, ζῆλος, ζηλοτυπέω, ζηλοτυπία, ζηλόω, ζήλωμα, ζήλωσις, ζηλωτέος, ζηλωτής, ζηλωτίκος, ζηλωτός; ὁμοζηλία; παραζηλέω, παραζηλόω, παραζηλώσις; ἀντίζηλος.

8. Ζῆλος often was paired with φθόνος (Lysias 2.48; Plato *Phileb.* 47E, 50C; *Leg.* 3.679C; *1 Macc.* 8:16; *T. Sim.* 4:5; *1 Clem.* 3:2; 4:7, 13; 5:2) or was used interchangeably with φθόνος in the same context

various attempts to sort out meanings and usage, especially of jealousy, competitiveness, and envy.[9] Aristotle defined φθόνος as "pain at the good fortune of others" (*Rhet.* 2.9, 1386b), noting that envy focuses on what others possess and how their good fortune is a reproach to us. "We feel it toward our peers, not with the idea of getting something for ourselves, but because the other persons have it" (*Rhet.* 2.10, 1387b). "We envy those whose possession of, or success in, something is a reproach to us" [and we consider it] "our own fault that we have missed the good thing in question; this annoys us and excites envy in us" (*Rhet.* 2.10, 1388a). He defined ζῆλος as "pain due not to the fact that another possesses [valued goods] but to the fact that we do not" (*Rhet.* 2.11, 1388a). This sense of ζῆλος is best rendered not as *jealousy* but as *emulation* (Latin, *aemulatio*) or *competitiveness*.[10] A recent study on envy in the New Testament by Anselm Hagedorn and Jerome H. Neyrey captures correctly various senses of ζῆλος and the defensive nature of jealousy: "ζῆλος can mean both [*sic*] attacking envy, good [i.e., positive] emulation, and defensive jealousy" (1998, 19). Envy, Aristotle observed (*Rhet.* 2.10–11, 1387b–1388b), is always negative, "a base feeling of base persons," whereas ζῆλος can be noble and praiseworthy when denoting competition for, and emulation of, something or someone virtuous. Envy, aggressive malice, was the disposition most frequently associated with the Evil Eye. Censure of the former went hand in hand with dread of the latter, just as the presence of the one generally implied the presence of the other. This was as true for Israel and the Jesus movement as it was for the world of the ancient Near East and circum-Mediterranean in general.

A further widespread phenomenon in the Greek world was dread not only of the envy of humans but fear, bordering on paranoia, of the envy of the gods, φθόνος Θεῶν. This divine envy, it was believed, is provoked by humans who attempt to

(Plato, *Symp.* 213D; *Leg.* 679C; Epictetus 3.22.61; Plutarch, *Frat. amor.* 16; *Mor.* 485D, E; *Mor.* 86C; 91B; *Tranq. an.* 16, 17; *Mor.* 470C; 471A; *T. Sim.*—for ζῆλ- terms see: 2:6, 7; 4:5, 9; for φθόν- terms see 2:13, 14; 3:1, 2, 3, 4, 6; 4:5, 7; 6:2). See also *T. Dan* 1:6 and 2:5; *T. Gad* 4:5; 5:3; 7:4; *T. Benj.* 4:4; and *1 Clem.* 3:1–6:4. Thus, their pairing often functioned as a hendiadys.

9. Aristotle, *Rhet.* 2:10–11; Chrysippus in Diogenes Laertius, *Lives of Eminent Philosophers* 7.111; Cicero, *Tusc.* 4.7.17.

10. Malina (2001, 127) suggests the felicitous translation "competitiveness" and sees this as a second type of jealousy (aggressive versus defensive jealousy). It is interesting to note, however, that a different term in Latin, *aemulatio*, rather than the Latin *zelus*, was employed to denote and distinguish this aspect of the Greek term ζῆλος (cf. Cicero, *Tusc.* 4.7.17). "Competitiveness [ζῆλος]," observes Aristotle, "is a feeling of pain at the evident presence of highly valued goods, which are possible for us to obtain, in the possession of those who naturally resemble us—pain not due to the fact that another possess them, but to the fact that we do not" (*Rhet.* 2.10–11). This feeling prompts a positive striving to attain goods or qualities for oneself. Thus competitiveness is "virtuous and characteristic of virtuous persons" since it involves striving for excellence and the valued goods of life. It is a healthy rivalry that prompts emulation of virtuous persons and their outstanding qualities (honor, courage, wisdom, wealth, authority) and so contributes to both individuals and the well-being of society in general. This competitiveness, so typical of, and so celebrated in, Greek agonistic society, is rarely mentioned in the Bible. The one possible exception is Rom 11:14, which I shall discuss below. Malina (2001), treating it as a form of jealousy, sees it mentioned in New Testament lists of vices (2 Cor 12:20; Gal 5:20; Jas 3:16). But these passages, the only ones he mentions, list negative actions to be avoided, not positive actions to be encouraged and praised. In each case the sense of the terms is not jealousy but envy. The modern sense of jealousy as competitive desire to possess what perceived rivals also possess approximates this aggressive aspect of ζῆλος.

rise above their allotted station in life and who seek more than their fair share of the goods at hand. The envy of the gods, sometimes also named *nemesis*,[11] consisted in their intense displeasure, indignation at, and intolerance of human hybris, immodesty, bragging, or ostentatious piety. Such action aroused divine envy, which would then, through a divine Evil Eye, strike down such arrogant persons, destroy their success, and reduce them to their proper place. This notion of the envy of the gods filled the Greek world with dread from Homer to Plato (de la Mora 1987, 6–7). Homer, speaking through the nymph Calypso, comments that "you gods are cruel and more inclined to envy than the rest" (*Od.* 4.118; 5.120). At the Isthmian games, a winning poet declares: "Let no envious god disturb the sweet rest I wish to live in" (Pindar, *Isthm.* 6.39). Herodotus insists, "I know for certain that the gods are envious (φθονερός)" (*Hist.* 3.40–47). He also knows that "[t]he vengeance of heaven fell upon Croesus as punishment for his pride of believing that he was the happiest of men" (*Hist.* 1.34).

Eventually skepticism concerning the gods' envying humans led to a critique of the notion of divine envy altogether. Aristophanes (ca. 445–385 B.C.E.), the iconoclast playwright, in the last of his comedies (ca. 388 B.C.E.) has the blind character Plutus declare: "Zeus has done this to me out of his envy toward humans. . . . He is particularly envious these days of persons with property" (Aristophanes, *Plut.* 87–91). Aristophanes' mocking of the gods and their envy is palpable. Plato (427–347 B.C.E.) divested the gods of passions altogether, so that envy is left an exclusively human vice. "Envy," he declared, "is outside the circle of the gods" (*Phaedr.* 247A); God "is free from envy" (*Tim.* 29 E). Aristotle (384–322 B.C.E.) concurs: "[T]he divine power cannot be envious" (*Metaph.* 1.983a). Hereafter the notion of envy of the gods waned to insignificance (Milobenski 1964; Walcott 1978; de la Mora 1987, 3–27; Dickie 1987; Schoeck 1987, 141–61; Rakoczy 1996, 247–70).

Where did Israel and the Jesus movement stand in regard to these notions of envy? They certainly had a lively fear of the Evil Eye, as I have shown in several studies.[12] Accompanying this fear of the Evil Eye was also an intense disapproval of envy, always viewed as a poisonous evil. What of zeal and jealousy? What terminology was employed in which social situations and what understandings of jealousy and zeal and envy lay behind these differences? We turn now to an examination of biblical texts.

קנא AND ζῆλος WORD FAMILIES IN THE OLD TESTAMENT

Biblical Hebrew has one chief set of terms for denoting the feelings of zeal (and related emotions), jealousy, and envy, namely, קנא and paronyms. Terms of the קנא family (verb, noun, and adjective) appear eighty-five times in the Hebrew Bible (most frequently in Num [15x] and Ezek [13x]).[13] Common to the diverse meanings of קנא is the sensation of *intense arousal, excitement, ardor,* or *strong feeling.* A comparison

---

11. Nemesis, personalized as a deity, was the Greek goddess of divine justice and vengeance who punishes human transgression of the natural, proper order of things and the arrogance that causes it.

12. On the biblical texts see Elliott (1988; 1990; 1991; 1992; 1994; 2005a; 2005b; 2006; 2007).

13. Sauer (1976). The German *Eifer, eifersüchtig,* Sauer's definition, is as broad in meaning as are קנא and ζῆλος.

with the Syriac cognate *qna* meaning "darkly colored" or " red" and the Arabic cognate *qn'* meaning "to become dark red" lends credence to the suggestion that the root meaning of קנא is perhaps "to become red in the face" (Good 1962, 806). Redness in the face is the external symptom of excitement and intense feeling of various kinds.

The verb קנא occurs thirty-four times. It appears thirty times in the piel form, meaning *be zealous*, or *be jealous*, or *be envious* (used of humans 24x, and of God 5x; cf. also Ezek 31:9). Four times it appears in the hiphil form, meaning *cause to be zealous or jealous or envious*, with humans (Deut 32:16; Ps 78:58), God (Deut 32:21b), or an idol (Ezek 8:8) as subject.

The noun קִנְאָה occurs forty-three times, with the possible meanings of *zeal, ardor, passion, wrath, fury, jealousy*, or *envy*. Nineteen of these concern humans as subjects; twenty-six concern the קִנְאָה of God.

There are eight occurrences of the adjective, with קַנָּא appearing six times (Exod 20:5; 34:14 [bis]; Deut 4:24; 5:9; 6:15) and קַנּוֹא occurring twice (Josh 24:19; Nah 1:2). Used only of God, the meanings vary from zealous to jealous. The Septuagint renders words of the קנא root almost exclusively with terms of the ζηλ- family.[14] These terms appear 118 times in the LXX and include ζῆλος (38x), ζηλοτυπία (4x), ζηλόω (49x), ζηλωσίς (4x), ζηλοτής (9x), ζηλωτός (2x); ὁμοζηλία (1x); παραζηλέω/παραζηλόω (8x); ἀντιζηλός (3x). Since these terms are as polysemic as those of the Hebrew קנא family, the context (cultural and literary) and social relations of the terms of both these word families determine whether their sense in a given passage is zeal, jealousy, or envy. The Septuagint never renders words of the קנא root with the standard Greek term for envy, φθόνος. LXX instances of φθόνος are discussed below.

ZEAL, JEALOUSY, ENVY—DETERMINANTS OF MEANING

Whether these terms have the sense of zeal or jealousy or envy is determined by a set of related contextual factors: the subject matter in view, the narrated social situation, the social relations and social dynamics that are stated or implied.

ZEAL (AND RELATED FEELINGS)

When the situation involves an event arousing excitement, intense feeling, ardent passion and when there is no issue of possession or aggressive malice in view, then the emotion is zeal or a related feeling, which can be weighted either positively or negatively. Zeal as earnest concern, or fervent devotion and commitment of a person or group to another person or group, is viewed positively, including human zeal for God, an honorable cause, or God's concern for humans. Fury stoking anger and wrath in the name of justice is praiseworthy. Fanaticism and zealotry, on the other hand, can lead to deadly consequences and are often censured as immoderate, exceeding acceptable limits. The fury or anger or wrath of God generally is said to be

---

14. There are only four exceptions. Once the verb קנא is rendered by παρώργισαν (Ps 105:16) and once by παρώξυναν (Deut 32:16). קִנְאָה is rendered once as καρδία αἰσθητική ("sensitive heart," Prov 14:30) and once by θυμοῦ ("wrath," Ezek 36:5).

directed against "the Gentiles/*goyim*" or the enemies of Israel. This fury can lead to annihilation and death.

JEALOUSY

When other conditions prevail, intense feeling or heated arousal can morph into the emotions of either jealousy or envy. *Heated* is the appropriate qualifier since the issue is an intensity of feeling that creates heat in the body and redness in the face.[15] When the scene involves two or more agents who are possibly rivals and a claim to ownership, loyalty, or possession is challenged, then the feeling is best rendered as jealousy, being jealous, provoking or being provoked to jealousy. Jealousy is sensing a challenge to one's claim of ownership of something which generally leads to a reassertion of ownership and control. On the human level and in the family circle, the classic example of jealousy in the Hebrew Bible is the husband who is jealous concerning his wife. He is anxious about her fidelity and the attempt of other males to gain control of her and takes steps to reassert his control. In biblical culture (in contrast to contemporary Western culture), jealousy was generally regarded positively as a desirable trait of a personage of honor defending and protecting those under this person's care and protection. In this positive sense, jealousy was attributed also to God, who was envisioned as jealous concerning his people just as a bridegroom is regarding his bride. Jealousy can concern other possessions as well. YHWH can be said to be jealous concerning his name (viz., his reputation), his land, and his house/temple. In contrast to zeal/anger/wrath and to envy, jealousy does not lead to destruction and death. It rather concerns retaining and protecting what one has.

ENVY

When the situation involves two agents or groups regarding themselves as rivals, one person/group viewing the sudden good fortune of the other and judging his own situation, by comparison, to be inferior, then the intense feeling of envy can arise in the person doing the comparing so that the envier feels pain at the other's success and wishes him or her to be deprived of that success or health or good fortune (so that they return to the state preceding the sudden good fortune). In accord with the prevalent notion of limited good, the envied person is assumed by the envier to have come to his good fortune at the cost of the envier. Envy is always directed toward or against someone or something and, in contrast to jealousy or zeal, is regularly linked with the Evil Eye as the mechanism by which envy is directed against others and even oneself, examples of which are Joseph envied by his brothers and Saul envious of David. Envy can even be self-damaging, self-consuming, and can result in the death of the envier as well as of the envied. Often in the Bible this link of envy and Evil Eye is expressly stated; in other instances it is implied.

---

15. The word "fury" derives from Greek πῦρ, "fire," and the expressions "hot under the collar," "hot-blooded," "(fire)-flashing eyes" all express a high level of feeling and arousal.

ZEAL, JEALOUSY, AND ENVY IN THE OLD TESTAMENT

Terms of the קנא and ζῆλος families, denoting *zeal* or the related feelings of *enthusiasm about something; earnest concern, setting one's heart on something, devotion to some person or cause*, or *ardor, anger, fury, wrath*, occur twenty-four times in the Hebrew Bible.[16] This set of emotions is attributed both to humans[17] and to God.[18] In regard to the zeal of humans, King Saul, for example, had zealous concern for the people of Israel and Judah (2 Sam 21:2). Phineas, Elijah, and Jehu are said to be zealous in their devotion to God (Num 25:13; 1 Kgs 19:10, 14; 2 Kgs 10:16). A psalmist sings of zeal for God's house (Ps 69:10, LXX 68:9). God, on some occasions, is said to feel zeal as an intense concern for his people (2 Kgs 19:31; Isa 26:11). In other instances God's zeal takes the form of anger at his people (Deut 29:20; Ezek 23:25) or fury or wrath at "the nations" (Ps 79:5), at Edom (Ezek 36:5), or at his adversaries (Isa 42:13; 59:17; Zeph 1:18—mostly with no mention of Israel as his possession).[19] Further instances in the LXX where ζῆλος has this range of related meanings also attribute the emotion to both humans and God.[20]

JEALOUSY IN THE OLD TESTAMENT

Terms of the קנא root with the sense of jealousy appear approximately thirty-two times in the Old Testament, with attribution to both humans[21] and God.[22] A classic instance of human jealousy is the case described in Num 5 when a husband is seized by a suspicious "spirit of jealousy" concerning his wife and is apprehensive about her possible infidelity. In social terms he is troubled that some male has laid claim to, and has alienated, his possession, namely his wife. Other passages also speak of jealousy in the context of marital and erotic relations.[23]

As applied to God, YHWH is said to be jealous[24] concerning highly valued entities belonging to him: his name (Ezek 39:25), his people (Isa 26:11), his land (Ezek 36:5; Joel 2:18), his city, Jerusalem and Zion (Zech 1:14; 8:2). God's very name is said to be "Jealous" (Exod 34:14). When the metaphor of marriage is employed to depict the

16. See Num 25:11, 13; Deut 29:20; 2 Sam 21:2; 1 Kgs 19:10, 14; 2 Kgs 10:16; 19:31; Pss 69:10; 79:5; 119:139; Isa 9:6; 26:11; 37:32; 42:13; 59:17; 63:15; Ezek 23:25; 35:11; 36:5; 38:19; 39:25; Zeph 1:18; 3:8.

17. See Num 25:13; 2 Sam 21:2; 1 Kgs 19:10, 14; 2 Kgs 10:16; Pss 69:10; 119:139 = 7x.

18. See Num 25:11a, 11b; Deut 29:20; 2 Kgs 19:31; Ps 79:5; Isa 9:6; 26:11; 37:32; 42:13; 59:17; 63:15; Ezek 23:25; 35:11; 36:5; 36:6 [?]; 38:19; Zeph 1:18; Nah 1:2 = 18x..

19. For God's zeal (abs.) see also Num 25:11b; Deut 29:20; 2 Kgs 19:31; Isa 9:6; 37:32; 63:15.

20. For humans see Sir 45:23 (of Phineas); 48:2 (of Elijah); 51:18; Jdt 9:4; 1 Macc 2:24, 26, 27, 50, 54, 58 (anger, "zeal for the Law," "zealous for the Law"). Exemplars of those zealous for the law: Caleb, David, Elijah, the three youths in the fiery furnace, and Daniel (1 Macc 2:52–61); 2 Macc 4:16. For God see Isa 11:11. Fourth Maccabees 13:25 speaks of a "common zeal" for doing what is right.

21. See Num 5:14 (bis), 15, 18, 25, 29, 30; Ps 106:16 (or envy?); Prov 6:34; 27:4 (?); Song 8:6; Ezek 16:38.

22. See Exod 20:5; 34:14 (bis); Deut 4:24; 5:9; 6:15; 32:16, 21a, 21b; Josh 24:19; 1 Kgs 14:22; Ezek 5:13; 8:3; 16:42; 36:6; 39:25 (or zealous?); Joel 2:18; Zeph 1:18 ? ("jealous wrath," RSV); 3:8? ("jealous wrath," RSV); Zech 1:14; 8:2 (bis).

23. See Prov 6:34; Song 8:6; Ezek 16:38; Sir 9:1.

24. See Exod 20:5/Deut 5:9; Exod 34:14 (bis); Deut 4:24; 6:15; Josh 24:19; Nah 1:2.

relation of Israel to YHWH, God is often portrayed as jealous or provoked to jealousy over Israel and her idolatry and infidelity.[25]

The Hebrew adjectives קַנָּא (Exod 20:5; 34:14 [bis]; Deut 4:24; 5:9; 6:15) and קַנּוֹא (Josh 24:19; Nah 1:2) are used only of God and always in contexts where Israel's exclusive devotion to God alone is in view and so always with the sense of God being jealous. God's jealousy concerning Israel is his insistence that Israel belongs exclusively to YHWH, with the demand for Israel's consistent fidelity. Accordingly, God is also said to be provoked to jealousy by an idolatrous, unfaithful people.[26] God is also depicted as provoking Israel to jealousy (Deut 32:21b). The rare expression "image of jealousy" (occurring only in Ezek 8:3, 5) most likely refers to an image of a foreign god that provokes God to jealousy.[27]

ENVY IN THE OLD TESTAMENT

Terms of the קנא and ζῆλος families with the sense of envy appear seventeen times in the Old Testament and only in relation to humans.

The Philistines envied Isaac and his great possessions (Gen 26:14). Rachel, the barren one, envied Leah, her fertility, and her blessing from God (Gen 30:1). Joseph's brothers envied Joseph and his greater favor with Jacob (Gen 37:11). Men in the camp were envious of Moses (Ps 106:16). "I was envious of the arrogant," the psalmist confesses, "when I saw the prosperity of the wicked" (Ps 73:3). Often the warning is issued not to envy: "do not envy a man of violence" (Prov 3:31). "Do not let your heart envy sinners" (Prov 23:17). "Do not envy the wicked" (Prov 24:1, 17). "Do not envy wrongdoers" (Ps 37:11). Envy, Israel is told, is a killer: "Envy makes the bones rot" (Prov 14:30). "Envy slays the simple" (Job 5:2). "Wrath is cruel," laments the sage, "anger is overwhelming, but who can withstand envy?" (Prov 27:4).[28]

In the LXX, the standard Greek terms meaning exclusively *envy*, φθόνος and paronyms, appear ten times and only in the Apocryphal writings.[29] According to 3 Macc 6:7, it was envy and slander that caused Daniel to be thrown to the lions. Envy, Wisdom observes, has plagued the creation from the very beginning and "through the devil's envy death entered the world" (Wis 2:24; cf. *1 Clem.* 3:4).

The common association of envy with the Evil Eye finds explicit expression in Sir 14:10 which speaks of one with an "envious Evil Eye" (ὀφθαλμὸς πονηρὸς φθονερός) begrudging bread at a meal. Tobit likewise shows the association of envy

25. See Deut 32:16; Ps 78:58; Ezek 5:13; 16:38, 42; cf. Ezek 8:3, 5.

26. Deut 32:16, 21a; 1 Kgs 14:22; Ps 78:58.

27. Further instances in the LXX where terms of the ζῆλος family have the sense of *jealous, jealousy* in relation to humans include Wis 1:10 (or envious?); 5:17; Sir 9:1; 30:24 (or envy?); 40:5 (or envy?); 1 Macc 8:16 (or envy?).

28. For further references to envy in the Hebrew Bible see Num 11:29; Eccl 4:4; Isa 11:13b; Ezek 31:9. Additional instances in the LXX where ζῆλος has the sense of "envy, envious" include Gen 49:22 LXX (Joseph the envied [ζηλωτής] son ?); Prov 4:14; Wis 1:10 (or jealousy?); Sir 9:11; 30:24 (or jealousy?); 37:10 ("not jealous," RSV); 40:5 (or jealousy? among seven vices); 45:18 (Aaron was envied); 1 Macc 8:16 (or jealousy?)

29. See φθονεσάτω (Tob 4:7, 16 BA); φθονερός (Sir 14:10); φθόνος (Wis 2:24; 6:23; 1 Macc 8:16; 3 Macc 6:7); ἀφθόνως (3 Macc 5:2; 4 Macc 3:10); ἀφθόνως (Wis 7:13); καταφθονεῖν (Dan Theod. Bel 12, v. 1).

and Evil Eye: "[D]o not let your eye begrudge [lit., be envious, φθονεσάτω] the gift when you make it" (Tob 4:7, 16). This suggests that to the list of passages referring to envy, all texts mentioning the Evil Eye should also be appended[30] while also remembering, however, that envy and Evil Eye are related but not identical.[31]

ZEAL, JEALOUSY, AND ENVY IN THE NEW TESTAMENT

In the New Testament, terms of the ζῆλος family appear forty-one times denoting zeal and related feelings of jealousy or envy.[32] Here, as in the LXX, the sense common to all three meanings is *intense feeling, strong arousal,* which then takes the form of zeal, or jealousy with either positive or negative force, or the form of envy with always negative force. Using the criteria as set forth above, the New Testament texts can be classified as follows.

The New Testament has eighteen instances where the sense of ζῆλος and paronyms (ζηλεύω, ζηλόω, ζηλωτής) is that of *zeal,* or the related feelings of *enthusiasm for, devotion to* someone or something, *eagerly seek, earnestly desire.*[33] The subjects are predominantly human and the emotions have predominantly positive force. Once ζῆλος has the sense of *fury* in the expression "fury of fire" or "furious fire" (Heb 10:27).

Judeans are said to be zealous for the law (Acts 21:20). Paul confesses once being zealous for the traditions of his fathers (Gal 1:14) and zealous in persecuting the church (Phil 3:6). Subsequently he was zealous for God (Acts 22:3). Paul speaks of Israel's zeal for God (Rom 10:2); the Corinthians' zeal for Paul (2 Cor 7:7); the Corinthians' "enthusiastic response to" the collection for the needy in Judea (2 Cor 9:2). The Corinthians are encouraged by Paul to "fervently desire" the better charisms (1 Cor 12:31), the spiritual gifts (1 Cor 14:1), and especially the gift to prophesy (1 Cor 14:39). The Corinthians' zeal can lead to repentance (2 Cor 7:11). In Rev 3:19 God urges the believers to "be zealous for me"/"set your heart on me."

Ζηλωτής with the genitive denotes *being zealous, enthusiastic, eager for something:* for the law (Acts 21:20); for God (Acts 22:3); for spiritual gifts (1 Cor 14:12); for the traditions of the fathers (Gal 1:14); for good deeds or what is good (Tit 2:14; 1 Pet 3:13). Ζηλωτής used absolutely theoretically could have the sense of either *jealous* or *zealous.* In the case of Luke 6:15 and Acts 1:13 (Simon the Zealot), usage and tradition argue for the latter. Here the zeal most likely had political coloration.

---

30. See Deut 15:9; 28:54, 56; Prov 23:6, 28:22; Wis 4:12; Sir 14:3, 6, 8, 9, 10; 18:13; 31:13; 37:11; Tob 4:7, 16; Ep Jer 69; and 4 Macc 1:26, 2:15.

31. See also 1 Sam 2:32, RSV: "envious eye."

32. See ζηλεύω (1x); ζῆλος (17x); ζηλόω (11x); ζηλωτής (8x); παραζηλόω (4x).

33. See ζηλεύω, Rev 3:19; ζῆλος, John 2:17; Rom 10:2; 2 Cor 7:7, 11; 9:2; Phil 3:6; ζηλόω, 1 Cor 12:31; 14:1, 39; ζηλωτής, Luke 6:15; Acts 1:13; 21:20; 22:3; 1 Cor 14:12; Gal 1:14; Tit 2:14; 1 Pet 3:13.

JEALOUSY IN THE NEW TESTAMENT

In seven instances the sense of ζηλ- root terms is that of jealousy.[34] Paul, as the one who has presented the Corinthians to Christ "as a pure bride to her husband," states that he is jealous (ζηλῶ) concerning them with the jealousy (ζῆλος) of God (2 Cor 11:2), that is, the jealousy of the deity concerning that which belongs to him. The marital metaphor makes the meaning *jealousy* more likely than *zeal* and concerns the Corinthians' exclusive relation to Christ. First Corinthians 3:3–4 also has to do with the issue of belonging and loyalty so that the ζῆλος raging among the Corinthians most likely denotes jealousy rather than envy. The list of vices in Gal 5:19–21 includes both ζῆλος (5:20) and φθόνοι (5:21). Since the terms do not form a hendiadys and since ζῆλος with the sense of envy would be redundant, it probably denotes jealousy here.

Paul uses the verb παραζηλόω, "provoke to jealousy," four times of both humans and God.[35] He speaks of Israel being provoked to jealousy through his ministry to the Gentiles (Rom 11:14) and by the salvation of the Gentiles (Rom 11:11b). He warns the Corinthian believers to avoid provoking God to jealousy (1 Cor 10:22). To the Judean believers of Rome he recalls the word of God transmitted by Moses, "I will provoke you [Israel] to jealousy through those who are not a people" (Rom 10:19).[36] In each case Israel as God's special possession and the covenantal relation are in view.

ENVY IN THE NEW TESTAMENT

Envy is mentioned or alluded to no less than twenty-four times in the New Testament. Ζῆλος or ζηλόω mean "envy" (Acts 5:17; 13:45) or "to envy" (Acts 7:9; 17:5; 1 Cor 13:4; Gal 4:17 bis, 18; Jas 4:2) in nine instances. The verb φθονέω occurs once (Gal 5:26) and the noun φθόνος eight times.[37] Given the close connection of envy and the Evil Eye in the Bible and the ancient world generally, the five explicit references to the Evil Eye in the NT[38] should be added as well. Finally, an idiom for envy occurs in Acts 8:23 according to Louw and Nida (1988, I:88.166). The apostle Peter denounces Simon Magus for wanting to purchase a blessing of the Holy Spirit with money and urges Simon to repent and seek forgiveness, "For I see that you are bitterly

---

34. See ζηλῶ in 2 Cor 11:2 and Gal 5:20 ("jealousy" because φθόνοι is also mentioned); ζηλόω in 2 Cor 11:2; and all four occurrences of παραζηλόω, "provoke to jealousy" (Rom 10:19, 11:11, 14; 1 Cor 10:22). All but ζῆλος θεοῦ in 2 Cor 11:2 have humans as subject.

35. Once with God as subject (Rom 10:19) and once with God as object (1 Cor 10:22).

36. On "provoking to jealousy," see BDAG (763) on παραζηλόω at 1 Cor 10:22, where Danker aptly explains the social dynamic. According to Danker, God would be insulted if the Corinthians sacrifice to mere secondary deities. Or, viewed another way, God's claim to exclusive possession of the Corinthians would be provoked by their idolatry and infidelity. On Rom 10:19 compare KJV: "provoke to emulation," which does not mean *emulation* in the modern sense of *imitation* but which is an archaic English cognate of the Latin *aemulatio* (Vulg Rom 10:19) with the sense of "provoke to vigorous competition."

37. For φθόνος see Mark 15:10/Matt 27:18; Rom 1:29; Gal 5:21; Phil 1:15; 1 Tim 6:4; Tit 3:3; 1 Pet 2:1. Although Nestle-Aland[27] reads φθόνος in Jas 4:5, it is most likely an aural scribal error for τὸν θεόν, as I indicate below.

38. For references to the Evil Eye see Matt 6:22–23/Luke 11:34–36; Matt 20:1–15; Mark 7:22; Gal 3:1.

envious (ἐις γὰρ χολὴν πικρίας, lit., "you are in the *gall of bitterness*"). In all of these instances, this negative emotion is attributed only to humans and never to God.

Envy recurs often in lists of vices that followers of Jesus are urged to avoid.[39] In Jas 4:2 envying is paired with murdering (φονεύετε καὶ ζηλοῦτε).[40] The most dramatic pronouncement on envy in the NT occurs in the passion narratives of Mark and Matthew (Mark 15:10/Matt 27:18). Pilate, we are told, "perceived that it was out of envy (φθόνος) that the chief priests handed him over [for execution]." According to the narrative of Acts, it was also envy that drove those seeking the arrest of the apostles (Acts 5:17, ζῆλος) and of Paul (Acts 17:5, ζηλώσαντες). Paul charges that even some Christ followers at Philippi preached Christ out of envy (Phil 1:15). The classic example of sibling envy and the survival of envy and the Evil Eye in the Bible, namely the powerful story of Joseph and his brothers (Gen 37, 39–47), is recalled in Acts 7:9–16 where ζηλόω also has the sense of envy.[41]

These conclusions vary from most of the lexica which do not distinguish jealousy from envy and instead regard them as synonyms.[42]

DIFFICULT DECISIONS

In some cases decisions on translation cannot be made with certainty, especially when the original terms are used absolutely or when the context is vague. Thus sometimes terms of the קנא or ζηλ- families can plausibly be rendered as either *zeal* or *jealousy* (e.g., Num 25:11a, 11b; Qoh 9:6; Song 8:6; Ezek 36:5, 6; 39:25; Zech 1:14; 8:2). Romans 11:14 is one instance in which παραζηλόω has been thought to have had the sense of *jealous competitiveness* of which I spoke earlier. Paul, addressing the Gentiles, says he intends to provoke to jealousy his fellow Israelites (lit. "my flesh") so as to save some of them. Jerome translates the verb παραζηλώσω with *ad aemulandum provocem*, which perhaps influenced the KJV rendition, "provoke to emulation." The terms *aemulandum* (gerund of *aemulor*) and its English cognate *emulation* would seem to suggest that both Jerome and the KJV translators regarded the Greek verb as having the sense of *jealous competition* (and with positive force). If so, this would be a singular occurrence in the Bible of jealousy with this sense.

In other cases, either *envy* or *jealousy* could fit the context: for example, Job 5:2;

---

39. See Rom 1:29; Gal 5:21; 2 Cor 12:20; 1 Tim 6:4; Tit 3:3; 1 Pet 2:1; cf. Rom 13:13; 1 Cor 3:3.

40. See the similar pairing of φθόνου φόου ἔριδος in Rom 1:29. Ζῆλος is paired with ἔρις, "strife," in 2 Cor 12:20 and Gal 5:20.

41. On Joseph as envy's victim see also *T. Sim.* 2:6, 7, 13, 14; 4:5; *T. Gad* 3:3; *T. Jos.* 1:3. The topic of envy runs throughout the *Testament of the Twelve Patriarchs*; Joseph is its chief target. The appearances of ζηλόω in Gal 4:17–18 within a text segment concerning the Evil Eye tips the scales in favor of *envy* (Elliott 1990).

42. BDAG (427, 763, 1054), for example, explains ζῆλος as: (1) "intensive positive interest in someth[ing], *zeal, ardor,* marked by a sense of dedication"; (2) "intense negative feelings over another's achievements or success, *jealousy, envy*"; ζηλοτυπία as "jealousy"; and παραζηλόω as "provoke to jealousy, make jealous." Φθόνος is defined as "envy, jealousy." Louw and Nida also do not distinguish between "jealousy" and "envy" and use both as translations not only of terms of the ζηλ- family (§88.162, 163, 164) but also, and incorrectly, of φθον- (§88.160, 161) and of ὀφθαλμός πονηρός (88.165); so also *EDNT* 2 (1991, 100–110—sub ζῆλος); *EDNT* 3 (1993, 427—sub φθόνος).

Ps 106:16 [LXX 105:16]; Qoh 9:6; Ezek 39:25 (God is zealous/jealous concerning his name); Rom 13:13; 2 Cor 12:20; Gal 5:20; Jas 3:14, 16. Usually the verb παραζηλόω means *provoke to jealousy*. This may be its sense in Sir 30:3: "[H]e who teaches his son provokes his foe to jealousy." However, "provoke to envy" would perhaps better fit the context. The advantage gained by a son through his education would more plausibly arouse a foe's envy than his jealousy. In 1 Cor 13:4, since ζῆλος is contrasted to "love," *jealousy* (which could be viewed as an expression of love) is less likely than *envy*, a clear antithesis to love. In 1 Macc 2:58, φθόνος and ζῆλος are combined. In such cases, ζῆλος could be rendered "jealousy" with φθόνος meaning "envy" ("there is no envy or jealousy [φθόνος οὐδε ζῆλος] among them"). Or the combination could represent a hendiadys since ζῆλος and φθόνος often are used interchangeably and synonymously in the same context (1 Macc 8:16; *T. Sim.* 4:5; *1 Clem.* 3:2, 4:7; 5:2).

James 4:5 is especially problematic. Some translations render the phrase πρὸς φθόνον "with jealousy," " jealously";[43] others, "with envy," "enviously."[44] The former is impossible and the latter, implausible. Φθόνος, always a vice, always means envy and never jealousy. Therefore, translations referring to jealousy are simply erroneous. But the translation, "He [God] yearns with *envy* over the spirit he has made to dwell in us" would produce the only instance in the entire Bible where the vice of envy would be attributed to God or a spirit from God, and would illogically portray God as envious of something he himself conferred. Sophie Laws (1980, 177–78) and Luke T. Johnson also reject this association of envy with God. They instead take "spirit" as the subject of the verb ἐπιποθεῖ and regard the statement as a rhetorical question expecting a negative response: "Does the spirit he made to dwell in us crave enviously?" (cf. similarly NEB). The major problem with this, as Johnson concedes, is "the absence of the particle μή, which customarily introduces questions expecting a negative response" (1995, 267, 281–82). It seems likely, therefore, that J. J. Wettstein was correct in suspecting a textual corruption. Although Nestle-Aland[27] reads φθόνος in Jas 4:5, it is most likely an aural scribal error for τὸν θεόν. The thought of 4:5b is introduced by the phrase "Scripture says," and the language of the verse appears to derive from or allude to Ps 41:2b LXX (ἐπιποθεῖ ἡ ψυχή μου πρὸς σε, ὁ Θεός, "my soul yearns eagerly for you, O God"). With πρὸς Θεόν instead of πρὸς φθόνον Jas 4:2 most likely reads, "The spirit that he [God] has made to dwell in us yearns eagerly for God."

CORRECTING BIBLICAL VERSIONS

The consideration of social context and social dynamics I have undertaken here gives us a firmer basis for determining sense in original context and appropriate translation. As a result, I suggest that we need to challenge the rendition of these terms in some modern Bible translations as socially implausible and conceptually misleading.

---

43. See, for example, RSV, NRSV; BDAG (377—sub ἐπιποθέω).

44. See, for example, Vulg (*ad invidiam concupiscit*), KJV ("lusteth to envy"), NEB ("turns towards envious desires"), and Stumpff (1964, 888), who proposes "to strive with envious greed."

In several cases, *zeal* or *zealous* better fit the context than *jealousy* or *jealous*. For example, in Num 25:11–13, the stress on God's *wrath* against Israel and absence of any issue of possession or envious malice favors *zeal* over *jealousy* (against RSV): "he [Phinehas] was *zealous* with my [God's] *zeal*" (25:11) . . . he was zealous for his God" (25:13). Similarly, in 1 Kgs 19:10 and 14, Elijah is "zealous for the Lord" (not *jealous*, RSV). The RSV version of Zeph 3:8 opts for "jealous wrath" but there is no implication of jealousy here; "*fire* of my [God's] wrath" makes better sense here and in Zeph 1:18 (cf. also Ps 79:5). On the other hand, RSV Ezek 36:6 "jealous wrath" captures well the implications of both zeal and jealousy in this passage (Ezek 36:5–7) (cf. also Ezek 38:19). Ezekiel 5:13, "I, the Lord, have spoken in my *jealousy*," accords better with the context than "in my zeal" since the topic is God's punishment of an unfaithful people (Ezek 5:5–17).[45]

In other passages, content, context, and social relations make *envy* more likely than *jealousy*. Joseph is the biblical example par excellence of a victim of sibling envy who survived and flourished (Gen 37, 39–50). The KJV and *La Biblia* accurately translate Gen 37:11 as "envy" (*envidia*) in contrast to RSV, NRSV ("were jealous of"). Numbers 11:26–30 tells of the prophesying of Eldad and Medad in the camp. When Joshua objects, "My lord Moses, forbid them" (v. 28), Moses responds, "Are you *envious* for my sake?" (v. 29, so KJV). Moses suspects Joshua of resenting the spirit and gift of prophecy enjoyed by Eldad and Medad and of wishing the gift squelched. This is the nature of envy, not jealousy (against RSV, NRSV, "are you jealous"; cf. *La Biblia*, *celos*). Similarly, it was their noxious *envy* (so KJV, *La Biblia*), not their *jealousy* (so RSV, NRSV) of Moses and Aaron that motivated the rebellion and punishment of Dathan and Abiram (Ps 106:16). Since envy (and the Evil Eye) were thought to wither the body or cause death even to the envier, the preferred translation of Prov 14:30 is "*envy* makes the bones rot" (so also *La Biblia* and against RSV "passion"). The same holds for Isa 11:13a, which refers not to the *jealousy* of Edom concerning Judah but rather the end of Edom's *envy* of Judah (so also *La Biblia* and against RSV).

In the NT, Acts 7:9 refers to the classic case of envy in the OT, stating that the patriarchs *envied* Joseph (not *were jealous of*, RSV). It is also envy rather than jealousy of which Acts 5:17 speaks as it recounts the *envy* that the high priests and Sadducees had toward the apostles because of their healing power (so also *La Biblia* and against RSV, NRSV *jealous*). Paul (and Silas) as successful missionaries were victims of Judean envy (KJV, *La Biblia*), not jealousy (so RSV) (Acts 13:45, 17:5). The RSV rendition of ζηλόω in Gal 4:18 as "to make much of" has no parallel anywhere else in the Bible and little to commend it. The verb rather refers to being *envied* in a context (4:12–20) where Paul is defending himself against an accusation of his opponents that he had injured the Galatians with an Evil Eye (Gal 3:1; see Elliott 1988; 1990; 2005).

---

45. Romans 10:19 (quoting Deut 32:21) speaks of God (as recounted by Moses) *provoking* Israel *to jealousy* and anger with what is "no people" and "a senseless people" (viz., the Gentiles). The RSV translation misconstrues the syntax. The Gentiles here are not the *object* of Israel's jealousy. The Gentiles rather are the *means* of the provocation. God uses those who are no people to provoke Israel to jealousy. When provoked, Israel will not be jealous *of* the Gentiles but rather jealous *through the mediation. of,* or because of, the Gentiles. Jealousy here would be distress concerning the loss of what belongs to Israel such as God's favor and blessing. This would also be the case in Rom 11:11 and 11:14.

SUMMARY AND CONCLUSIONS

The Hebrews did not devise terminology that precisely distinguished feelings of zeal from feelings of jealousy or feelings of envy, in contrast to English. A certain overlapping of usage also is evident with respect to the Greek term ζῆλος and its paronyms. But this does not mean that the biblical authors were unconcerned with these distinctions. It is apparent that as high-context societies they relied on social context and social dynamics to make clear the specific feeling intended or implied. In this essay, I have suggested more precise definitions and proposed new criteria based on social factors that aid our understanding and translation of terms in several ways.

First, a more precise definition and delineation of the concepts of *zeal, jealousy,* and *envy,* and of the differing social relations and dynamics they presuppose, enables greater precision in the understanding and use of these terms in common parlance, in biblical translations, and exegetical studies.

Second, the polysemic nature of such terms as those of the קנא and ζῆλος word families requires for their understanding close attention to the literary and social contexts in which they are embedded and employed. Close consideration must be given the subject matter of the texts in which they appear, the indicated social situations, and the social relations and dynamics they presuppose. When this is done in the case of the קנא and ζῆλος word families, it becomes clearer than heretofore when the terms have the sense of zeal or jealousy or envy.

Third, conclusions drawn in this study move us beyond the discussion of these terms in the standard lexica, exegetical dictionaries, and commentaries where jealousy and envy are usually treated as synonymous and where mention is rarely made of the connection of envy and the Evil Eye.

Fourth, we have encountered some texts where a definitive decision concerning sense and translation cannot be made and where yet other factors must be considered. Nevertheless, even here we have been able to suggest further determinants of meaning.

Fifth, our investigation has identified certain incorrect or misleading translations of modern versions insensitive to the specific nuances of zeal, jealousy, and envy. As an interesting general rule, I have found that the King James Version and the Spanish translation of *La Biblia* are in more frequent agreement with my proposed translations than the RSV or NRSV or NEB. I suspect that this may be due in great part to the fact that the KJV and *La Biblia* are closer culturally to the original biblical writings than are other modern Western translations. Distinguishing between biblical instances of jealousy and envy should be particularly helpful to modern Bible readers who usually equate the terms in everyday parlance.

Sixth, the emotion of envy, with which we are primarily concerned, has been identified as an intense feeling like zeal and jealousy, but different from them in several ways. Envy is never viewed positively but always negatively as malice directed against perceived rivals and their success and well-being supposedly gained at the envier's expense. It is linked, as zeal and jealousy are not, with the vicious Evil Eye through which envy operates and works its damage. It is regularly condemned by the biblical authors either explicitly or implicitly. At the same time they acknowledge that envy reared its ugly head repeatedly in Israel's history. Patriarchs and matriarchs, kings, prophets, and commoners were both the perpetrators and the victims of this noxious evil. The censure of envy expressed by biblical writers mirrors the disapproval registered by Greeks and Romans as well. In the intertestamental period, envy was linked for the first time to the devil, whose envy of Adam and Eve was said to have introduced death into the world (Wis 2:24). Followers of Jesus claimed envy to be the cause of his death and of the establishment's opposition to members of the Jesus movement. Envy and its partner, the Evil Eye, were condemned by Jesus and his followers. The emotion was both personally malicious and socially divisive and hence inimical to community cohesion. It was not until the patristic period, however, that Christians linked it explicitly with the devil.

Seventh, in regard to our initial question concerning God and envy, two things have become clear. First, Israel and the Jesus movement conceived of YHWH in anthropomorphic terms, including ascribing to YHWH zeal and jealousy. While describing God as greatly aroused over, or intensely dedicated to, or furiously angry with, or fervently jealous concerning some group or object, they nevertheless did not portray God as envious or provoking to envy. Of the eighty references or allusions to envy in the Bible, neither envy nor its malignant cousin, the Evil Eye, is attributed to YHWH.

This is in dramatic contrast to the Greek conception of the envy of the gods who directed their envy and Evil Eye as punishment against human hybris and overweening ambition. What prevailed in the Greek world from the beginning until Plato, however, never gained a foothold in Israelite or Christian thought. As far as we can ascertain, biblical communities never conceived of envy as an *external* force, whether from a god or a *daimon*, threatening a person from without. It was rather regarded as an *internal* human disposition, which arose in the human heart and was expressed through a noxious Evil Eye. In this respect Israel and the early church viewed envy just as they did the Evil Eye. In the Bible the Evil Eye is never portrayed as an external demonic force—in contrast to the surrounding cultures—but always as human characteristic and moral defect (Elliott 2005, 163–67).

The adjective ἄφθονος, *without envy*, is not used of God in either LXX or New Testament, even though this divine quality is everywhere implied.[46] In the post-biblical period, however, the church fathers gave extensive consideration to the ἀφθονία of God (Unnik 1971; 1973). Since envy was equated with stinginess, begrudging, and lack of generosity, to be without envy was equivalent to being *generous, liberal,* a

---

46. Philo recalled Plato's position and applied it explicitly to YHWH as well. Thus he states, "[W]e have it on the sacred authority of Plato that 'envy (φθόνος) has no place in the divine choir,' and 'wisdom is most divine and most free-handed.'" At another point he makes it even clearer by declaring, "For there is neither doubt nor envy (φθόνος) in God. It is true that the Deity neither doubts nor envies. . . . The Deity . . . is without part in any evil and is not envious of immortality or anything else whatever in the case of the good man" (*Quest. Gen.* 1.55 on Gen 3:22). See also Pseudo-Phocylides 70–75, where envy is excluded from the heavenly realm.

quality of God mentioned often in the Bible[47] and perhaps most prominently in the parable Jesus told of the workers in the vineyard (Matt 20:1–15).[48]

Second, on the basis of a clearer delineation of the nature and insidiousness of envy, as distinct from jealousy and zeal, we can now better appreciate why Israel and the early Church never spoke and probably never conceived of their God as envious. Imagining God as capable of jealousy, zeal, ardor, or anger posed no problem but the line, apparently, was drawn at envy. The reason for this, I suggest, lies in the way envy was understood in antiquity—namely as an attack on another fed by a perception of rivalry, a grief over a rival's happiness, a notion of limited good, a sense of inferiority by comparison, and a wish that the happiness of the other be destroyed. Inasmuch as envy was felt toward peers of similar status, how could it be attributed to YHWH, who was held to be exalted above all creatures in majesty and transcendence? To what entity, divine or human, could YHWH have felt inferior by comparison? Moreover, of what valued good would the Creator of the world and the source of all life have been deficient? How could YHWH be imagined to be envious of the happiness of mortals when He was worshipped as the source of all that exists and the fount of every blessing? In terms of the divine enforcement of justice and the natural order, Israel and formative Christianity spoke of the zeal and jealousy of God but never of divine envy. God often was said to oppose the arrogant and give grace to the humble, to remove the mighty from their seats and exalt those of low degree; but never was envy said to lie behind this action. Instead YHWH's affect and action were stated to be prompted by his commitment to the covenant and fidelity to his promises. Rather than feared as an envious deity, YHWH is worshiped as a constantly generous, merciful and liberal God, qualities that are envy's opposite.

Eventually the envy so alien to YHWH was connected to God's cosmic adversary, the Devil. In the first century B.C.E. envy was first linked by an Israelite with the Devil and death (Wis 2:24). By the fourth century of the Common Era, the Church as well had begun to view both envy and the Evil Eye as the Devil's doing.[49] In the popular mind, this unholy linkage of devil and envy has continued ever since. Envy, then, is not God's but the devil's domain. Envy, as Jesus warned his followers, lurks in every creature's heart (Mark 7:18–23). The recipe for resisting it is not ritual but repentance (Elliott 2005b, 165–67), sharing of precious resources, and imitation of an envy-less God who is liberal, hospitable, and generous in abundant measure.

---

47. For generosity as a desirable and honorable quality see Deut 15:14; Tob 4:5–11, 16; Matt 20:15—all as opposed to having an Evil Eye. See also Prov 11:24–26; 14:31; 19:17; 21:26; 28:27; Sir 4:4–6; 2 Cor 8:1–5; 9:6–7, 11–15.

48. On this parable of "invidious comparison" and the generosity of the owner, see Elliott 1992. For God as generous see also Rom 10:12; 2 Cor 9:8–11; Phil 4:19; James 1:5.

49. See, for example, Basil of Caesarea, Homily 11, "On Envy" (PG 31. 372–386); Limberis (1991); also Cyprian, *De zelo et livore*. CSEL III.1.13.417–32.

The Usefulness of the Meaning Response Concept for Interpreting Translations of Healing Accounts in Matthew's Gospel

John J. Pilch

When presented with a blind and dumb demoniac (Matt 12:22), Jesus[1] restored him to well-being. In some translations, Jesus is said to have cured the man (NRSV, NAB, JB, NJB, NEB), while in others he is reported to have healed him (KJV, RSV, TEV, CEV). One and the same Greek word, θεραπεύω, is translated as *cure* and *heal* without distinction.[2] Dictionaries tend to agree (Liddell and Scott 1996, a.v.; Louw and Nida 1988: I:23.139). Acknowledging that three Greek words in the NT (θεραπεύω, ἰᾶσθαι, and σοζείν) are frequently translated *heal* interchangeably, scholars rightly caution against "making refined distinctions on grounds of etymology" (Hemer 1986, 54). Such ambiguous translation characterizes the entire semantic field of health, sickness, and related terms in the Bible.

The risk of misunderstanding and misinterpreting the Bible because of such imprecise translations is especially acute in the contemporary Western world where many ordinary readers have a rather sophisticated understanding of health and sickness issues. This knowledge, however, is tainted by the modern triumph of a "universalist biology" which "tends to blind us to the dramatic variation in the ways that people experience their own physiology based on who they are and what they know" (Moerman 2002, 70). This universalist conviction persists even though anatomy students learn that the illustrations in their textbooks can be verified in perhaps only 30 percent of human beings. Thus, readers of the Bible often believe that the words *blind, deaf, paralyzed,* and so on meant in antiquity exactly what they mean in the modern world.

For this reason, I published an article in 2000 urging that translators of the Bible adopt the definitions of *health, sickness,* and related terms that are standard in medical anthropology (Pilch 2000a). Anthropology in general bridges cultures, and medical anthropology in particular identifies and explains commonalities and differences

---

1. By "Jesus" I mean here and throughout the essay the way in which the author of Matthew chose to portray Jesus.

2. Θεραπεύω occurs forty-five times in the New Testament.

97

concerning human health and sickness issues across cultures. In that discipline, disease and illness are explanatory concepts of the reality called *sickness*. Disease is an explanatory concept representing a biomedical understanding of a sickness event, while illness is an explanatory concept that reflects a sociocultural understanding of a sickness event. Given the absence of scientific technology in antiquity, it seemed best to speak of illnesses rather than diseases in the Bible, even though diseases certainly existed at the time.

Further, medicine seeks cures (the control of a disease). While every sick person hopes for a cure, when that is elusive one hopes at least to regain and maintain meaning in life. This is the function of healing: to restore and maintain meaning in life. Again, it seemed that *healing* was the better word to describe events in the Bible in which sick people were restored to well-being. In a book published in 2000 and in subsequent publications, I used and continue to use those definitions and distinctions from medical anthropology in my analysis of the healing and sickness reports in the Bible (Pilch 2000b). I have incorporated these concepts and distinctions in twenty-one articles related to sickness and similar terms that were submitted for publication in the *New Interpreter's Dictionary of the Bible* (Sakenfeld 2006). While some scholars have adopted these definitions (Estévez Lopez 2003), contemporary medicocentric interpretation of ancient texts nevertheless still prevails and is abetted by imprecise translations.

In this essay, therefore, I propose a concept that can be employed in the interpretation of sickness and healing reports in the Bible however misleading the translation may be. This concept should help exegetes and Bible readers to remedy their frustrations with medicocentric translations. The concept, *meaning response*, was coined and described by the medical anthropologist Daniel Moerman (2002).[3] His very first article on this topic, "Anthropology of Symbolic Healing" (1979), proved richly insightful for the analysis of healing reports in the New Testament, especially the man born blind (John 9; Pilch 2000b, 32–34, 132–38). Some twenty-five years of continued research, discussion, and reflection since then have sharpened the concept we now explore for its usefulness in understanding biblical reports of healing.

Meaning Responses

Humans beings have three possible responses to injury: autonomous, behaviorally specific, and meaning responses (Moerman 2002, 16). Among the most important responses to injury are the autonomous ones. As the name indicates, these responses are part and parcel of the human body and its physiology. They are automatic and beyond the control of the subject. The human body is well equipped to heal itself. Its key tool is the immunological system, but other related systems play a role, too. In other words, an injured body immediately seeks to initiate a healing process. A cut

3 Daniel Moerman is the William E. Stirton Professor of Anthropology (emeritus) at the University of Michigan–Dearborn.

and bleeding finger can clot and heal quickly.[4] Colds and headaches are other examples. In other words, most sicknesses for ordinary, healthy people are self-limiting.

Behaviorally specific responses include the ways the human body responds to medical treatment. A severe case of sinusitis—a bacterial infection that causes pain in the throat which in turn causes a pain in the ears when swallowing—responds with amazing speed to an antibiotic. Similarly, pressure on the cut finger of a person on aspirin therapy is another example of a behavior-specific response. Such pressure eventually stops the bleeding. A Band-Aid also helps in this case.

A meaning response describes the way a person interacts with the total context in which a therapeutic intervention occurs. Moerman defines the meaning response as "the psychological and physiological effects of meaning in the treatment of illness" (2002, 14). The key word is *meaning*. Human beings provide the meaning since they are meaning-seeking and meaning-creating beings. Thus, "[W]hat people know and understand about medicine, what they experience about healing, and what healing processes mean can enhance both autonomous and behavioral healing processes" (Moerman 2002, 20). A retired, wheelchair-bound Franciscan friar who lost a leg to diabetes regularly took aspirin to assuage his pain(s). Aspirin, of course, serves this purpose. But when this friar sent someone to purchase a new supply of aspirin, he specified the brand name: Bayer. In fact, he would draw the aspirin face with Bayer printed vertically and horizontally, sharing the letter "y." Any other brand did not treat his pain effectively. This illustrates a human meaning response. If other brands of aspirin did not alleviate his pain, it may be that the meaning he gave to this specific brand of aspirin is what brought relief. Perhaps aspirin itself was actually ineffective.

Moerman's investigations centered on placebos, that is, inert materials that have been considered to cause a healing. He argues that if something is inert, then in reality it can cause nothing! How, then, can one explain scientifically measurable improvements in sickness conditions, including proven cures, when the *materia medica* is inert (a placebo)? The answer lies in the many elements that contribute to the formation of a meaning response. With the aid of this insight about meaning responses to sickness experiences, let us review Gospel healing reports about Jesus with a particular focus on Matthew.

HEALERS

According to Moerman, all healers or therapists play a very important role in the formation and effectiveness of a healing response (Moerman 2002, 32–46). The nature, character, personality, behavior, and style of healers can wield enormous influence on a human meaning response. This is true not only with regard to inert *materia medica* but also to active medication. One review of the medical literature reporting treatments for angina pectoris found that drugs were no more effective than placebos. The physicians made the difference. Enthusiastic physicians could heal 70 percent to 90 percent of their patients with placebos, while skeptical physicians could only heal

---

4. Unless one is on aspirin therapy. Aspirin functions as an anti-clotting agent. This will be discussed below.

30 percent to 40 percent (Moerman 2002, 38–39). Certainty stands out as the most powerful aspect of a healer's demeanor. This certainty and self-confidence derives from the healer's conviction that the techniques are indeed powerful and effective. When the healer can convey this certainty to patients, the techniques are very likely to work effectively. The personality of the sick person appears to have little to do with the outcome.

Jesus is most appropriately identified as a folk healer (Pilch 2000b, 85–86). In general, a folk healer's power is viewed as real and effective but is not necessarily accepted by everyone as legitimate. Many reports of Jesus' healing activity are brief (Matt 12:22 presents the diagnosis and the healing). The ensuing controversy between those who recognized his power as legitimate and those who did not is frequently longer than the report of the healing.[5] Jesus' certainty about and his clients' faith in his healing powers are rooted in his status as a holy man (Pilch 1998, 53–55; 2002, 106–8). In the Synoptic tradition, this is the very first identification of Jesus. " 'I know who you are,' said the unclean spirit, 'the Holy One of God' " (Mark 1:24).[6] All cultures identify a holy person (man/woman) as someone who has direct experiential contact with the realm of the deity or the spirit world and who brokers favors (especially healing) from that realm to human beings. The characteristics of a holy man are direct contact or communication with spirits (Matt 3:16–17; 17:1–8); control or power over spirits (Matt 8:28–34); control over alternate states of consciousness experiences (ASCs), the means by which a holy person contacts the spirit world (Matt 14:23–33); a *this worldly* focus on the material world, that is, the holy person uses his or her abilities for the benefits of individuals or the community and not for personal gain (Matt 9:30); the ability to journey to the sky and the spirit world (2 Cor 12:2–5); the holy person has no fears of being possessed by demons he exorcizes (Matt 8:28–34); the holy person can remember at least part of his or her ASC experiences (Matt 17:1–8); and healing is the major focus of the holy person's activity (Matt 3:24).

The ethnography indicates that there is a process by which a holy person becomes a healer. This is how Jesus experienced that process. After being contacted by a spirit which identified itself (Matt 3:13–17, God, father*)*, Jesus the holy man had to acquire necessary ritual skills. Successfully passing the test of his loyalty by Satan (Matt 4:1–11) in which Jesus demonstrates mastery of the challenge-and-riposte procedures, a basic cultural ritual skill, he is prepared to continue to hone these skills and acquire still others. This requires tutelage by a spirit and real-life teacher. Mark reports that angels ministered to Jesus (and undoubtedly tutored him) after he passed the test of his loyalty (1:13). Tradition also reports that Jesus was a disciple of John the Baptist who surely tutored him in the additional skills needed by a holy man (John 3:22–24). The Baptist himself was recognized as a holy man (Matt 11:7–11). Evidence indicates that, throughout his life, Jesus experienced a growing familiarity

---

5. Matthew 12:23 presents the controversy over Jesus' healing power, leading eventually to a direct challenge to the legitimacy of his power or authorization for his healing activity in Matt 21:23.

6. Matthew 9:8 expressed this idea after an exorcism performed by Jesus when the crowd acknowledged Jesus as "one empowered" or "authorized" to do such things by God (Malina and Neyrey 1998, 155–57).

with his possessing/adopting spirit (Matt 17:1–19). Moreover, he continued to have ongoing ASC experiences (Matt 11:25–27). Jesus was certain that God always heard him (John 11:41–42), and he communicated with God often (John 12:27–30).

Such experience gave Jesus rock-solid confidence in his skill as a holy man/healer. This confidence appears to have been recognized by sick people as well. When two blind men followed Jesus and begged him for mercy, Jesus asked: "'Do you believe that I am able to do this?' They replied: 'Yes, Lord.' Then he touched their eyes, saying, 'According to your faith be it done to you.' And their eyes were opened" (Matt 9:27–31). Medicocentric approaches to interpreting this event identify the specific eye problem as cataracts and Jesus' touch as couching the cataracts (Howard 2001, 242). This explanation is highly speculative even if this procedure is well described by Aulus (Aurelius) Cornelius Celsus (25 B.C.E.–50 C.E.) reflecting the medical knowledge of the Alexandrian school.[7] The value of Moerman's hypothesis about the importance of meaning response is that whether or not one accepts a medicocentric explanation of the healing of the two blind men, the potential effectiveness of Jesus' strategy is heightened by his confidence in what he does and the strength of the faith in him and his activity that Jesus inspired in his clients. The reason for this is that Jesus is a vehicle of God's power. He required faith in the God of Israel who acts through holy men such as he himself was. To blaspheme the spirit is to dishonor God by rejecting or denying divine activity. Spirit is best interpreted as God acting (Matt 12:31–32).

A study of troubled students, half of whom were assigned to psychotherapists and the other half to warm, trustworthy, and caring professors from a variety of disciplines, concluded that "positive changes experienced by our patients, whether they were treated by a [therapist] or a [professor], are generally attributable to the healing effects of a benign human relationship" (Strupp and Hadley 1979, cited by Moerman 2002, 92–93). The effective healer is one who can evoke meaning responses in the sick person. This would apply to healers in the ancient world and especially Jesus in the New Testament.

A healer's strategy is similar to the psychotherapeutic process. Each has four key elements. The therapist has a theory. He creates and maintains a specific interpersonal context characterized by empathetic listening. He strives to understand the meaning of client's reports. Finally, he attempts to reinterpret these reports so the client can gain new understanding and create new meaning. From the client's perspective as a sick person, s/he appreciates the therapist's familiarity with her or his problem. Clearly others with the same or similar problems have approached the therapist, so this sick person is one among many. The sick person further appreciates a caring listener, who takes the report seriously and tries to reinterpret it together with the sick person (Moerman 2002, 95–96).

This process can be found in the reports about Jesus' healing activities. The summary healing reports in Matthew indicate that Jesus' reputation as a healer was widespread (Matt 4:24; 11:4–6; 14:35; 15:30–31). Moreover, when word of a particular healing was broadcast, others quickly brought their sick to be healed (Matt 8:14–16). Jesus was

---

7. Couching is the manual displacement of the lens of the eye into the vitreous humor.

known to be compassionate and sympathetic (Matt 9:36; 14:14; 20:34). The case of the blind and mute demoniac (diagnosis) healed by Jesus (therapy) illustrates Jesus' masterful ability to reinterpret sickness episodes (Matt 12:22–45). The blind and mute man could certainly hear all along, but now he could also speak and see. Immediately after his healing, he witnesses and hears the heated conflict between Jesus and the Pharisees. The man hears the Pharisees' question about the source of the healer's power (v. 24). He hears Jesus' warning about the terrible consequences of blasphemy against the Spirit (vv. 31–32). He hears Jesus' exhortation to good speech and a warning against bad speech (vv. 34–37). Finally he hears Jesus' reassessment of the healed condition (the prognosis). The expelled demon may try to return, perhaps with companions. If the healed person wants to remain whole, that is, to retain the ability to speak, he is best advised to heed Jesus the healer's advice about good speech, lest a worse condition than the first result (vv. 43–45).[8]

KNOWLEDGE AND ILLNESS

"The biomedical model of disease is so pervasive that we often fail to see it as such but view it as reality" (O'Boyle 1993, cited by Moerman 2002, 67, but omitted in his bibliography). Moerman uses this quotation to introduce a very important idea in his sixth chapter, "Knowledge and Cultures; Illness and Healing." He reminds us that we do not really know the world "as it is," but rather as we experience and interpret it. To illustrate the point, he summarizes classic research about food and what we know about eating. In the United States, cows and pigs are edible although dogs and horses are not. We consider this only natural. Yet Hindus do not eat cows, Muslims do not eat pigs, many Native Americans eat dogs, and the French consider horse to be a delicacy. The point is that human eating has two dimensions: the nutritional and the meaningful. All the animals mentioned are nutritional, but cultures assign different meanings to the animals that determine whether or not they should be eaten in a given culture. These meanings are interpretations, and interpretations are not the entities interpreted.

As already noted above, the chemical reality of aspirin is essentially acetylsalicilic acid. The meaning of the pill (that it is an analgesic) and its brand name (e.g., Bayer) are interpretations. Aspirin, however, is not analgesic in relationship to the pain of a bacterial infection, hence the interpretation needs qualification. The proven effectiveness of generic medications underscores the fact that considering brand names alone to be effective is an interpretation.

"Much of the meaning of medicine, of the meaning response (and in the narrowest sense, the placebo effect), is a cultural phenomenon engaged in a complex interplay on the meanings of disease and illness. The modern triumph of a universalist biology tends to blind us to the dramatic variation in the way that people experience their own physiology based on who they are and what they know" (Moerman 2002, 70). As Moerman observes later in a footnote about the 1987 edition of the *Merck Manual*, "biology is cultural" (Moerman 2002, 73 n. 25).

Knowing is a very complex cultural phenomenon, and country is not a very use-

8. For a similar analysis in John's Gospel, based on a model of symbolic healing, see Pilch 2000b, 32–34, 131–38.

ful way of identifying and understanding culture. Northern and southern parts of one and the same country exhibit variations in its culture, for example, in lifestyles, diet, and language. Medical research ordinarily conducted in national laboratories or university hospitals will tend to have homogeneous subjects: those participating in the research are relatively cosmopolitan and relatively urban. Therefore, conclusions drawn in these studies may have limited applicability.

Moerman concludes this chapter by noting that the illnesses from which human beings suffer at the present time, and which are diagnosed and understood according to widely shared conventional scientific medicine, still vary significantly. They have different meanings in different places. Conviction about the malicious effects of the evil eye, which characterizes about 36 percent of the world's cultures, and especially the illnesses (including death) that it is considered to have caused, is viewed as superstition in the West, especially in scientific medicine (Pilch 2004).

One final point about knowledge (Moerman 2002, 84). Knowledge is not a synonym for belief. For many people, knowledge is what is true and real. But it is important to distinguish two kinds of knowledge: experiential and empirical. All human beings have knowledge that is experientially true but not necessarily empirically true. Some cultures (German, Austrian, Polish) believe one can catch a cold by standing in a draft. Some of these people do experience that consequence. On a train trip from Krakow, Poland, to Czechoslovakia in 1925 to play the trumpet in an orchestral concert, my late father as a young student enjoyed feeling the wind on his face as he stuck his head out the window or stood elsewhere in the draft. Sure enough, he got sick and could not play in the concert. His experiential knowledge that drafts cause colds played a role in his sickness. He was cautioned to avoid drafts by his teachers, but he gave no heed. Of course, no empirical knowledge would support this explanation of his cold. To further complicate matters, the experiential knowledge of people in one culture will differ widely from similar experiential knowledge of people in another culture.

SICK PEOPLE AND THEIR ILLNESSES IN THE NEW TESTAMENT

These insights from Moerman contribute to a better understanding of taxonomies of illness reported in the New Testament (Pilch 2000b). For example, there are two areas in Matthew's Gospel that might reveal the taxonomy recognized by his community: thirteen summary reports or references to healing of illnesses scattered throughout the Gospel; and a cluster of ten demonstrations of power (δυνάμεις, see Matt 13:54, 58)—mainly healings—in Matt 8–9 (Pilch 2000b, 80–84).

Summary reports of healings list illnesses that Jesus or his disciples remedied. Four of the thirteen mention that people were possessed by a demon or unclean spirit (4:24; 7:22; 8:16; 10:8). In Matt 4:24, demoniacs (participle) are listed along with the moonstruck and paralytics (nouns), suggesting that to be possessed by a demon was itself considered an illness.[9] At the same time, this culture firmly believed

---

9. It is medicocentric and anachronistic to translate this word *epileptic*; *lunatic* is better, but also misleading (Pilch 2000b, 19)

that spirits—including God (Exod 15:26)—were personal agents who could inflict illnesses.[10] In assessing the other specific illnesses mentioned in summaries (Matt 11:4—the blind, the lame, those with a repulsive scaly skin condition [leprosy], the deaf, the dead; Matt 15:36—the lame, the maimed, the blind, the mute, and many others; Matt 21:14—the blind and lame), two things should be noted. One, the afflicted person is described (e.g., the blind) rather than the affliction (e.g., blindness). This reflects the culture's preference for concrete thinking rather than abstractions. It also reflects the experiential knowledge of these sick people in this culture. People experience a condition that affects their being. It is not the condition that is the main concern, it is the person's experience and interpretation of that condition. Recall that biology is cultural. It is not easy to demonstrate conclusively that these conditions (blind, paralyzed, etc.) are the same known in the contemporary Western biomedical understanding. Moerman notes that

> in so far as a culture (German, Navajo, Zulu) is a skein of meanings, understandings, beliefs, and knowledge, stitched together somehow by metaphors, institutions, and memories, and in so far as these things can affect individual lives, it seems reasonable to anticipate that these factors will work themselves out differently in different places in the world, even places as similar as Germany and Holland, Britain and the USA. (2002, 84–85)

The differences between the contemporary Western world and the ancient Middle Eastern world are surely even more pronounced.

In previous research (Pilch 2000b, 81–84), I had proposed a taxonomy for the cluster of ten demonstrations of Jesus' power in Matt 8–9, reflecting a cultural concern for boundaries and their violation.[11] This interpretation still seems to be plausible and valid. In each instance, Matthew's report appears to confirm that *biology is cultural*. The so-called leper in Matt 8:1–4 whose irregular skin condition removed him from the community (Lev 13:45–46) was brought by Jesus back within the boundaries of the community. This is based on understanding leprosy as a cultural interpretation of a physical condition rather than a purely physical condition that is definitely not Hansen's disease (Pilch 2000b, 39–54).

The paralysis that incapacitated the centurion's servant (Matt 8:5–13) signaled a misalignment of the body's three symbolic zones, another cultural interpretation of the human body (Malina 2001, 68–71; Pilch 2000b, 106–11). In this case, hands-feet (locomotion; purposeful activity) were not in sync with mouth-ears (self-expressive speech) and heart-eyes (emotion-fused thinking). This lack of synchronicity indicates trouble within the boundaries of the body, which Jesus remedies in this instance even at a distance. The same misalignment of symbolic body zones characterizes the case of another paralytic (Matt 9:1–8, hands-feet) and the two blind men (9:27–31, heart-eyes; compare Matt 20:29–34).

---

10. See, for example, Matt 17:18, where a demon appears to be the cause of or is associated with the moonstruck condition and its consequences mentioned in v. 15; cf. Ps 121:6.

11. This includes the boundary of the sea in Matt 8:23–27 as well as those of the human body elsewhere in this cluster.

By restoring Peter's mother-in-law to wholeness (Matt 8:14–17), the ruler's daughter to life (Matt 9:18–19, 23–26), and the woman with the severe menstrual irregularity to well-being (Matt 9:20–22), Jesus once again shores up and strengthens boundaries. Home is the appropriate locus for women. Despite her anomalous presence in her son-in-law's home (a daughter left her family—the *in-laws*—to live with her husband in the patriarch's compound), the illness (described as fever) of Peter's unnamed mother-in-law puts the household at risk. She certainly played some role in the functioning of the household (Prov 31:10–31). Upon being restored to well-being, she immediately resumed her important role.

The death of a marriageable daughter also poses a risk to the household (Matt 9:18–26; Pilch 2007). The family loses an opportunity to become stronger because this death negates the possibility of a patrilateral parallel cousin marriage. Even if that marriage were not imminent, the family lost a valuable pair of working hands. The girl's death weakens the family. Restored to life, the girl is not the only beneficiary of Jesus' power. The family is made whole again, too, and its potential growth in well-being is set back on track.

The woman with the menstrual irregularity (Matt 9:20–22) is found outside the domestic setting (the home) but with her feminine power run amok. With this condition, she is definitely out of place in the public sphere, and she poses a threat to order and tranquillity even though driven to the public arena by a desperate hope for help. The distinctive aspect of this story (reported in greater [i.e., interpretive] detail in Mark 5:24–34) is that Jesus has effective power but is apparently not always in control of it. Even so, since his power is from God, this healing is God's will (the passive voice confirms this), and Jesus approves: " 'Take heart, daughter; your faith has made you well.' And instantly the woman was made well" (Matt 9:22; Greek is literally *saved*).

Healing the demoniacs (Matt 8:28–34; 9:32–34) involves an even larger group than family. The two demoniacs in the country of the Gadarenes posed a threat to the safety of the community and all passersby (Matt 8:28–34). By casting out their demons, Jesus restores the two men to normal existence. Moreover, the demons are completely expelled from the region, once again securing its boundaries and making it completely safe. The brief account of the healing of the mute demoniac (Matt 9:32–34) not only gives further testimony to the power of Jesus but also suggests potential benefit for all of Israel, making secure even broader boarders. This report also witnesses to the never-ending conflict of opinion about Jesus' healing power. No one ever denied his power and effectiveness. The conflict centered on the source of his power: was it God? or was it the prince of demons?

The seemingly anomalous report in this cluster is that of Jesus calming a storm (Matt 8:23–27). While at first glance this does not appear to be a healing, perhaps it can be so interpreted. If healing is the restoration of meaning to life, then the sea which was overstepping its divinely ordained boundaries was interrupting the order that God imposed on chaos at the very beginning (Gen 1). The sea was put back in its place and healed on this occasion.

A literary-theological interpretation of these ten demonstrations of Jesus' power relates them to the ten plagues of the Exodus (Exod 7:8–11:10). As the Lord God threw creation back into chaos (at least in Egypt) to allow the Israelites to escape captivity, so Jesus restores order to chaos in human life by offering liberation from enslaving human conditions (Matt 8–9). This is certainly an appropriate interpretation. Perhaps a medicocentric focus on identifying the real sickness conditions that Jesus addressed misses the main point. As should be clear by now, biology is cultural, and the specific biological sickness issues that Jesus remedied require a cultural interpretation.[12]

POWER OR AUTHORITY?

While contemporary interest tends to focus on the sickness events in these healing reports, the main point seems to be rather the power (ἐξουσία) of those who can overcome them. The Greek word can be translated both *authority* (e.g., Matt 7:29, Jesus teaches with authority) and *power* (e.g., Matt 9:8, Jesus has power to heal a paralytic; 10:1 the disciples are empowered to heal and exorcize). Most translations consistently translate the word as *authority*. The JB translates it as *power* in Matt 9:8 (but unfortunately not in Matt 10:1 where it would also seem to be appropriate in English). The report in Matt 9:1–8 nevertheless seems to favor power over authority. Jesus claims that if he says "your sins are forgiven," who can tell whether they are or not? But if he says "rise and walk," and the person stands up and falls on his face, clearly Jesus does not have the *power* he claims to have. Danker in *The Greek-English Lexicon* (2000) would seem to agree that the word is best translated *power*.

In a social-scientific register, *authority* is the socially acknowledged right to command, direct, or order people. This is true of Jesus' teaching. *Power*, on the other hand, must be distinguished. Power over adult people is the ability to have effect with the sanction of force for non-compliance. Thus, Jesus has power over spirits, who are other-than-human persons. Power over things and children is the same as force. Jesus exhibits such power over the roiling sea, suggesting that translations of ἐξουσία need to be revisited.

OTHER HEALING REPORTS IN MATTHEW

There are six other healing reports in Matthew's Gospel outside the cluster in Matt 8–9. These include the healing of a man with a withered hand (Matt 12:9–14); sick people gaining healing just by touching the fringe of Jesus' garments (Matt 14:34–36; compare Matt 9:20; see Num 15:38); healing of the Canaanite woman's possessed daughter (Matt 15:21–28); healing of the moonstruck and possessed young man (Matt 17:14–21); healing of the two blind men near Jericho (Matt 20:29–34); and healing of the blind and lame in the temple (21:14). All of them exhibit elements of the human meaning response.

Three of these reports (the withered hand; touching the garment fringes; blind

---

12. It would seem that the models I proposed in 2000b are still plausible—though not necessarily the only—cultural interpretations. That the models are cultural and not medicocentric is in their favor.

and lame in the temple) are very briefly reported. They are high-context reports.[13] The passive voice in the story of the man with the withered hand as well as sick people touching the fringes identifies God as the agent. The context could contribute to the formulation of a meaning response in each case. In the men's community center (synagogue), Jesus makes a good case for doing good even on the Sabbath (the pretense on which Jesus' enemies wanted to entrap him). The sick man would be heartened by Jesus' answer more than he would be frightened by the obvious attack on Jesus. Similarly, the people at Gennesaret knew of his reputation as a holy man/ healer, and that anything—even an article of clothing—associated with such a person could and would transmit the power of God who was the one and only healer in the Israelite tradition (Exod 15:26; Sir 38:2; Acts 19:11–12). This is a central element in the Israelite meaning response to illness.

Mention of Jesus healing the blind and lame in the temple (Matt 21:14) has too little information to make a judgment about a meaning response. Some traditions (2 Sam 5:8 LXX) excluded such from the temple, and, according to Lev 21:17–24, priests who were blind or lame were disqualified from entering the sanctuary. Scholars are agreed this is a polemical statement in Matthew's narrative.

The story of the Canaanite woman's possessed daughter (Matt 15:21–28) testifies to Jesus' reputation as a holy man/healer. Even a non-Israelite appreciated Jesus' power, and she addressed her request to him with respectful titles: Lord, Son of David. Despite an insulting response from Jesus, she persisted and obtained what she requested. The passive voice (v. 28) once again indicates that the God of Israel is the healer. Whether or not the Canaanite woman understood this is beside the point. Her confidence was in Jesus as Israelite holy man (Son of David) and devotee of the God of Israel, and it remained unshaken to the end. Actually, in this instance Jesus' behavior would seem to blunt the formation of a meaning response, even though the beneficiary is the woman's absent possessed daughter. The daughter is the one who would have to construct a meaning response. Yet it is plausible to suspect that her mother has helped the daughter to construct one. In order for it to be effective, Jesus the healer must cooperate with it, which is what the mother's persistence seems to achieve. One can imagine how she related this encounter to her healed daughter and how much she (and perhaps the daughter, too) relished repeating it for others. The mother bested Jesus in a challenge-and-riposte contest (the only person reported to have done so in Jesus' career), and Jesus—as a good loser—granted her request.

The report about the possessed moonstruck young man (Matt 17:14–20) once again recounts the healing itself in a single verse (v. 18, θεραπεύω). Though it adds significant details (falling into fire and water), the diagnosis is also brief and reported in a single verse (v. 15). The greater part of the report compares Jesus with his disciples as healers. Though empowered by Jesus to heal (Matt 10:1, 8) and quite likely

---

13. A text sketches in outline and leaves out what it is assumed the reader already knows. It is left to the imagination of the reader to fill in the gaps. The author of Matthew depends upon the general cultural knowledge of the readers to supply from their own cultural and social resources to complete the text. While for most people of the world, the term "9/11" is a high-context one that does not require filling in the gaps because of its international exposure, the term "ground zero" referring to the same thing, but internal to the United States, is a term requiring additional information for it to make sense to them.

tutored by him in appropriate techniques, they are unsuccessful in this instance. Jesus explains why. They are lacking in confidence in the God of Israel (faithless and perverse generation, v. 17; little faith, v. 20). As noted above, the most important characteristic of a healer that will enhance therapeutic effectiveness is self-confidence and certitude. This is the healer's most important contribution to the formation of a healing response in a sick petitioner. In this report, Jesus is keenly aware of a key to his own success as a healer, and he chides the disciples for not developing that element.

Finally, the healing of the two blind men (Matt 20:29–34) contains some key elements that contribute to the petitioners' successful formation of a meaning response. They cry out to him with honorable titles: Son of David, Lord (vv. 30, 31). This indicates that even if they have never met him before, they know about him and have confidence in him. When rebuked by the crowd to shut up, they shout all the louder. Such persistence testifies to their faith in the healer. In response to Jesus' inquiry: "'what do you want me to do for you?' they reply: 'Let our eyes be opened.'" Once again the passive voice indicates that these blind petitioners recognize Jesus as a holy man who has the ability to broker that gift of healing from the world of God. By touching their eyes, Jesus channels to them healing energy from God which proves to be immediately effective. The certitude of Jesus in his abilities communicated to these petitioners who are equally stubbornly committed to him as the healer/holy man works welcome results.

CONCLUSION

As mentioned above, enough has been written about the problems of ambiguous or misleading translations relative to healing, sickness, and related notions in the Bible to encourage more respectful and plausible representations of the ancient Mediterranean world. Given the translations that exist, this article proposes a fresh insight from medical anthropology, namely, the meaning response, as a better way to interpret sickness and healing reports in the Bible. This preliminary application to the Gospel of Matthew tests and demonstrates the usefulness of this concept. Medical anthropology and its insights are not intended to replace traditional historical-critical exegesis. The intention is rather to enrich and give increased Mediterranean cultural plausibility to the interpretation of healing stories.

Translating the Hebrew Body into English Metaphor
Carolyn Leeb

Language is a social enterprise, and understanding meaning in language requires an understanding of the social systems that underlie the language. Translation of biblical Hebrew has not always taken account of the social systems in which the biblical texts were produced. Anthropology—the critical study of human beings in their social milieu—is a crucial resource in determining what words mean in speech between two native speakers of a language and thus is vital to translation. We understand intuitively that words which refer to abstractions, such as values or practices, are culture-dependent. But words which refer to concrete physical objects must be defined in ways which reflect their symbolic value to a particular culture as well. In no area, perhaps, is this more apparent than when the physical reality referred to is the human body. Social systems divide the activities of human beings in various ways, and these activities are seen as connected with particular parts of the body. Furthermore, various parts of the body may symbolize particular values in these social systems. How human beings were envisioned and how their activities were *embodied*, that is assigned to particular parts of the body, was not the same in the ancient world as it is for much of the world today.

We live in a world where modern science, especially medicine, has unlocked many of the secrets of the human body. When we read a word which describes a body part, we tend to assume first that the referent is the anatomical structure which it indicates and further that all symbolic meaning has developed secondarily. While this may be true for visible, external body features such as hands and noses, for internal, invisible body parts it was certainly not the case. Ancient peoples had only limited understanding of anatomy and physiology and understood neither the precise relationships among the organs which were revealed when an animal was slaughtered nor the particular bodily functions those organs performed. Innards were associated with various human experiences and activities on a less than scientific basis. The heart, for instance, was not recognized as a pumping organ until quite late, in William Harvey's 1628 *Exercitatio anatomica de motu cordis et sanquinis in animalibus*.

Complicating our cross-cultural conversations with the ancient world still further is the fact that we group and divide human activities and responses into different categories, according to different criteria, from those assumed by much of the ancient world. By contrast with the comparatively recent fragmentation of humans as body, mind, and soul/spirit, the ancient world viewed human beings more holistically. What's more, we tend to classify human responses based on the supposed *quality* of those responses: rational or emotional, thoughts or feelings (with perhaps a third category of autonomic responses). Actions then spring from, are motivated by, responses to either emotions or rational decisions and thoughts in our modern view. For the ancient world, the *locus* of interior experience, rather than its *quality* was determinative in evaluating it. They made little distinction between the perception, realization, or knowledge of a situation and what we would call the *emotions* associated with that experience. In this study, I shall deal with the way one set of human responses is *embodied*—that is, symbolized by reference to the human body—by an idiom which includes the Hebrew words widely translated *heart*, לב/לבב.[1]

DOES HEBREW לב MEAN HEART?

We have long known that Hebrew לב designates an amorphous interiority rather than our modern anatomical sense of heart, and this interiority was not specifically understood as an emotional, much less romantic, locus. BDB describes לב and לבב as "inner man, mind, will, heart," with its first description of the human heart as "*the inner man* in contrast with the outer" (1907, 524). It lists such things as mind, knowledge, thinking, reflection, memory; inclinations, resolutions, and determinations of the will; conscience, moral character; seat of appetites; the man himself; and "seat of the emotions and passions."

Cognates in other Semitic languages point to a similar semantic domain, suggesting words like body, interior, center of personal action, thought, mind, interior core (*CAD* 9 164–76; *DISO* 1965, 134; *WTM* 463–64). Notably absent are words describing affect or feelings, except insofar as the English word *heart* is included in all the definitions. That inclusion encourages English-speaking interpreters to import into the texts, anachronistically, all those things which the word *heart* signifies in English.

Heinz-Jusef Fabry points out, "It is generally assumed that the primary meaning of *lēb* is the organ we call the heart but this cannot be proved. The anatomical reference of *lēb* is quite vague in all the Semitic languages . . . the OT scarcely ever uses *lēb* for the 'heart' as a physical organ" (1974, 411). He suggests, instead, English terms such as "Personal Identity," "Vital Center," and "Affective Center" (1974, 412–14).

Harold Louis Ginsberg comes to a similar conclusion: "But it is the *lēbāb* that figures most often in references to the inner life, both emotional and—and this is its special sphere—intellectual" (1972, 509). Of the tendency of translators and interpreters to assume—or even assert—an anatomical sense of the word, he notes rather wryly: "The corresponding Hebrew words (i.e., *lēb* and *lēbāb*) only sometimes have the meanings in question, but many translators and writers on the Bible are, or act as if they were, largely unaware of the fact" (1972, 508).

That the word Hebrew לב does not principally reference the seat of *romantic* feelings, or even of feelings generally in contrast to thoughts or reasoning, has been

---

1. I shall treat לב and לבב as variant spellings of a single word.

pointed out consistently over the years. Already in 1881, Daniel Goodwin described Hebrew לב (and Greek καρδία as well) as standing for "the central part in general, the inside, and so for *the interior man* [emphasis in original] as manifesting himself in all his various activities. . . . [I]t is not especially confined to the feelings and moral acts in distinction from the intellectual . . ." (1881, 67). He goes on to say "Thus לב and καρδία are the subject or seat, not only of the affections, but of thought, imagination, meditation, memory, perception, reflection, knowledge, skill, belief, judgment, reasoning, consciousness" as well as "the affections and all the moral activities"(1881, 70). He further observes, "The ancients did not make the nice mental and linguistic analyses of modern thought. They used לב, καρδία, בִּינָה, and νόυς for the whole inner man, now with special reference to one special faculty, or state, and now another. . . . [S]tanding as it does for the inner man, καρδία is never contrasted with anything else within, but with what is without" (1881, 71).

Nearly a century later, Hans Walter Wolff came to essentially the same conclusion, while observing "that the usual translation 'heart' for *lēb(āb)* . . . leads our present-day understanding astray" (Wolff 1974a, 40). He observes how little understanding of anatomy and physiology are reflected by Hebrew Bible usage. "The heart is always recognized as being an inaccessible, hidden organ inside the body" (1974a, 42–43). Hence, ". . . the heart stands for the inaccessibly unexplorable—for anything that is quite simply impenetrably hidden" (1974a, 43). While acknowledging that the heart is also the locus to which feelings are imputed in the Hebrew Bible, Wolff says, "in by far the greatest number of cases it is intellectual, rational functions that are ascribed to the heart . . ." (1974a, 46). Thus, "In our language *mind* is exactly the right word at this point" (1974a, 47). "The *heart* in Hebrew," Wolff continues, "describes the seat and function of the reason. It includes everything that we ascribe to the head and the brain—power of perception, reason, understanding, insight, consciousness, memory, knowledge, reflection, judgment, sense of direction, discernment. These things circumscribe the real core meaning of the word *lb*" (1974a, 51).

In spite of this consensus, in a 1998 article Mark Smith asserted that "biblical Hebrew לב commonly expresses emotion" and suggests that "emotions are associated with the hearts and innards because they are physically experienced there" (429, 427). This clearly assumes a specific connection between the anatomical heart as we know it and the ancient Hebrew understanding of the word. More recently Marjorie O'Rourke Boyle, in two outstanding articles in which she considers the use of Hebrew לב in idioms about *broken* or *stopped* "hearts," has convincingly demonstrated the volitional and ethical sense, relating to the will and the intellect rather than merely to affect, in which the Hebrew Bible uses the word. Her careful chronicling of the progress of ancient medical knowledge was immensely helpful in clarifying how little the ancient understanding of Hebrew *heart* was related to the actual organ which is designated by our use of that word (Boyle 2001).

IDIOMATIC USES OF לב

Biblical Hebrew uses לב in various idioms, such as "hard of heart," "clean heart," "broken-hearted," and "circumcise the heart." Hebrew also includes two distinct idioms with the verb דבר, to *speak*. When one is said to דבר בלבו, "speak in one's own heart," the phrase indicates speaking to one's self, that is, thinking. Translations of this idiom have been consistent and without controversy.

In ten instances, one is said to דבר על לב/לבב, "speak upon/against/over/concerning the heart." One of those cases—Hannah praying silently in the temple (1 Sam 1:13)—is intermediate between the two idioms. She is praying silently, as in the case of one who "speaks in her own heart," but she is addressing not herself but God. The other nine uses of this idiom, in which the speaker addresses another individual, are the subject of the present study. Unfortunately the translation of the phrase does not often reflect what we have learned about the significance of לב in a Hebrew cultural world. As a result, the interpretation/meaning of the narratives in which the idiom is embedded is contested.

The simplest strategy—one claimed by a number of translators—would be to translate the phrase literally as "speak to the heart." In doing so, the word *heart* is freighted with the denotations and connotations, the values and significations, of the word *heart* in our social world. As we saw above, those are not identical to the ideas represented by לב in the ancient world. The failure to propose and articulate an explicit model of the social world whose values and practices will inform our study leads to assumptions and definitions derived from the implicit model from which we instinctively operate—the model of our own social world.

A survey of English translations in English Bible versions is revealing.

Genesis 34:3
(KJV) *spake kindly* unto the damsel.
(NJB) *tried to win her heart*.
(JPS) *spoke comfortingly* unto the damsel.
(NRSV) *spoke tenderly* to her.

Genesis 50:21
(KJV) *spake kindly* unto them.
(RSV) *comforted* them.
(NJB) by *speaking affectionately* to them.
(JPS) *spoke kindly* unto them.
(NRSV) *speaking kindly* to them.

Judges 19:3
(KJV) *to speak friendly* unto her
(NJB) *to appeal to her affections*
(JPS) *to speak kindly* unto her
(NRSV) *to speak tenderly* to her

2 Samuel 19:7
(KJV) *speak comfortably*
(NJB) *reassure*
(JPS) *speak to the heart*
(NRSV) *speak kindly*

Hosea 2:14
(KJV) *speak comfortably* unto her.
(NJB) *speak to her heart*.
(JPS) *speak tenderly* unto her.
(NRSV) speak tenderly to her.

Isaiah 40:2
(KJV) *Speak ye comfortably*
(NJB) *Speak to the heart*
(JPS) *take heart*
(NRSV) *Speak tenderly*

2 Chronicles 30:22
(KJV) *spake comfortably*
(NJB) *encouraged*
(JPS) *spoke encouragingly*
(NRSV) *spoke encouragingly*

2 Chronicles 32:6
(KJV) *spake comfortably*
(NJB) *spoke to them to encourage*
(JPS) *spoke encouragingly*
(NRSV) *spoke encouragingly*

The usual translations turn soft in translation and ignore what is known about לב in Hebrew. *ThWAT* (and, in English, *TDOT*) likewise move away from their presentation of לב as the inner core of the personality to a more emotional, even romantic sense when the word is used in the idiom (Schmidt 1973, 105), with the following suggestions: "common idiom for wooing affection"; "to comfort and cheer" although not restricted to "the circle of the family"; "seductive"; and "seductive persuasion" (Schmidt 1973, 412–34, 417–18).

Wolff ignores his own solid anthropological work on the meaning of לב and suggests of the idiom: "Sie gehört hauptsächlich zur Liebessprache . . ." (1973, 86). He describes the phrase as belonging to the "language of love," but that it is "an appeal which is an attempt at a change of will (Hos 2.16f.; Gen 34.3)," an "appeal to the conscience," and "invitation to a decision," an effort "to move someone to decision" (1973, 52).

A few authors have pointed out the inconsistencies but have been ignored by interpreters of biblical texts. J. Alberto Soggin suggests what may be a very appropriate translation, *to reason with*, but reintroduces English *heart* into a supposed *literal* translation: " 'Reasonably': literally, 'to his heart,' which in the metaphorical usage of the context in the Semitic languages is the seat of the reason and not the motions, cf. Hos 2.16; Isa 40.2 and other passages" (1981, 285). Georg Fischer takes issue with the notion that "דבר על לבה . . . ist speziell in der Liebessprache zu Hause, in der die Wendung das Verhältnis des Mannes zur Frau charakterisiert" and reports (1984, 244–50, 244) that the first publication of this now common interpretation is found in Artur Weiser (1949, 30). He suggests that דבר על לבה never indicates a tête-à-tête between two lovers, but is always found in situations in which there has been a serious breech or transgression. The phrase then, in his view, reflects seeking pardon, perhaps forgiveness (Fischer 1984, 249–50).

A sampling of the way the phrase has been translated in commentaries is instructive:

Genesis 34:3
"spoke reassuringly to her" (Wenham 1994, 305)
"spoke tenderly" (von Rad 1972, 328)

"sought to win her affection" (Speiser 1964, 262)[2]

Judges 19:3
"speak reasonably with her" (Soggin 1981, 283)
"speak intimately to her" (Boling 1975, 271)

Hosea 2:16
"romance her" (but first "seduce her") (Stuart 1987, 43)
"woo her heart" (but first "allure her") (Wolff 1974b, 31)[3]
"spoke wooing words" (Mays 1969, 35)
"speak intimately" (but first "entice her") (Andersen and Friedman 1980, 215)[4]

Isaiah 40:2
"speak tenderly" (Childs 2001, 293)
"speak to Jerusalem's heart" (Watts 1987, 76)
"speak tender words to Jerusalem (Blenkinsopp 2002, 177)

An occasional interpreter has been skeptical. Fokkelien van Dijk-Hemmes, in her reference to the use of the idiom "to speak to her heart" in texts of "sexual violence," says, "[T]he translation in the RSV 'and I'll speak tenderly to her' seems to be slightly out of place, to say the least" (1989, 85).

The nine passages which include the idiom דבר על לב share certain contextual commonalities. The passages include Gen 34:3 (Shechem and Dinah); Gen 50:21 (Joseph and his brothers); Judg 19:3 (Levite and his concubine); 2 Sam 19:8 (David and his troops); Hos 2:16 (Yahweh and Israel); Isa 40:2 (Yahweh's agent and Jerusalem); Ruth 2:13 (Boaz and Ruth); 2 Chr 30:22 (Hezekiah and Levites); and 2 Chr 32:6 (Hezekiah and his military officers).

In every case, the speaker is a man or the deity conceived as male. In more than half of them, the addressee is either a woman or the nation conceived as feminized. Each situation involves a large asymmetry of power, with a powerful speaker and powerless hearer. In every case, the person(s) addressed has been (or is about to be) the victim of debasement or humiliation. In a world in which honor is construed as masculinity, while that which is female is subject to shame, situations of dishonor effectively render even male subjects *feminized*. In most of the texts, the dishonor is

---

2. E. A. Speiser's translation of vv. 2–3 is worth quoting in full: "Shechem son of Hamor the Hivite, head of the region, saw her, seized her, and slept with her by force. But being deeply attracted by Dinah daughter of Jacob, and in love with the maiden, he then sought to win her affection" (1964, 262). In note 3, he goes on: "he then sought to win her affection. Literally 'he spoke at/upon her heart,' not so much to comfort her as to persuade her" (1964, 264).

3. ". . . but Yahweh will speak a new, indeed, a tender and loving word to Israel in the wilderness" (Wolff 1974b, 41). "This expression (דבר על לבה) belongs to the language of courtship. Shechem 'spoke to the heart' of Dinah, since 'his soul was drawn to her and he loved her' (Gen 34:3). Ruth (2:13) was amazed that Boaz 'spoke to her heart' as though she enjoyed his special confidence. Such a manner of speaking brings comfort (cf. also Isa 40:2). The Levite in Judg 19:3 most accurately reflects Yahweh's attitude. He speaks 'to the heart' of his wife who had gone astray, with the intention of bringing her back. The reason for 'speaking to the heart' is therefore love and the awareness of belonging together; its object is to overcome sorrow and resentment (cf. also 2 Chr 32:6), obstinacy and estrangement" (Wolff 1974b, 42).

4. Verse 16: "Therefore, behold, I am going to entice her. I will lead her through the wilderness and speak intimately to her" (215). In his commentary on this verse he reports: "speak . . . the reference is to speaking endearingly in courtship (Gen 34:3; Ruth 2:13; Isa 40:2)."

of a sexual nature—or at least is described in those terms. There is a broadly shared, sexually charged vocabulary in these texts: ענה, to "humble, a woman by cohabitation" (Gen 34:2, Judg 19:24); נבלה "disgraceful folly, esp. of sins of unchastity" (Gen 34:7; Judg 19:24); or נבלות "immodesty, shamelessness." Other words indicating shame and humiliation are prominent as well—for example, כלם and בוש. Recent scholarship has expressed concern over the metaphoric sexual treatment of women as symbols for a faithless nation in the prophets (Setel 1985; Carroll 1985; Brenner 1993; Weems 1995). Despite our reluctance to accuse Yahweh of rape, the public stripping and exposure described in those passages would certainly be experienced by the female character as a sexual assault.

None of the women characters in the passages under study is portrayed as properly under the supervision and oversight of an adult male, a circumstance which was so vital to a woman's reputation in the ancient world of honor and shame. Metaphorical women, that is, the collectivity of Judah or Jerusalem, are portrayed as "whore" (זנה) and "adulteress" (נאף). Nonmetaphorical women characters are likewise insufficiently controlled and protected by male overseers. Ruth, Dinah, and the Levite's concubine are all termed נערה, a word unfortunately too often translated as *maiden*, but which in fact generally describes serving women, working unprotected in the fields or someone's household. It is never used for proper young women, except in those cases when they find themselves outside their own households, away from or estranged from the בת־אב, without proper chaperonage. Such exposure always carries with it the presumption of unchastity. The Hebrew word נערה is usually translated "girl, damsel, maid, or young woman" precisely because in our cultural world *age*, rather than *status*, is the attribute by which we categorize people. In fact, few named characters are described by this word, which is nearly always reserved for servants. In addition to the three characters mentioned above, we have only Abishag (a woman in explicitly *sexual* service), Esther (also displaced from her father's house and in sexual service in the harem of a foreign king), and Rebekah (first introduced chatting with a stranger at the well). Additionally, the term appears in the legislation of Deut 22 in reference to women whose sexual purity may have been compromised by seduction or rape.[5]

In nearly all of the texts surrounding the phrase דבר על לב, the addressee suffers a grievous hurt or wrong, generally at the hand of the speaker. The question of sexual assault is overt in the stories of Dinah and the Levite's concubine. The "idyllic" nature of Ruth's tale is not a story of sexual assault, but rather of being forced by circumstances to barter her attractiveness and sexuality in exchange for the means of survival for herself and her mother-in-law. Both Isaiah and Hosea contain, prior to the passages in question, highly sexualized descriptions of Yahweh's punishment of the nation by stripping and exposure (Hos 2:2–13; Isa 3:16–4:1; cf. also Isa 47). Although the passages in Chronicles are not portrayed in sexual terms, the defeat of Judah and capture of many of her citizens by then-stronger Israel, as well as the siege of Jerusalem by Sennacherib, were clearly experienced as humiliation and emasculation. The Hebrew Bible is replete with images of conquered Judah as

---

5. A fuller discussion of this term appears in Leeb (2000).

the "seduced and abandoned" woman. Only the stories of Joseph and his brothers and of David and his troops, among these texts, is free of sexual connotations, and, even in those cases, shame and disgrace are central to the narratives. The brothers have been forced by famine into begging for support from their powerful brother, a situation not entirely unlike Ruth's, because in an honor-shame world, dependency is feminization and feminization is shame. Likewise, David's men have been dishonored by David's choice to grieve his son rather than celebrate their military successes.

DIFFERING INTERPRETATIONS RESULTING FROM DIFFERING TRANSLATION OF THE IDIOM

Several of the texts which feature the term "speak to the heart" involve actions which are sometimes referred to as "rape," or at the very least "sexual assault." Different translations of the idiom lead to disputed interpretations of the narratives in which it is found and differing evaluations of the perpetrator of the sexual activity. In particular, the character of Shechem and the nature of his actions with Dinah have been the subject of scholarly disagreement (van Wolde 2002, 537; Fewell and Gunn 1991, 196; Sternberg 1992, 463–88; Bechtel 1994, 19–36). The decision for, or against, a charge of rape against Shechem has sometimes hinged on the way the interpreter translates דבר על לב. Those who view it as *love-talk* tend to see the incident as courtship or seduction. Others consider it sexual assault. A few even call it rape but discount the severity of the assault because Shechem is such a nice guy in the aftermath. Fewell and Gunn write:

> All of the verbal expressions in this verse [Gen 34:3] are terms of affection at home in contexts where a commitment to another person is being made. Indeed, they are noticeably the terms of courtship and marriage. Moreover, the last expression—"to speak to the heart of"—may move us beyond the account of Shechem's affections to those of Dinah. It appears to function as a perlocutionary expression, that is one describing a speech act that produces consequential effects on the feelings, thoughts, or actions of its hearers—in other words, a successfully completed action, like the verbs "convince" or "compel" in English as distinct from "urge" or "advise." In our present context, therefore, the expression, "he spoke to [her] heart," indicates both Shechem's action and Dinah's positive response. (1974, 196)

Indeed, *convince* or *compel* would perhaps be better translations, since Hebrew did not distinguish feelings from thoughts. The idea is to produce actions. Dinah's *feeling* about the matter—positive or negative—is precisely irrelevant.

Some of the discussion about how to characterize Shechem's actions has centered on the Hebrew words שכב (qal, lie with/"lay") and ענה (piel, afflict, humble). Ilona Rashkow argues for rape in Shechem's case, based largely on this verb, rather than any argument based on inferences about his character based on his "sweet talk" after the assault. "In biblical Hebrew, the normal grammatical construct šākab 'm (lay with) is used to convey cohabitation, a mutually agreed upon act. However, šākab or šākab 'et ('lay' used with a direct object rather than a preposition) is used when the act is forced, a rape" (1990, 226). In English, too, to say that *he lay with her* is merely quaint, whereas to say that *he laid her* sounds like taking sexual advantage. Nevertheless, Rashkow follows other interpreters in her understanding of the Hebrew idiom:

> The narrator also reports that Shechem "spoke to the heart" of Dinah, catching the reader's attention with that phrase since it appears in the Hebrew Bible only eight other times, and each time in situations putting or showing the speaker in a positive or favorable light. Shechem raped Dinah, and his action was deplorable. Although v. 3 does not cancel the impact of v. 2, it provides another dimension to Shechem's character. Just as the narrator uses three verbs to shock the reader, the narrator again uses 3 verbs to suggest the replacement of violent behavior by equally strong emotion. (1990, 227)

In a footnote, she makes this "favorable light" more explicit: "Since to 'speak to the heart' is to 'comfort,' 'appease,' or 'soothe' (Judg 19:3; Hos 2:16; 2 Sam 19:8; 2 Chr 30:22, 32:6; Isa 40:2; Gen 50:2; Ruth 2:13), Shechem's sincerity and love are clearly emphasized by the use of this expression."

Gordon J. Wenham, too, suggests a reading of *laid her*: " '*Laid her*' instead of the more usual 'lay with her' implies forcible illegitimate intercourse. 'Shamed her' is another term always used to describe intercourse without marriage (e.g., Deut 21:14; 22:29; 2 Sam 13:12)" (1994, 305). Of course, in a social world in which marriage itself is designated by *taking a woman*—indeed consummation seems to be marriage—the question of *legitimacy* of intercourse is of enormous consequence. Wenham goes on to say, "Yet we learn that Shechem was not your callous anonymous rapist, so dreaded in modern society, but an affectionate young man, who 'loved the girl and spoke reassuringly to her' " (1994, 317). This statement is, of course, both amazing and horrifying. Wenham has already noted that this was "forcible illegitimate intercourse," yet this act of violence is somehow mitigated because of Shechem's feelings of affection. His assertion that Shechem was not "anonymous" is also curious; the narrative is clear enough that Dinah's transgression was in her "going out," and, thus, one wonders how Shechem would have been known to her. Perhaps Wenham means only that Shechem was not hooded or masked as he violated Dinah. Even allowing for the different expectations of an earlier decade, our understanding of the effects of date rape and acquaintance rape make these seem very cavalier assertions.

Biblical Hebrew lacks a word which clearly and consistently means rape. In the disputed passages, the word at issue is ענה, which in prior centuries was translated by words suggesting abuse or violation. Gerhard von Rad sums up earlier arguments this way: "The verb which is usually translated 'humble' (*'innâ*) indicates the moral and social degrading and debasing by which a girl loses the expectancy of a fully valid marriage" (1972, 331). More recently, Ellen van Wolde has examined the semantic arguments and suggests: "The conclusion is clear: *'innâ* is an evaluative term used in a judicial context which marks a debasement of the social status of a woman with effects on the debasement of the men related to her within the whole social structure of Israelite society" (2002, 537). The precise nature of the activity which leads to this "debasement" is left unspecified, as van Wolde rightly indicates that the verb refers not to the act itself, but to the consequences (2002, 541–42). We lack, in our social world, an exact equivalent to this circumstance in which one's social standing is determined by what has been done to an individual, rather than what that individual has done.[6]

Thus our understanding is complicated by the fact that the target language for our translations (English) has a word for a category of sexual activity (*rape*) which did not exist per se in the source language (Hebrew). In using a word which denotes a social reality which was unknown in the ancient world we retroject our values and associations along with the word or phrase. In order to understand this assertion—that ancient categories of sexual activity did not include an exact equivalent for what we would consider rape—we must consider carefully and articulate explicitly (1) what we mean by rape in English and (2) whether that definition would have been meaningful in the ancient world.

RAPE IN ENGLISH

What, then, constitutes *rape*? The first edition of the *Random House Dictionary of the English Language* (1966) says:

1. the act of seizing and carrying off by force.
2. the act of physically forcing a woman to have sexual intercourse.
3. See *statutory rape*, which entry says, *U.S. Law*, sexual intercourse with a girl under the age of consent, which age varies in different States from 10–18 years.

Reflecting a more contemporary understanding, *Merriam-Webster Online* describes rape as follows:

> unlawful sexual activity and usually sexual intercourse carried out forcibly or under threat of injury against the will usually of a female or with a person who is beneath a certain age or incapable of valid consent—compare SEXUAL ASSAULT.

Sexual assault is then described in that same reference as:

> illegal sexual contact that usually involves force upon a person without consent or is inflicted upon a person who is incapable of giving consent (as because of age or physical or mental incapacity) or who places the assailant (as a doctor) in a position of trust or authority.

Our contemporary understanding of rape has expanded considerably over the past four decades. As a result, even two contemporary native speakers of English may be describing different circumstances when using the word *rape*. In 1966, force and intercourse were necessary to merit the label. In 2007, other forms of sexual activity may be included in the category of rape, and the inability to give real consent has

---

6. On the other hand, the fact that we still suppress the names of rape victims suggests that there remains, in our culture, a tendency to impart shame to those who have suffered from sexual assault.

been substituted for the use of force. Interestingly, prior to 1976 physically forcing a woman to have sexual intercourse did not constitute rape if she was your wife.[7]

If rape is sexual intercourse accomplished by force or threat of force, many marriages in the ancient world could be called rape. If rape is sexual intercourse without valid consent, rape in the ancient world is a crime by men against men, since the consent that was needed for sexual activity between a man and a woman was not the woman's, but her guardian's, that of the head of the household to which she belonged. Her thoughts or feelings about the matter were irrelevant. A father (or brother or other male relative) could require her to submit to sexual intercourse in an arranged marriage at any age agreeable to the men involved, or the father could forbid sexual intercourse. What mattered were his wishes, his will, not hers. If rape is sexual intercourse without the woman's valid consent, then *rape* is a term which is not meaningful in a discussion of events in the ancient world, because in the world of ancient Israel and Judah, a woman was almost never a competent actor, capable of giving consent.

Based on mid-twentieth-century definitions of what constitutes rape, some commentators have argued that the presence of the verb חזק indicates physical force and that its absence, for instance in the story of Dinah, suggests mutuality and consent. Danna Nolan Fewell and David M. Gunn nevertheless suggest that Shechem has in fact used force, observing that "a woman is defiled when she sleeps with anyone outside the proper boundaries of marriage; see Num 5:13–31; Lev 21:7, 13–14" (1991, 207). They go on to say, "Note that the issue is not that their sister has been raped but that she has been 'lain with.' The fact that she has been forced seems immaterial" (1991, 199). Indeed, in this social world, it is immaterial. What is significant is whether the men who control her sexuality, who permit or limit access to her, have given their consent to intercourse with her. However, Fewell and Gunn seem to suggest, based on their translation of the phrase דבר על לב, that after the violation Dinah could simply go home, if she chose, to resume her life as it was before she was "lain with": "The language used earlier in v. 3 to describe Shechem's attitude toward Dinah (his soul clung to Dinah, he loved the young woman, and he spoke to the young woman's heart) hardly suggests that he is at the same time forcibly holding her hostage" (1991, 200).

Michael Parsons decries the fact that both Luther and Calvin assert that "Jacob and David are the primary victims of the crime" (2002, 142). But the esteemed Reformers are, in fact, correct in that assessment. In a social world in which women existed in a state of perpetual minority—that is, never given adult autonomy, always expected to be under the protection and tutelage of an adult male—the crime of *rape* is a crime against the brothers or fathers whose consent for intercourse would have made the act a marriage rather than an outrage.

---

7. "Until 1976, marital rape was legal in every state in the United States. Although marital rape is now a crime in all 50 states in the U.S., some states still don't consider it as serious as other forms of rape. The only states that have laws that make no distinction between marital rape and stranger rape are Colorado, Delaware, Florida, Georgia, Indiana, Massachusetts, Montana, Nebraska, New Jersey, New Mexico, North Carolina, North Dakota, Oregon, Texas, Utah, Vermont, Wisconsin and the District of Columbia. These states have no marital rape exemptions" (Stritof 2007).

AN ANTHROPOLOGICALLY INFORMED TRANSLATION OF THE PHRASE דבר על לב

Bruce J. Malina, employing the insights of cultural anthropology, has clarified how the ancient Mediterranean world viewed the human person. Human responses were not categorized based on *quality* (i.e., emotional or rational), but on *location* (i.e., interior or exterior). This interior/exterior, public/private bifurcation was reflected in the value symboled by various body parts (2001, 68–71). He describes persons—as understood in that world—as comprised of three zones:

1. A "zone of emotion-fused thought," which comprises an individual's interiority. The phrase "emotion-fused thought" highlights the lack of a perceived separation between thinking and feeling. This zone relates anatomically to "eyes, heart, eyelid, pupil" and their activities such as seeing, knowing, understanding, thinking, remembering, choosing, feeling, considering, and looking at.

2. A "zone of self-expressive speech," which includes mouth, ears, tongue, lips, throat, teeth, jaws, and their activities: speaking, hearing, questioning, singing, instructing, praising, blaming, cursing, swearing, obeying, disobeying, ignoring.

3. A "zone of purposeful action" which describes the hands, feet, arms, fingers, legs, and their activities: doing, accomplishing, intervening, touching, coming, going, giving, taking, making, and so on.

Building on this model of the first-century personality for our study of the Hebrew idiom, I propose three realms (which reflect, but do not precisely correspond to, the zones in Malina's model):

1. The interior realm
2. The exterior directly observable realm
3. The exterior symbolic realm

The interior realm involves responses and activities which occur *within* an individual, which are thus not directly observable by others. This is, more or less, the *central processing unit*. For the ancient world, this interior realm was not strongly divided, as it is with us, into emotional and rational categories. To this realm belong thoughts and feelings, will, resolve, courage, fear. This realm is represented by all interior bodily organs, such as heart and liver. Access to this interior realm is gained through the eyes and ears.

The directly observable realm includes what human beings do, that is, actions which can be observed directly and immediately: gestures, behaviors, activities, accomplishments, actions. This realm is usually represented by hands and arms, legs and feet.

The exterior symbolic realm includes all forms of human communication through languages, both verbal and non-verbal. This realm is highly context dependent and is most closely associated with the parts of the body involved in producing or receiving sound: ears, mouth, and so on.

Each of the exterior realms—directly observable and symbolic—is involved in both input into and output from the interior realm. In both cases, the principal forms of input are visual and auditory, although other senses play a limited role in human communication.

SUGGESTING A NEW TRANSLATION

In my model, the heart is part of the interior of a human being, a locus of both reason and feeling, and all of the basic philological research on Hebrew לב is in agreement. The so-called *heart*, then, represents this inner core of a human being that is hidden from the outside world, except of course when the individual communicates or takes action based on what has been worked out within. The heart is private and therefore unguarded, uncensored. Honor and shame are awarded based on what is public about a person—what is said and what is done. The workings of the heart bring neither honor nor shame from other people until they are translated into words or actions. God, of course, who is able to view this quintessentially private inner being judges the heart as well as the words and deeds, although the ability of God to see the interior of a person may have been a late development in Judah's theology. With this understanding of the sense of the word *heart* in Hebrew, how should we translate the idiom דבר על לב? Clearly "to speak to the heart" is to address the inner core of a person, the mind, the will, the very thoughts. The preposition על frequently has an adversative sense, which suggests that an appropriate rendering of the phrase is *reasoned with*, or *argued with*, or *explained*.

The related idiom "to say in his [own] heart" means to talk to oneself, that is, "to think." By analogy, to speak to the heart no doubt reflects an entirely private conversation, without witnesses and without chaperones. The cultural implications of this could be enormous. Without witnesses, an individual can speak to another frankly and perhaps honestly, without posturing for approval from onlookers, but also without risking censure for words which should not be spoken. Similarly, such a conversation might transgress cultural limits: a man in the ancient world should not boldly and directly address another man's wife or daughter in private. To do so is to commit a social penetration, resulting in an offense as serious in that social world as bodily penetration is in ours, in other words *taking an indecent liberty* with a woman. Perhaps it is to this social penetration which Dinah's brothers refer when they ask, "Shall our sister be treated like a whore?" In the world of ancient Israel and Judah, only prostitutes and women without guardians were addressed privately and intimately by those who were not part of their immediate family.

Because of the adversative nature of the preposition על in this idiom, our anthropologically informed translation must include the idea of addressing someone's intellect and will with the intent to change preexisting thoughts, beliefs, intentions. It means to reason with, argue with, persuade, or, perhaps better, dissuade. It means to talk into or out of something.

The phrase surely also means addressing an individual in a way that reaches that inner core, volitional center, mind, will of the person addressed. In other words, it means, at the very least, to *get through to* them. When we say in English that we plan to have a heart-to-heart talk with someone, we don't mean that we will address them romantically. We mean that we will speak in words that they will understand and *lay out the consequences*, always with an eye toward affecting the will and changing behavior. It means *to get real, not to sugar-coat it, to make them an offer they can't refuse.*

An anthropologically informed translation of the phrase דבר על לב influences our reading of the narratives, sometimes subtly, sometimes more significantly. Let us examine the relevant passages in the order of their increasing importance to the central points of this argument.

GENESIS 50:15–21

Joseph's brothers quite rightly fear retribution for their earlier treachery against him. Now in fear and dependency, they grovel before him like slaves. He reassures them, by *speaking directly and privately* (as is appropriate when someone has suffered a loss of honor) to *change their minds* about the presumed outcome.

2 SAMUEL 19:2–9

Absalom's attempted usurpation of the throne had led to his death, but David's troops had to "steal into town" humiliated (הנכמים) like an army that had run away in battle (19:4). Joab accuses David of shaming them, by loving his enemies more that those who had been faithful[8] to him, and advises David that failure to act will result in mass defection (19:6–8). Joab's advice: Speak directly and frankly to your officers to *reason with them,* to *talk them out of* defecting.

RUTH 2:1–13

When Boaz first sees an unknown, unchaperoned woman in his field, he asks whose serving woman she is (2:5). Discovering that she is without a male protector and is apparently healthy and hard-working (2:6–7), he places her under his own tutelage, along with his other agricultural servants. He even warns his male farm workers that, despite appearances to the contrary, this woman is no longer "fair game" (2:9). He *directs (persuades, compels, convinces)* her to restrict herself to his fields to seek her food and drink. Ruth shows her gratitude for his assistance and protection by debasing herself by prostration and expresses surprise that he has explained all this to her *privately and directly,* "even though I am not one of your servants," in other words *just as if she were one of his servants.*

JUDGES 19:1–5

One may appropriately, if uncomfortably, observe that according to one possible definition of rape, namely sexual intercourse without the consent of the *individual whose consent is required,* the assault on the Levite's concubine is not rape, since her master has offered her to the men who take her life. This subsequent action on his

---

8. The verb אהב here should be understood as to show faithfulness or loyalty, rather than to have romantic or sexual *feelings* for someone.

part makes it difficult to see romantic motivation behind the words he speaks in the opening verses of the story. The concubine has left her house, and whether we read "went whoring" (זנה) with MT or "became angry" with LXX (ὠργίσθη), she is guilty of leaving his supervision, and her chastity is automatically impugned. Even before this incident, she is apparently of such low social standing that her father has been able to arrange not *marriage* but *concubinage* for her. Nothing about her master's behavior, either when he reaches her father's house or when he is in Gibeah, suggests that *love-talk* was on his mind. He has instead gone to her father's house to *explain the consequences* of her departure and to *compel her* to return with him, perhaps even to face punishment.

GENESIS 34:1–3

Unlike Amnon, who lured his half-sister Tamar into his home for the purpose of sexual assault, Shechem sees Dinah in the countryside, where presumably any cries for help would not be heard. Also unlike Amnon, after sampling the merchandise he wanted the whole package. And so he *privately reasoned with* her, *explaining* how, now that the deed was done, he would "make an honest woman of her." Dinah's changing fortunes—or perhaps we should say changing status—is reflected by the changes in the terms by which she is named. In the beginning (34:1) she is daughter of Leah, perhaps less closely supervised as daughter of the less-valued wife, or perhaps less attractive. After Shechem has seized and violated her, she is spoken of—by the narrator, but the focalization is clearly Shechem's—as an unchaperoned woman (נערה), perhaps to minimize his offence (34:3). However, when he approaches his own father for help in arranging the marriage, he asks, "Get me this *girl*" (ילדה, girl-child presumably kept chaste under her father's supervision) to convince his father that this would be a suitable union. When Jacob hears of the defilement of his "daughter" (34:5), he does not act immediately, but his sons are incensed because of the "outrage" (נבלה) which has been committed against their honor by Shechem's sexual activity with "the daughter of Jacob" (34:7). Shechem's father, Hamor, approaches the Israelite men and speaks in properly familial terms, appropriate to negotiating a marriage. "My son wants your daughter" (34:8, plural pronoun, indicating that the honor of the sons as well as Jacob is involved). He makes, indeed, a proposal for widespread intermarriage between the two peoples. Since that negotiation is not immediately successful, Shechem himself speaks up, addressing all the men of Dinah's family (34:11). "Get me this *unchaperoned woman* (נערה) for a wife" (34:12). The message is clear: if she had been properly protected, this might not have happened, but at this point she is damaged goods. Dinah has no doubt committed a violation of her culture's standards for a daughter's behavior, and she may have willingly assented to the sexual activity, but that does not make Shechem's words to her "sweet nothings." Both of them know the societal ramifications of what has just happened, and Shechem is attempting to *convince her to make the best of a bad situation.*

HOSEA 2:16–17

The second chapter of Hosea describes Yahweh's rejection of Israel on grounds of prostitution and adultery (2:4). As a result, he punishes her by disowning her children (2:6), stripping and exposing her (2:5; 2:12), imprisoning her (2:8), and repossessing all the garments with which she might protect herself from the leering public (2:11). The familiar vocabulary of shame and disgrace is prominent (הבישה 2:7 and נבלתה 2:12). Now after committing this sexual assault—and in Hosea it is clear that Israel *was asking for it*—Yahweh will *seduce* her and lead her into the wilderness, that place where a man could *have his way with* a woman and her cries would not be heard (Deut 22:25–29). The outcome of this wilderness assault, as prescribed by Deuteronomy, depended upon whether the unchaperoned woman (נערה) was already promised/espoused (מארשה) to another man. If so, the assault was a capital offense against her father (22:25–27). If not promised, however, the perpetrator has only to compensate her father for his economic loss. Her assailant has, as we say, *bought the ranch*, and the woman's compensation for her considerable loss of status is a guarantee against future divorce by him (22:28–29). In the wilderness, Yahweh will *speak directly and privately* to Israel and *explain the consequences* of her prior conduct. Indeed, Yahweh will dictate her response (Hos 2:17) and her manner of addressing him (2:18). Only after he has thus reasoned with her will Yahweh make a permanent commitment of espousal to Israel (2:21–22).

ISAIAH 40:1–2

That these verses have come from a different author than most of the book's first thirty-nine chapters is uncontested. Those earlier chapters, however, are known to the exilic author, indeed are the pre-text to which he is responding. Jerusalem has been called a whore (1:21). In language which is perhaps less sexually charged than Hosea's, but equally punitive, she is promised stripping and public shaming (3:16–4:1). Surely this must reflect the way that the exilic community—as well as many back in Judah—must have felt: violated and shamed. Loss of independence and power has left them feminized and dishonored, without hope for any improvement in the future. Regarding this despair, Yahweh speaks: Pity my people. *Let them in on a secret*, which the powers of Babylon do not yet know. *Reason with them. Explain to them. Persuade them* that there is an end in sight. Although they got only what they deserved, they have already made the two-fold repayment which I required of them.

CONCLUSION

Our investment in keeping this idiom within the semantic domain of love-talk is clear from these final two examples, especially those in which God is the speaker. After all, God could not possibly be a rapist or one who would sanction or promote rape. Yet, in order to preserve aspects of our theology, we disregard our knowledge of the anthropology of the ancient world and of the clear evidence of the semantic value of the noun. Our notion of a loving God is challenged by lumping him into the same category as rapists and others who take advantage of their positions of power. We avoid this cognitive dissonance in some cases by rehabilitating the other characters. Boaz is doing a noble thing by addressing this unprotected women so sweetly. Shechem did not really rape Dinah so much as win her heart. Our tendency has been to turn the idiom into love language in order that we can salvage our view of God as a speaker of love language. If Shechem is just *telling it like it is*, then so is Yahweh, which fails to fulfill our wish to see God not so much as being unconditionally loving but as acting in ways which make us feel unconditionally loved. We prefer "nice talk" to "straight talk," especially when it comes to God.

As C. S. Lewis quipped:

> We want, in fact, not so much a Father in Heaven as a grandfather in heaven—a se-
> nile benevolence who, as they say, "liked to see young people enjoying themselves,"
> and whose plan for the universe was simply that it might be truly said at the end of
> each day, "a good time was had by all." (1962, 40)

We translate in ways which will protect God's reputation at all costs, and by that we mean our own view of the nature and actions of God. This reflects a particular approach to the biblical text as divine words chronicling past events in a way that is normative and prescriptive. An anthropologically informed approach to translation allows us to accept that the biblical texts arise out of concrete social worlds in which real human beings have experienced God's self-revelation in the events of their lives. Their accounts of that self-revealing God are descriptive of their experiences in a concrete historical context. And these texts serve us best when our knowledge of that context—teased out with the help of methods borrowed from the social sciences—are translated and interpreted in ways that are informed by the meanings and values carried by the words and phrases by which these ancient authors chose to record their apprehension of the divine self-revelation.

Relexicalizing Leviticus in 4QMMT:
The Beginnings of Qumran Anti-language?

Robert A. Kugler

4QMMT (henceforth "MMT") remains one of the most fascinating texts among the Dead Sea Scrolls.[1] It is generally regarded as a two-part letter or treatise from the leader of a Jewish community who explains his group's views on Jewish law relating to the purity of temple practice and personnel to an addressee whose decrees could apparently determine the implementation of such laws. The first part of the letter (Part B)[2] begins with the declaration that אלה מקצת דברינו, "These are some of our rulings" relating to matters of purity (B 1–3) (VanderKam 1998a; 1997, 179–94); Fraade 2003; Grossman 2001). Twenty such rulings follow in B 3–82. The author uses the phrase אנחנו חושבים, "We reckon," to introduce his own group's views, and he employs אתם יודעים, "You know," to suggest to the letter's recipients the inevitability of their agreement with his legal reasoning. The second part of the letter (Part C) is addressed to a single recipient, and it exhorts him to accept the authorial group's views articulated in Part B. The author states that because of his group's views they had separated מרוב העם, "from the multitude of the people" (C 7), and that the recipient can find in his group's positions no מעל ושקר ורעה, "treachery, deceit or evil." Indeed, his group's legal understanding is the correct one, and the recipient knows (ידע) this to be true (C 8–9). Next the author states that he composed the treatise to encourage the single recipient to investigate in "the book of Moses (ספר תורה), in the books of the prophets (בספרי הנביאים), and in David (בדויד)" to discover God's plan that the recipient disobey God's law for a time and experience misfortune, but also return to the God's law in the End of Days (C 10–16). The author then recalls the fates that befell Israelite kings as proof that some of the blessings and curses had

---

1. For the *editio princeps* see Qimron and Strugnell (1994). The secondary literature on MMT is abundant. See especially Kampen and Bernstein (1996) and the contributions by Brooke and Harrington in Bernstein, Martínez, and Kampen (1997); on general interpretive issues and the specific question of legal hermeneutics in MMT, see also Fraade (2000, 507–26); idem (2003, 150–61); Grossman (2001, 3–22); Høgenhaven (2003, 187–204); Kugler (2000, 90–112); Sharp (1997, 207–22); Steudel (2006, 247–63); Weissenberg (2003, 29–45).

2. So-called Part A is a calendar that appears in 4Q394 before the beginning of Part B; for the text, see Qimron and Strugnell (1994, 44–45). It is not clear whether the calendar in 4Q394 was an integral part of MMT as a complete work; in any case, the matter is not of concern in this study.

already come to pass (C 16–21). He announces that the End of Days has come and that God's promises of judgment for the righteous and wicked will not be canceled, as the fates of Israel's kings also prove (C 21–26). Thus it is for the recipient's and the people's welfare that אנחנו כתבנו אליך מקצת מעשי התורה שחשבנו, "We have written to you some precepts of the law according to our thinking." Following those precepts, suggests the author, will put the recipient and the people on the right side of God at the final judgment (C 26–32).

Not surprisingly, one of chief questions scholars seek to answer about this work is the identity of the sender(s) and recipient(s).[3] Most agree that the second-person singular addressee was probably a Hasmonean ruler, but the identities of the sender and his group and of the second-person plural addressees of part B are not so clear (Steudel 2006; Fraade 2003; Grossman 2001).

The best evidence for addressing the latter mystery are the strategies for legal reasoning vis-à-vis the scriptures exhibited by the authorial group and the addressees in comparison with the strategies of named groups evident in texts of the same period. Regrettably, however, little of the available evidence is reliable. Other Dead Sea Scrolls help fill out the portrait that begins to emerge in MMT, but they never answer the question of identity directly, and the variegation in modes of legal reasoning among the Scrolls deepens the mystery more than they clarify it. Worse, the other roughly contemporaneous sources are so sparing and tendentious in depicting Jewish groups engaged in legal reasoning as to be of little or no use in establishing the identities of the parties to MMT (New Testament; Josephus; Philo).

By contrast, although it is later than MMT by two centuries and more, the testimony of the rabbinic canon to types of Jewish legal reasoning vis-à-vis scripture in late antiquity identifies parties by name and by consistent modes of argumentation. As a consequence the temptation to rely on the evidence of rabbinic texts to identify the parties to the debate in MMT proves irresistible. The lateness of rabbinic texts vis-à-vis the Scrolls is excused on the assumption that they nevertheless preserve traces of Jewish groups from the time of the Dead Sea Scrolls and the authors of MMT. Yet this approach, while occasionally promising, has achieved no consensus and in fact seems to be moving most recently in the opposite direction.[4]

---

3. Among other key questions two especially draw substantial attention: (1) the document's date and purpose relative to the Qumran community's development over time (see esp. the articles by Fraade 2003 and Grossman 2001); and (2) the implications for the growth of the canon of Hebrew Scriptures for the reference to the "the book of Moses (ספר תורה), in the books of the prophets (בספרי הנביאים), and in David (בדויד)" in C 10 (Ulrich 2003; Bertholet 2006).

4. For a most recent entry into this debate, see Yadin (2003, 130–49), who signals the crumbling of what could at one time have passed for an emerging consensus. That consensus was that MMT reflects the restrictive legalism of the Sadducees over against the Pharisees' more lenient interpretation of the law; for this view, see especially Schiffman (1994, 83–95), but see also the moderating perspective of Baumgarten (1996, 512–16); idem (2003, 33–41); see also Regev (2005, 158–88), who argues that the "halakhic relationship between the Sadducees and Qumranites may be . . . explained as two divergent branches of a primordial tradition that developed independently" (161). Yadin (2003) departs from this loose consensus by suggesting that the Qumranites were not related to the Sadducees so much as they were the forebears of the legal traditions associated in the rabbinic canon with R. Ishmael, a figure whose rulings appear frequently and are distinct from the Sadducean and Pharisaic traditions depicted by the rabbinic testimony.

This essay is a test probe for a different approach to understanding the legal rhetoric and reasoning of MMT. I propose assessing in its own right MMT's legal reasoning vis-à-vis scripture, without the specific and narrow influence that comes from consulting later Jewish groups' models for comparative evidence. I am not so naïve, however, as to assume that I am the first to consider this path, or that I can investigate MMT without any interpretive framework (Kugler 1997): as biblical scholars working with social-science models are wont to point out, the choice is not between having an interpretive framework or not, but between choosing one consciously or unconsciously, reflexively or critically. Mindful of that caveat, I propose adopting a generic interpretive framework that has proven useful in investigating linguistic phenomena across time periods and cultures, and that is responsive to and coherent with the specific rhetoric of MMT: the sociolinguistic concept of anti-language.

The first portion of the essay explains the concept of anti-language and what led me to use it to investigate MMT's legal reasoning from scripture. This leads in turn to a selection of three test cases to determine if anti-language proves itself in actual practice to be a useful aid for understanding the nature of scripture-based legal reasoning in MMT. I conclude with an evaluation of the test cases and thoughts on the study's implications for a notion that surfaces in the course of working through the three test cases: the idea that developing an anti-language, although apparently a matter of interpretation, is more akin to translation, at least from the standpoint of the community that develops the anti-language.

WHAT IS ANTI-LANGUAGE AND WHY MIGHT IT HELP
IN INVESTIGATING THE LEGAL REASONING OF 4QMMT?

The sociolinguist M. A. K. Halliday coined the term *anti-language* in a 1976 article that investigated insider-outsider prisoner languages in Poland and the United States (Halliday 1976). Halliday argued that an anti-language provides oppositional subgroups within society a linguistic identity that is transparent to insiders but opaque to normative society. Halliday also delineated the selective nature of anti-languages: they typically are not comprehensive in their coverage, but rather attend only to those aspects of society that most concern the oppositional group vis-à-vis the rest of society. Halliday and his successors further circumscribed the means by which an anti-language accomplishes this purpose. First, anti-languages create a specialized vocabulary relating to a subgroup's principal area(s) of interest by relexicalizing society's normative code relating to the subgroup's chief concern(s); this they do either by introducing new, invented vocabulary, or by converting existing terms to bear new meaning (Halliday 1976, 571; Irvine 1989, 253). Second, anti-language assists a subgroup to develop its oppositional identity through "conspicuous avoidance and violation of forms recognized as 'standard'" (Irvine 1989, 253).

That the people of the Dead Sea Scrolls produced an anti-language to address their concerns for religious purity and impurity especially as it relates to temple personnel and practice has long been known to readers of the Scrolls, if only intuitively. The prevalence of dualistic and "specialized" language, the anachronous use of Hebrew, the tendency toward full orthography, and the use of archaic and cryptic scripts made it hard to miss the fact that the people of the Dead Sea Scrolls had developed the hallmarks of an anti-language, their own *linguistic identity* that was *transparent among them but opaque to outsiders*. Recently William Schniedewind made a formal case for "Qumran Hebrew" as an anti-language, suggesting that several "lines of evidence point to the conscious creation of an anti-language by scribes within the Qumran community," including "Avoidance of Aramaic and Colloquial Language," "Classicizing Tendencies," "Orthography and Paleography," and "Use of Code and Symbolic Terminology" (Schniedewind 1999). Perhaps unwittingly he also pointed to the origins of anti-language at Qumran in *rejecting* MMT as an example of it. Not finding in MMT the characteristics of Qumran Hebrew that he identified as evidence of anti-language, he declared it devoid of the phenomenon and attributed that to its likely early date and conciliatory character (Schniedewind 1999, 251–52). Yet as we have seen already, MMT was created to express a self-defining subgroup's perspective on purity issues as they relate to temple practice and personnel in opposition to the perspective held by another party. Further, as the following analysis of three legal rulings in MMT based on scripture will demonstrate, to circumscribe its author's views on purity and practice MMT redefines existing terminology, introduces new vocabulary, and violates and even avoids forms likely recognized as "standard" by the wider Jewish community. All that MMT lacks vis-à-vis the hallmarks of an anti-language is a clear intent to be opaque to opposing groups. But MMT suggests that anti-languages do not necessarily begin with that purpose but rather develop toward it over time. Thus, MMT proves to be good evidence of the origins of anti-language at Qumran.

In light of these observations, I turn now to three case studies to test the capacity of the anti-language concept for illuminating MMT's legal rhetoric and reasoning vis-à-vis the scriptures, and Leviticus in particular, the biblical book upon which MMT draws most heavily. I begin with a legal ruling about the proper place of animal sacrifice and slaughter in which the use of a standard formula, כתוב, "what is written," is generally thought to precede a simple rephrasing of Lev 17:3–4 that adds nothing to the biblical text (4QMMT B 27–33). I continue with a passage in which כתוב precedes a term absent from the scriptures, but which probably recalls Lev 22:28 on the slaughter of a parent beast and its offspring on the same day (4QMMT B 36–38). I conclude with a ruling in which no formula introduces a discussion about animal hides and bones and carrying handles that most commentators explain by reference to later rabbinic discussions, but which can also be understood more simply as a clarification of ambiguous syntax in Lev 11:25, on carrying the carcass of an unclean animal (4QMMT B 21–24).

THREE TEST CASES: LEVITICUS INTERPRETED IN MMT

4QMMT B 27–33

Our first test case takes up Lev 17:3–4 and its insistence that all slaughter take place at the tent of meeting, and that none be undertaken in the camp or outside the camp.[5] The ruling clarifies what each of those places is: the sanctuary is the tent of

---

5. Qimron and Strugnell (1994, 156) call this a paraphrase of Lev 17:3, as does Bernstein (1996, 39). Brooke (1997, 72) takes issue with the use of the term "paraphrase," noting rightly that the language of

meeting and the holy of holies, Jerusalem is the camp, and "outside the camp" refers
to the settlements in the land outside of Jerusalem.

27 [ו]ע[ל שא כתוב] איש ישחט במחנה או[

28 [ישחט]מחוץ למחנה שור וכשב ועז כי [   ]

29 ואנחנו חושבים שהמקדש] משכן אוהל מועד הוא וי[רושלי[ם]

30 מחנה היא וחו[צה] למחנה] הוא חוצה לירושלים [הוא מחנה

31 ער[י]הם חוץ ממ[חנה   החטאת ו]מוציאים את דשא

32 [ה]מזבח ושור]פים שם את החטאת כי ירושלים [היא המקום אשר

33 [בחר בו מכול שבטי ישראל

[And concern]ing that which is written: [if a person slaughters inside the camp, or
slaughters] outside the camp cattle or sheep or a goat: for [. . . .] And we think that
the sanctuary [is the place of the tent of meeting, and J[erusale[m] is the camp, and
out[side] the camp [is outside Jerusalem,] that is, the encampment of their settlements. It is outside the c[amp . . . the purification offering and] take out the ashes of
[the] altar and bu[rn the purification offering, for Jerusalem is the place which [he
chose from among all the tribes of Israel.]

This ruling clarifies the authorial group's view of Lev 17:3–4: since the group views
the camp as Jerusalem and "outside the camp" as the area outside of Jerusalem, profane slaughter is prohibited in all those places. The opponents take a more lenient
view of sacred space, inasmuch as the phrase in B 35, "they are not slaughtering in the
sanctuary" (אי[נם שוחטים במקדש]), is understood to permit slaughter "in the camp"
and "outside the camp."[6] Aharon Shemesh and C. Werman point out the further
exegetical move in B 31–32 meant to ensure this narrow reading: alluding to Lev 6:4
and its requirement that certain organs be taken "outside the camp" for disposal, the
author counts on the "blanket agreement that they [the organs] are burned outside
Jerusalem" (2003, 121–22). That the ruling closes with the additional echo of Deut
12:5 to mark Jerusalem as the place of God's choosing also cleverly subsumes under
this conservative view of profane slaughter the more liberal perspective articulated in
Deuteronomy that allows slaughter apart from the sanctuary (B 32–33).

The habit of advancing our comprehension of MMT with the help of rabbinic debates has produced strikingly conflicting interpretations of this passage. Lawrence H.
Schiffman, on the one hand, points not only to 11QT 52:13–16 as text that clarifies
the distance that constitutes "outside the camp" (three days' journey); he also cites
Sifre Deut 75 as tannaitic support of this reading and as further evidence of what he
understands to be the Sadducean predilection of MMT over against the Pharisaic
views (as they are reconstructed from the later rabbinic texts) (Schiffman 2001, 275;

MMT is entirely that of Leviticus; thus, it is a reordering, not a paraphrase. But see also Parry (1997, 448),
who observes that the allusion to Lev 17:1–4 makes the following changes: 4QMMT reads "Israelite" as
"person"; 4QMMT lists "cattle or sheep or goat" to MT's "ox lamb, or goat"; there is a shift in the order
of prepositional phrases ("inside/outside the camp"); 4QMMT ignores the "Revelation Formula," "and
Yahweh spoke to Moses saying" (17:1), and the "Commission Formula," "This is the word which Yahweh
has commanded." Parry concludes, perhaps too confidently, that "[t]he author of MMT deliberately omits
the revelatory speech forms to avoid using the Tetragrammaton" (448).

6. On expanded notions of sacred space at Qumran, see Harrington 1997, 114–16, 123–24; Schiffman 1996, 88–89; Schiffman 1985, 308–9; Schiffman 1989; Bernard 2001, 80.

see also Nahmanides on Deut 12:20). By contrast, Azzan Yadin reads B 25–28 in light of a debate between R. Ishmael and R. Akiba to argue that the text is about *ḥullin* (non-sacral slaughter), and that MMT and R. Ishmael agree in reading Lev 17:3 as prohibiting the consumption of *ḥullin*, against R. Akiba who regards the verse as prohibiting only "the slaughter of *qodashim*—the sacrifice of sheep or goat or oxen—outside the Tent of Meeting" (Yadin 2003, 143; see also Eshel 1995; Kister 1999, 337 n. 84).

But what comes of the passage when we interpret it with the help of the anti-language concept and leave behind the bias of the rabbinic testimony? Keeping in mind the origins of an anti-language—a group's reinvention of a normative code to express its members' own linguistic identity—we see that process underway in this passage. The phrase שׁ־ חושבים ואנחנו in B 29 states boldly the group's claim on the ruling as distinctively their own,[7] and its plain sense is to establish the geographical referents the group attaches to the terms "camp" and "outside the camp." Recalling the essential features of anti-language, this is a case of creating specialized vocabulary related to the Qumran group's principal interest in purity and sacrifice by relexicalizing Judaism's normative code on the topic, the book of Leviticus, and of doing so by converting existing terms to bear new meaning. And although the use of a formula to introduce the rearranged quotation of Lev 17:3–4, כתוב, does not violate what seems to be a standard form (Qimron and Strugnell 1994, 140; Fitzmyer 1960; Bernstein 1994; VanderKam 1998b; VanderKam 2006), the ruling does move in that direction by reinscribing what is written with new meaning. That the ruling does not conceal meaning from outsiders, but rather aims to reveal it to them further indicates that we see here only the nascence of an anti-language; in this sense, Schniedewind is correct to judge MMT as lacking a fully developed anti-language. Yet we may see in this an originary moment for the group's anti-language, an instance where its members begin to lay out the alternative language, which for them was clearly little more than a true *translation* of the normative code.[8]

4QMMT B 36–38

While it is largely reconstructed and anything said about it must be tentative, 4QMMT's editors and most commentators are confident of the general contours of the next ruling we investigate.

36 [על העברות אנחנו חושבים שאין לזבוח א[ת האם ואת הולד ביום אחד

37 [ועל האוכל אנח]נו חושבים שאיאכל את הולד

38 [שבמעי אמו לאחר שחיטתו ואתם יודעים שהו]א כן והדבר כתוב עברה

---

7. The phrase appears again in the legal section to function in the same way at B 36, 37, 42, 55, 64–65, 73 (with אומרים instead of חושבים in the last two instances); see also Qimron and Strugnell (1994, 99), who argue that attaching this meaning to this phrase is unique to MMT vis-à-vis biblical and Mishnaic Hebrew; this may count as further evidence of nascent anti-language in MMT.

8. As for the text's relationship to later rabbinic discussions regarding the consumption of *ḥullin* or the proper locus of non-sacral slaughter, this tradition may have figured into the thinking of those who engaged in those debates and recorded them, but we hardly need to—nor should we—predicate our reading of 4QMMT on the terms of those debates, especially when the concept of anti-language clarifies so simply the plain sense of the text.

[And concerning pregnant animals: we think that one should not sacrifice th]e mother and its fetus on the same day. . . . [And concerning consumption {of the fetus}: w]e think that the fetus may be eaten, [the one that was in the womb of its mother, after it has been slaughtered. And you know that thi]s is so, for it is written {concerning} a pregnant one {animal}.

It is generally agreed that the background to this ruling must be Lev 22:28, the prohibition against slaughtering (שחט) a parent animal (שור או שה) and its offspring (בנו) on the same day (ביום אחד). By contrast, if we accept the editors' reconstruction of B 36, על העברות אנחנו חושבים שאין לזבוח, and its replacement of שחט with זבח,[9] the first part of the ruling actually addresses *sacrificing* a *mother* and its *fetus* on the same day. And inasmuch as the reconstruction of B 38, שבמעי אמו לאחר שחיטתו, is correct in light of what does appear in B 37, the second part of the ruling permits the priests or the one making sacrifice to eat the fetus after properly *slaughtering* it rather than let it go to waste.

That said, commentators are troubled by the following claim, והדבר כתוב עברה, "And the matter is written about a pregnant one" (Qimron and Strugnell 1994, 50–51 n. 38). Even though the preceding material reflects some sort of interpretation of Lev 22:28, they are nearly united in judging that the quotation formula כתוב is poorly used before a nonbiblical word for a pregnant animal (Bernstein 1996, 41; Brooke 1997, 73).[10]

Puzzlement over its use in this case set off a quest to locate a rationale for the use here of כתוב that does not rely exclusively on Lev 22:28. Schiffman relates the ruling to 11QT 52:5–7 and 4Q270 2 ii 15; the former prohibits the sacrifice (זבח) of a pregnant beast and the sacrifice (זבח) of a parent beast and its offspring on the same day, while the latter prohibits ישחט הבהמה והיה עבר]ה, "slaughtering a beast with a living fetus" (2000, 143; Qimron and Strugnell 1994, 157–58, 157 n. 115).[11] Schiffman goes further and also calls to mind *m. Ḥul.* 4:5, a text that adjudicates the disposition of dead and living eight- and nine-month-old fetuses *found* in a slaughtered animal (all eight-month-olds and dead nine-month-olds are to be torn from the mother's womb

---

9. It is certainly the most likely reconstruction; Qimron and Strugnell (1994, 157–58) explain that they posit העברות because of the same word in the singular at the end of the ruling (B 38). Moreover, they supply לזבוח in B 36 because in a similar ruling in 11QT 52:5–7 the texts uses זבח instead of the שחט of Lev 22:28; also, the previous ruling dealt with matters relating to animal sacrifice and the sanctuary (see במקדש in B 35); and the second part of this ruling—using the word אכל—has clearly shifted to the question of non-sacral slaughter.

10. The harshest judgment on 4QMMT's author comes from Bernstein (1996, 41), who writes, "The 'argument' of MMT (if we may dignify it with that name) . . ." Brooke expresses discomfort with the term's use here. For more on the debate about the meaning of כתוב in MMT, see the concluding remarks in this essay (Brooke 1997).

11. Schiffman says of 4Q270 2 ii 15, 11QT 52:5, and 4QMMT B 38: "All these texts share the notion that the slaughter of a pregnant animal violates the Torah's prohibition on slaughter of an animal and its young on the same day" (2000, 143). That judgment seems to overlook the differences in terminology I note among the three texts. Qimron and Strugnell (1994, 157–58) think that the 4QMMT ruling only aims to prohibit the intentional slaughter and sacrifice of a pregnant mother and its fetus on the same day. They relate their claim to the widespread debate in early Judaism as to whether a mother and its fetus are separate entities. For citations and secondary literature, see Qimron and Strugnell (1994, 157 n. 115).

and its blood removed; the live nine-month-old must be ritually slaughtered in light of Lev 22:28). Schiffman calls attention to the Mishnah text because it provides what he deems to be the more lenient, Pharisaic contrast to the Qumran ruling, inasmuch as the former permits "the slaughtering of pregnant animals, ruling that the fetus may be eaten without further slaughter," while he deems the Qumranites to prohibit slaughter of pregnant beasts (Schiffman 2001, 275; Regev 2003, 248; Harrington 1997, 125). Meanwhile, Yadin reads the ruling at a more abstract level, concluding from it that MMT parallels R. Ishmael's view that the fetus or embryo and the mother are of one being, against the Pharisaic view that they are separate beings (2003, 143–44).

None of these readings are particularly persuasive inasmuch as they overlook the clear differences between the Qumran and Mishnah texts, as well as the central assertion shared among all of them that probably lies at the heart of the 4QMMT ruling. As for the differences, only 4Q270 2 ii 15 seems to prohibit outright the slaughter of a pregnant beast as an intentional act, but it does so to include the act in a catalog of outrageously audacious intentional sins.[12] Inasmuch as 11QT 52:5–7 prohibits the sacrifice (זבח) of a pregnant animal in l. 5, and a parent beast and its offspring on the same day in l. 6, its concern is manifestly *not* with the possibility that someone would wittingly slaughter a pregnant beast; it assumes, instead, that slaughter has already occurred and it addresses whether the only-then-discovered fetus renders the beast an unacceptable sacrifice. Similarly, by using the verb מצא, *m. Ḥul.* 4:5 clearly refers to a pregnancy discovered only as a result of slaughter, but it addresses a different question, how one disposes of the fetus and what difference its status upon discovery makes for that disposition.[13]

As for the commonality among these texts, they are all rooted in what must have been an obvious principle of sound animal husbandry and its unhappy exception: one never intentionally kills a pregnant beast for food or sacrifice, but it can happen unexpectedly.[14] Although it does not speak directly to the case of surprisingly pregnant livestock, the prohibition in Lev 22:28 also seems to have elevated the importance of the matter to one of religious obligation and observance. Each texts wrestles with one or another of these practical and religious difficulties created by the human-caused death of a mother beast and its unborn offspring. 11QT 52:5–7 addresses the sacred status of the parent beast if it is only discovered to be pregnant in the course

---

12. They include יגלה את רז עמו לגואים, revealing the secret of one's people to the Gentiles (2 ii 13); סרה על משיחי רוח הקדש, rebelling against those anointed by the Holy Spirit (2 ii 14); תועה בחוזי אמתו, causing confusion in seeing God's truth (2 ii 14); בהמרותו את פי אל, rebelling against God's word (2 ii 14–15); ישכב אשה הרה מקיץ דם, lying with a woman at the end of her monthly period (2 ii 15–16); or ישכב עם זכר משכבי אשה, lying with a man as with a woman (2 ii 16–17).

13. The text reads: השוחט את הבהמה ומצא בה בן שמונה חי או מת או בן תשעה מת קורעו ומוציא את דמו מצא בן תשעה חי טעון שחיטה, "He who slaughters the beast and *found* in it an eight-month old [fetus], alive or dead, or a dead nine-month old [fetus], tears it [out] and drains its blood. [If] he *found* a living nine-month old, slaughter is required" (emphasis added) (Eshkol Edition).

14. Note in this regard that contrary to myriad commentators' judgments, *only* 4Q270 2 ii 15 actually entertains the question of whether slaughtering a pregnant beast is acceptable practice, and it does so to make it obvious that is not; the other texts simply take for granted that such practice is undesirable and unacceptable.

of a slaughter meant to lead to sacrifice. *M. Ḥul.* 4:5 answers the different question of whether in disposing of the unviable fetus found in the course of slaughtering an adult beast the stipulations for divinely acceptable slaughter must be observed. And 4Q270 2 ii 15 makes clear that in light of Lev 22:28 slaughtering a pregnant beast is not merely bad farm economics, it is also a crime against God.

We should read the ruling in 4QMMT B 36–38 against the backdrop of these religio-economic concerns that circumstance and biblical law imposed on Jews engaged in animal husbandry and temple sacrifice. And just as in the test case above, the concept of anti-language offers further assistance in understanding the author's legal reasoning. First, that the question is whether a mother and its fetus can be *sacrificed* on the same day indicates that the ruling addresses the problem posed by a beast that is brought for sacrifice, but is found to be pregnant upon *slaughter*. The answer MMT provides is in keeping with the judgment rendered by 11QT 52:5–7 (but it does not resolve the ambiguity left by 11QT 52:5–7 as to whether sacrifice of both mother and fetus or only the fetus is prohibited). Since the rulings in MMT are polemical in nature, one may also surmise that the opponents had adopted a contrary practice to permit the sacrifice of the mother and/or the fetus. Second, this ruling takes up a previously unmentioned question as well, whether in such cases of potentially complete loss of value—religious and nutritional—something can still be recovered. The (surprisingly) lenient ruling of the author is that after proper slaughter the fetus may, indeed, serve as a food source.

It is the third aspect of the ruling that most commands our interest: it concludes with the judgment that והדבר כתוב עברה, "The matter is written concerning a pregnant one." The use of the כתוב formula signals the author's view that his interpretation has precedent in scripture, most likely Lev 22:28: for this writer and his community the biblical law concerning a parent beast and its offspring embraces the case of a mother and its fetus, and its logic prohibits the sacrifice of both on the same day (against the opponents), but permits redemption of some food value after the proper slaughter of the fetus. Whatever one thinks of the quality of the author's logic, its foundation is clear: it depends on relexicalizing the Leviticus passage and on claiming that fresh vocabulary as the true translation of Leviticus' meaning.

As in our first test case, here too we see the emergence of a Qumran anti-language, the earliest stages of relexicalizing the "normative code" that pertains to the dissident group's primary interest in purity of sacrificial practice (Lev 22:28). This test case, though, adds a new layer of complexity to Qumran's emerging anti-language: in this instance כתוב does not introduce a merely rephrased version of the biblical text that retains its vocabulary word for word (Lev 17:3; B 27–32); instead, it introduces what most readers deem an interpretation of Lev 22:28 as a proper translation, saying, "The matter is *written* concerning a pregnant one." By doing this, the author subverts what seems certain to have been a standard form, the כתוב formula, thus adopting another aspect of anti-language for Qumran rhetoric. But as is true of our first test case above, because this ruling reveals rather than conceals a new linguistic reality to outsiders, it too records only an originary moment in the development of Qumran anti-language (Kugler 2000, 104–6).

4QMMT B 21–23

In what Schiffman calls "an almost certain restoration," MMT B 21–22 seems to prohibit the use of hide or bone from the carcass of an unclean animal to fashion a carrying handle (Schiffman 1996, 88; 1990; 1993, 191–98).

21　ה אף על עור[ות ועצמות הבהמה הטמאה אין לעשות]

22 [מן עצותמה] ומן ע[ו]ר[ות]מה ידות כ[לים

And concerning the hides and bones of unclean beasts: it is forbidden to make handles of vessels from their bones and hides.

The editors, though perhaps less confident of their own restoration than Schiffman (Qimron and Strugnell 1994, 49 n. 22, 155; Qimron 1996, 11–12), make the conjecture by comparison with 11QTᵃ 51:4–5, a text that prohibits carrying the flesh, hide, bones, or nails of an unclean animal (see also 47:7–15); with Josephus, who reports the decree of Antiochus III against bringing the hides of unclean animals into Jerusalem (*Ant.* 12.3.4); with *m. Ḥul.* 9:1–2, which rules that defilement comes from the flesh of unclean animals, but not their hide or bones; and with *m. Yad.* 4:6, which offers the apparently contrasting, strict Sadducean view that all parts of the animal cause defilement. Indeed, commentators agree that this ruling, like others in MMT, reflects a stricter Sadducean view over against that of the more lenient Pharisees: the latter prohibit only the carrying of the carcass as flesh, but not its hide or bones (*m. Ḥul.* 9:1–2); the former deem all of it—hide and bones, too—to be impure (B 21–22; *m. Yad.* 4:6) (Schiffman 1993, 442–48; Grabbe 1996, 95–97).

Once more, though, discussion of the MMT ruling seems to be unnecessarily biased by reliance on later polemical discussions in the rabbinic corpus. The debate referred to by Schiffman and others has to do with bringing hides and other body parts of unclean animals into Jerusalem, or with carrying the parts of slaughtered animals of any kind. By contrast, the remains of the MMT B 21–22 indicate that the ruling deals with hides of animals made into carrying handles (ידות), a much narrower concern than that of any of the supposedly related texts noted above. Where might the authors of MMT have come upon such a slender interest?

A peculiar use of the preposition מן in Lev 11:25 almost surely was the hook on which this ruling was developed. With respect to unclean animals the MT of the verse reads וכל הנשא מנבלתם יכבס בגדיו וטמא עד הערב, "And all who carry *from* their carcass shall wash his garments and remain unclean until evening." The use of the preposition מן with נבלתם is difficult, and making matters even more confusing is the subsequent inconsistency in its use when the question of carrying carcasses is addressed again in vv. 28 and 40. In fact, a summary of the versional evidence for vv. 25, 28, and 40 suggests strongly that this peculiar use of the preposition מן was perplexing to translators and tradents and puzzling to ancient readers. In v. 25 the Targums and some Syriac manuscripts omit the preposition while the Samaritan text retains it, and the Septuagint offers τῶν θνησίμαιων αὐτῶν, letting the ambiguity of a partitive genitive carry the weight of the omitted preposition (ἀπό) (Smyth 1920; §§1306–19). In v. 28 the Samaritan text supplies the preposition where it is absent in the MT מנבלתם), and once more the Greek offers only τῶν θνησίμαιων αὐτῶν. Verse

40 begins with a decree regarding the impurity of someone who eats *from* a carcass; the MT and the Samaritan text understandably use the preposition, as does the Greek text (ἀπο τῶν θνησίμαιων αὐτῶν). But in the latter half of v. 40 the question of carrying a carcass comes up again, and the MT and the Samaritan text do not introduce the preposition, but the Septuagint does!

Given this evidence for the translators' and tradents' obvious perplexity over מנבלתם in Lev 11:25 as well as the impertinence of the non-MMT evidence cited by previous commentators to explain B 21–22, one can justifiably speculate that MMT has simply devised its own way of managing the offending preposition on מנבלתם in Lev 11:25: "carrying *from* the carcass" is taken as a reference not to the carcass itself, but carrying by means of a part of the carcass, making from bone, hide, or other useful entrails a carrying handle, a יד (cf. 1QM 5:14) (Qimron and Strugnell 1994, 25, 49, 98; Waltke and O'Connor 1990, 213–14, §11.2.11.e).[15] And assuming the polemical nature of the ruling, it seems likely that the author and his community saw a contrary practice in the temple precincts, the use of derivatives of animal carcasses for carrying tools without regard for their origin or purity.

How does the anti-language concept explain this ruling better than reference to Josephus and the rabbinic materials? First, it provides an interpretive framework for understanding what transpired in MMT's translation of Lev 11:25 by interpretation. Here again we have an instance of relexicalizing the normative code, and this time by assigning new meaning to existing vocabulary and by introducing altogether new language. The troublesome preposition מן in Lev 11:25 is endowed with new meaning, and the non-biblical word for handle, יד, is added to the lexicon of terms pertaining to matters of temple practice and purity. Second, the absence of the כתוב formula, in spite of the similarity of this ruling to the previous two test cases, evinces the author's movement toward avoiding the use of accepted forms rather than merely overturning them or using them obliquely. And third, in this ruling we might think to see the first hints of the obscurantism characteristic of full-scale anti-languages: by omitting the כתוב formula and never speaking directly of Lev 11:25 the author adopts a concealing rather than revealing mode of discourse. It is worth noting, however, that given our suggestion thus far that the author treats his reading of Leviticus as essentially an act of translation, concealment was less likely the reason he overlooked the formula than that he viewed his *reading* of Lev 11:25 as self-evident, a mere matter of translation.

15. This explanation depends on the reconstruction and reading offered and defended by Qimron and Strugnell (1994). It should not pass without notice that the reading also has on its side the wordplay entailed in recalling a verse about *carrying* to speak about *handles* with a word that is a homonym for *hand*. Waltke and O'Connor (1990) note that the partitive use of מן is not unheard of. They also observe that in Exod 16:27 and Lev 5:9 we find just this use of the preposition with the same syntax that we find here, the preposition coming before the noun.

Evaluating the Test Cases and Thoughts
on Interpretation as Translation

What have our test cases indicated about the capacity of anti-language to illuminate the legal reasoning in MMT? Little more need be said than to observe that the anti-language concept proves at least as capable of explaining peculiarities in MMT's legal reasoning as recourse to the evidence of the later rabbinic canon, if not also more so. In particular, the later rabbinic evidence does not easily illuminate the seemingly odd understanding of the כתוב formula articulated in MMT, nor does it manage well the habit MMT has of relexicalizing Hebrew Scripture, the author's and opponents' normative code.[16] By contrast, explaining these things as features of anti-language in its developmental stages renders them readily understandable. Thus, what our three test cases point to is the possibility that by deploying more widely the concept of anti-language as an explanatory device in our study of Qumran legal rhetoric we may be able to better explain the legal reasoning in the Scrolls and to trace its developmental trajectory over time: the concept of anti-language could become a new and important tool for tracing the developmental history of Qumran legal reasoning as it is revealed to us in the Dead Sea Scrolls.

We have also learned that, at least from the standpoint of the community that develops it, an anti-language is more akin to translation than interpretation. As noted above, the use and non-use of the כתוב formula certainly points in that direction, as does an anti-language's insistence that it merely conveys the true meaning of words already accepted as normative. This study, brief and only suggestive as it may be, suggests that we ought to perhaps upend an old dictum about translation to see things in a new light: not only is all translation interpretation, but at least some interpretation is also merely translation.

---

16. Note especially the odd claims regarding the function of כתוב in MMT: Qimron and Strugnell (1994, 140) state flatly that the term never introduces a scriptural citation; Bernstein (1996, 38–46) is much more nuanced in his judgment, but is also puzzled by the apparent lack of direct quotations after the formula; Brooke (1997, 70–71) flatly contradicts the judgment made by Qimron and Strugnell (1994) to say that the formula nearly always introduces "scripture explicitly or in summary form" (71); Fraade (1998, 68 n. 35) declares that no instance of the formula introduces a scripture text, and B 38 may refer to a sectarian law. Yadin (2003, 148) does offer the innovative view that, like the phrase used by R. Ishmael, מאורסה הכתוב מדבר, the formula functions in MMT to clarify the nature of the subject of a biblical verse. Yadin comes close to circumscribing how the formula works in MMT, but it is neither necessary to link its use there with the formula used by R. Ishmael, nor is it clear that it *only* clarifies the status of a subject in a biblical verse.

COMMENTS FROM SOMEONE WHO ONCE
SHOOK HANDS WITH S. H. HOOKE

John Sandys-Wunsch

Nothing appeals more to human frailty than being put in a position of Olympian detachment from which one can comment on the work of others. To say then I am grateful for the invitation to contribute to this collection goes without further comment. I do think that it is very important to take into account cultural factors in the difficult task of understanding and translating the Bible. I commend the editor and his contributors for the time and energy they have put into their work

Now it will be apparent to the discerning reader that I am not in agreement with everything suggested in this book; but then I am far from infallible, and discussion amongst scholars is how matters are cleared up. I have simply been invited as a historical specimen to offer a different perspective from younger colleagues, leaving right or wrong to the judgment of posterity, and this I have tried to do.

Let me begin where I am in overwhelming agreement with the aim of the contributors to this volume. It strikes me that one of the curses—I employ the word advisedly—of some appeals to the Bible in public discourse in certain circles today is that the Bible is seen not as a source for reflection but as blanket endorsement of an interpreter's own prejudices. In other words, the scholarly work of the past five hundred years is being ignored. I find it quite likely that those who extol the Ten Commandments as the answer to everything have not bothered to read them recently—or is it that these upholders of the commandments have sufficient faith in the virtues of their grandparents that they feel they are immune to one of the provisions? The Bible is often an excuse for the Orwellian double-think only too obvious in the actions of someone who can recommend a culture of *life* in the case of stem cells and then sign death warrants for criminals, some of whom appear to have turned their lives around. Similarly, those who think the Bible is against contraception do not have the consistency to endorse easily available health care for the children they insist should be born.

The careful study of the Bible done in the past few centuries has shown that far from being an infallible record of eternal verities, it is instead a very human record of the meeting between a human tradition and the transcendent, however you wish to describe it/him/her. In this encounter the human side saw the situation through its own cultural presuppositions, not all of which were admirable. The proof of this assertion is that no one really wishes to enact without exception all the laws and practices described and required in the Bible, apart from the case of individuals ready to swallow contradictions, ignore common sense, and set up legal procedures for those bent on executing their teenaged children—a temptation known to many parents but rejected by an overwhelming majority.

As a commentator on this book there are obviously two entities involved on which I have to comment, namely the social sciences and translation. Each of these requires some discussion.

SOCIAL SCIENCES: THE NATURE AND LIMITATIONS OF SOCIAL SCIENCE

The social sciences present two initial problems: what disciplines are social sciences, and what is social science anyway in distinction to the *hard* sciences of physics, chemistry, and so on? The problem was neatly stated by the great eighteenth-century author Georges-Louis Leclerc, Comte de Buffon (1707–88), author of the thirty-five-volume *L'Histoire Naturelle,* who prefaced his section on the natural history of *l'homme* with the with the astute remark:

> However much interest we have in understanding ourselves, I suspect we are better at knowing what is not us. Furnished by nature with organs designed for our survival, we use them to receive information about what is outside us. We only expand our attention on the exterior world and we live outside ourselves. Too occupied in multiplying the functions of our senses and extending the expansion of the exterior part of ourselves that we rarely make use of that interior sense that reduces us to our true dimensions. (1749, 429)

The glory of the natural sciences is their ability to predict results. Barring the intrusion of impurities, when one reduces table salt into its component parts one can be sure before one begins about the weight of the sodium and the chlorine one will produce. The social sciences are nowhere near as reliable, and their specialty is explaining results after the fact rather than predicting outcomes. The trouble is that human beings are far from predictable, and this is why when one talks about, say, a culture as being *patriarchal*—and *patriarchal* can be used of very different cultures—this does not mean that every woman in that culture behaves the same way. History is full of examples of women from Bathsheba through Lucretia Borgia to Queen Victoria who were quite adept at making their influence felt in cultures that were far from being devoted to the doctrine of equal opportunity. Human beings are infinitely variable, and, while knowing the outlines of the culture in which an individual lives may throw some light on why this individual behaves as he or she does, it does not mean we can assume without evidence what this individual would inevitably do in a given situation.

The actual bounds of social sciences, and even the classification and nomenclature, are far from standard. Anyone besieged by a phalanx of social scientists knows that the best defense is to throw their ranks into confusion by asking for clarification about the difference between anthropologists and sociologists. In reading the contributions in this book I feel very much like Monsieur Jourdain, the hero of *Le Bourgeois Gentilhomme,* who was astonished to discover that he had been speaking prose all his life, for in reading Carolyn Leeb's examination of the different range of meanings of biblical words in a way most of us old-timers thought of as the occupation of a philologist, I have discovered that all my life I have been talking anthropology.

In the case of ancient societies the application of social-scientific theory is limited by the paucity of data. Social history is a relatively modern invention. Even the most banal everyday data is missing in ancient and even not-so-ancient records. For example, when the seventeenth-century Swedish warship *Vasa* was raised, social historians were interested in the clothing fragments recovered because up till then there were no surviving records of what Swedish sailors wore at the time of the *Vasa.*

In modern social science it is possible to take surveys of public opinion and private attitudes on various matters such as Reginald Bibby's work on the changing Canadian attitudes toward religion (1987). In ancient cultures nobody was much interested in such matters before Herodotus, and so the written material scholars are left with embodies more prescription than analysis. This means that when one talks about patriarchy in ancient Israel, the reconstruction has to be based on laws, exhortations, and the occasional narrative; nobody knows how many Israelite men helped their wives butcher the sheep for dinner in a given period; even less is one in a position to know how customs varied from region to region or from time to time.

Language in particular is unreported in a scholarly fashion. The distinction between *sibboleth* and *shibboleth* in Judg 12:6 is one surviving example of what must have been many differences in Hebrew pronunciation. We have to face the reality that many problems of interpretation may turn on dialectical differences lost to history. Worse still, one cannot assume that in the case of words found in the Hebrew Bible the absence of evidence is the evidence of absence. Estimations of good scholars suggest that only 20 percent of the words in use in ancient Israel have been preserved in its official documents; it is also likely that some words which were current in Hebrew in the biblical period may have gone underground only to be preserved in oral discourse and appear in later in rabbinic usage.

In fact, the whole normal process of social science is reversed in biblical studies; instead of a great deal of evidence throwing light on an individual feature of a culture, a few instances, such as that of the Levite's concubine in Judg 19, have to be expanded to general conclusions that are far from certain.

THE HISTORY OF THE APPLICATION OF SOCIAL-SCIENTIFIC CONSIDERATIONS TO THE INTERPRETATION OF THE BIBLE

As a historian of Western thought as shown in the permutations of biblical scholarship, I cannot resist pointing out that there is a long and honorable tradition of using human sciences as a means of understanding the Bible. I am sure the contributors to this collection are quite aware of this, but for the sake of their readers they should lift their mortarboards to pay tribute to the admonitions of Ecclesiastes, who claimed there was nothing new under the sun, as well as those of Jesus ben Sirach, who advised readers to praise famous men and our fathers who begat us. The awareness of *culture* in the modern sense of the term goes back to the eighteenth century at least. The most notable awareness of the differentness of the thinking of ancient cultures was the use of the word *mythology* in an extended meaning to cover the different type of thinking found in antiquity. In the late eighteenth century, Eichhorn[1] used this category to make sense of Genesis, and it only took a hundred years for the awareness of this term to gain complete respectability in Gore's article in *Lux Mundi* (1779, 129–256).

Certainly in Britain alone in the late nineteenth century and throughout the twentieth century, one only has to think of the work of scholars such as Robertson Smith (1889), Sir James Fraser (1918), Alfred Guillaume (1938), S. H. Hooke (1958), and A. R. Johnson (1964)—and the list could be much longer without mentioning work done in other countries—to see how prolific the discipline had become. It is for this reason that the opinion of Richard L. Rohrbaugh that it is over the past thirty or forty years that the social sciences have contributed a great deal to the understanding of the Bible might perhaps be better as an opening statement to a presentation of the evidence rather than as an invocation of a self-evident truth.

<h2 style="text-align:center">GENERALIZATIONS</h2>

A term often used in this book is *Mediterranean anthropology*. I presume this relates to Mediterranean culture rather than the work of scholars based there. But when one talks about the culture of sizeable areas such as the Mediterranean, it is my opinion that one should be wary of the generalizations. Generalizations can easily turn into a snare and a delusion, for they give the illusion of knowledge rather than its substance. There are essentially two navigation points for judging a generalization, namely geographical and chronological, both of which require discussion.

I am not sure the whole of the Mediterranean can be taken as a single cultural area—it is both too large and ironically too small to be of help in understanding and translating the Bible. In the biblical period there were contacts between Israel and its immediate neighbors as well as with Egypt, Greece, Rome, and perhaps Carthage. But can one say these countries exhibited a common cultural basis? For example the Egyptian notion of the afterlife mediated through the pharaoh is one important difference between Egypt and the surrounding people. But *Mediterranean anthropology* is also too restricted a term, for Israel was also influenced by the cultures of the peoples of Mesopotamia and Persia, who were a long way from the Mediterranean.

The other threat to the accuracy of generalizations is the matter of chronology. In a word, cultures can change. There is ample evidence for changes within the Old Testament as a result of the Babylonian captivity, and the influence of Hellenistic culture after Alexander the Great caused a great deal of realignment of culture across the ancient Near East and even further East.

But there is a third danger in generalizations, namely one that occurs when cul-

---

1. J. G. Eichhorn published his work as an article in his *Repertorium für biblische und Morgenländische Litteratur* (1779, 129–256). A translation of his opening passage along with a discussion of his work can be found in John Sandys-Wunsch (2005, 250).

tures are named by their putative attributes. It may be correct in some sense of the term to refer to Israelite culture as one of shame and honor, but what is meant? Shame and honor exist in many cultures to the point that one would be hard-pressed to find a group devoid of these very human characteristics. It is indeed true that some cultures take honor and shame more seriously than others, such as traditional Japanese culture, which took honor seriously to the point where suicide was the only way to atone for failure. But in the Hebrew Bible this is not the reason for notable suicides. Saul indeed falls on his own sword, but this was in a situation where he was going to die soon anyway, and suicide as an honorable exit was better than being killed slowly by the Philistines. Similarly, when Samson committed suicide it was because he had been suffering what Saul had avoided, only Samson in his particular method of self-slaughter was able to take his enemies with him as a practical gesture. I think there is a need to define more closely what exactly was shame and honor within Israelite culture. This to some extent has been done in a number of recent works on ancient Israelite culture (Esler 2005).

TRANSLATION

Translation is one of the most difficult of the arts, for before any creative transpositions can be made one has to get the grammar and idioms of the original language correct. The most famous howler in Western theology is of course Augustine's interpretation of Paul in Rom 5:12, in which the good bishop interpreted the Greek expression *eph ho* as "in him." Augustine used this translation to prove his point that Adam's descendants were "in him" when he committed the first sin and were therefore guilty of it. In fact *eph ho* was a Greek idiom that meant "because," although philologically it looks like "in him" if you do not know Greek well. This is the equivalent of translating the French *pas de deux* as "father of twins." But this mistake in translation was to cause a great deal of needless grief in the history of the church, where parents whose children died before they could be baptized had the additional torment of thinking their child might have been sent to hell for Adam's sin.

The simplest example of the disasters that accrue from a failure to understand idiom was provided by Mark Twain as part of his attack on the cultural pretensions of Europe. Twain exploited the nature of idiomatic expressions in his ridicule of the French translation of his story *The Celebrated Jumping Frog of Calaveras County*. His method was to give a literal translation of the French version, or, as he put it: "In English. Then in French. Then clawed back into a civilized language once more by patient, unremunerated toil" (1935).

Here is the first line of his original version followed by his retranslation of the French edition:

> Well, thish-yer Smiley had rat-tarriers, and chicken cocks, and tom-cats, and all of them kind of things, till you couldn't rest, and you couldn't fetch nothing for him to bet on but he'd match you. He ketched a frog one day, and took him home and said he cal'klated to edercate him; and so he never done nothing for three months but set in his back yard and learn that frog to jump. (1935, 1072)

> Eh bien! this Smiley nourished some terriers à rats, and some cocks of combat, and some cats, and all sorts of things; and with his rage of betting one no had more of repose. He trapped one day a frog and him imported with him (et l'emporta chez lui), saying that he pretended to make his education. You me believe if you will, but during three months he not has nothing done but to him apprehend to jump (apprendre à sauter) in a court retired of her mansion (de sa maison). (1935, 1078)

It is not surprising that this spoof of Twain's is the unwelcome ghost at the banquet of fanciers of computer translation. Obviously Twain carried this out tongue in cheek, but there have been similar translations of biblical texts done in all seriousness.

But after the idioms and the syntax have been mastered there is another source of misunderstanding. This is when, in the editor's words, "the Bible was written by, for, and about people whose worldview, culture, social values, and aspirations differed radically from those of the modern reader." A good example already alluded to in this article occurs in the Ten Commandments where it is stated that God will visit the sins of the fathers unto the third and fourth generation of them that hate him. To put it mildly we find it difficult to think that we deserve punishment from God for what our great-grandfather may have done. This is because in our culture shame is not something that can be inherited, but in other cultures this appeared to be quite normal. In the Greek cycle of plays around the family of Atreus, shame followed the members of the family relentlessly all because of a grandfather who had made a god look foolish. Similarly in Josh 7, when Achan kept enemy property for himself rather than destroying it, it apparently made good sense that his whole family and even his livestock should all be executed.[2]

Sometimes the best intentions of modern translations detract from the intent of the Bible writers. One particular case is Heb 2:5–9, which in the asv (along with its British cousin the rv) is translated:

> For not unto angels did he subject the world to come, whereof we speak. But one hath somewhere testified, saying, What is man, that thou art mindful of him? Or the son of man, that thou visitest him? Thou madest him a little lower than the angels; Thou crownedst him with glory and honor, And didst set him over the works of thy hands: Thou didst put all things in subjection under his feet. For in that he subjected all things unto him, he left nothing that is not subject to him. But now we see not yet all things subjected to him. But we behold him who hath been made a little lower than the angels, [even] Jesus, because of the suffering of death crowned with glory and honor, that by the grace of God he should taste of death for every [man].

This is a clear allusion to Ps 8:4–5.

> What is man, that thou art mindful of him? And the son of man, that thou visitest him? For thou hast made him but little lower than God, And crownest him with glory and honor. Thou makest him to have dominion over the works of thy hands; Thou hast put all things under his feet.

---

2. This firm moral conviction of parts of the Old Testament did not go unchallenged; Ezekiel is adamant that the Israelites will not be punished for the sins of their parents. This illustrates the necessity of bearing chronology in mind when one looks at a culture.

But for modern tastes, for which *man* is a four-letter word not to be used to describe humanity—or hupersonity if one wants to be consistent—the expression "son of man" sounds too sexist, so instead of "son of man" the nrsv of Ps 8 has:

> What are human beings that you are mindful of them, mortals that you care for them? Yet you have made them a little lower than God . . .

Following on from this, nrsv in Heb 2 replaces the mention of the son of man in the passage above, which completely obscures what the author of Hebrews was trying to say; the reference to Jesus as "Son of Man" (a designation not without its own problems) disappears in the text in Hebrews. In other words, a *politically correct* translation has failed to recognize a link between biblical texts which a more literal translation would have shown.

The situation is that given the choice of translating an expression so that it can be understood by the modern reader, or of rendering it literally, knowing full well the said modern reader will not understand it, one is faced with an insoluble dilemma only comparable to that of a man who sees his mother-in-law backing over a cliff in his new Porsche. It is possible that the best approach might be that of the rv or its cousin the asv; namely, you translate as accurately as possible from a philological standpoint and then leave commentators to explain why the meaning cannot be translated transparently into English. Or, you go the route suggested by Rohrbaugh in his essay "Foreignizing Translation" to provide a translation that stages a deliberately alien reading experience of the biblical text for the modern reader. Human experiences in the modern world differ so radically from the experiences of humans in the ancient world that the biblical text cannot be translated into an idiom that makes sense to the modern reader.

Essentially what is in play here is the distinction between the limits of translation and the function of commentary. Keeping these two different activities clearly distinguished might help to preserve a scholar's integrity. For example, if one is to take the suggestion that given the cultural background of the status of the rich, one should render "rich" as "greedy rich," then it follows that one should translate Matt 27:57 as "Joseph, a greedy rich man from Aramathea . . ."

On the other hand, perhaps one should wait until a philologically honed down translation is made, then the commentary can begin with a discussion of various possibilities that can be raised.

It is also possible that there are some things we shall never understand. Perhaps Paul's personality as reflected in his writing (or dictating) style may have made some of his comments unintelligible. I remember the excitement that broke out over the writings of Marshall McLuhan. I puzzled over his writings with little success as I tried to find out the general pattern of what he was saying until I had the pleasure of actually hearing him speak. I then realized that there was no point in looking for general patterns; his method was simply to produce an almost bewildering torrent of observations, all of which were brilliant and almost none of which were consistent. I suspect that Paul in a similar way reduced his amanuensis to despair, for footnotes had not yet been invented, and this lack in first-century book publication probably frustrated Paul as much as it has frustrated his readers ever since.

I leave the contributions of the various authors in this collection to the more or less tender mercies of their contemporaries. I think that some of the suggestions may help to clarify the biblical writings and that other suggestions may prove to be less convincing, but it is not my role to distinguish the sheep from the goats. All I can conclude is that it is not possible to render the Bible into modern English in a way that we as products of our culture can understand without the sort of explanation that should accompany any honest translation that is willing to admit its inadequacies.

Select Bibliography

Achtemeier, Paul. 1985. *Romans*. Atlanta: John Knox Press.

———. 1996. The Continuing Quest for Coherence in St. Paul: An Experiment in Thought. Pages 132–45 in *Theology and Ethics in Paul and His Interpreters: Essays in Honor of Victor Paul Furnish*. Edited by Eugene H. Lovering Jr. and Jerry L. Sumney. Nashville: Abingdon.

Adkins, Arthur W. H. 1960. *Merit and Responsibility: A Study in Greek Values*. Oxford: Oxford University Press.

Andersen, Francis I., and David Noel Freedman. 1980. *Hosea: A New Translation with Introduction and Commentary*. AB 24. Garden City, NY: Doubleday.

Aune, David E. 1980. Magic in Early Christianity. *ANRW* 23.2:1507–57. Part 2, *Principat*, 23.2. Edited by H. Temporini and W. Haase. New York: de Gruyter.

Balch, David L. 2004. Philodemus, "On Wealth" and "On Household Management": Naturally Wealthy Epicureans against Poor Cynics. Pages 177–96 in *Philodemus and the New Testament World*. Edited by John T. Fitzgerald, Dirk Obbink, and Glenn S. Holland. NovTSup 111. Leiden: Brill.

Bammel, Ernst. 1997. Rechtsfindung in Korinth. *ETL* 73:107–13.

Barna, Laray M. 1998. Stumbling Blocks in Intercultural Communication. Pages 337–46 in *Intercultural Communication: A Reader*. Edited by Richard E. Porter and Larry A. Samovar. Belmont, WA: Wadsworth.

Barr, James. 1961. *The Semantics of Biblical Language*. Oxford: Oxford University Press.

Barrett, C. K. 1968. *A Commentary on the First Epistle to the Corinthians*. HNTC. New York: Harper & Row.

Bassler, Jouette M. 1993. Paul's Theology: Whence and Whither? Pages 3–17 in *1 & 2 Corinthians*. Vol. 2 of *Pauline Theology*. Edited by David M. Hay. Minneapolis: Fortress.

Bassnet, S. 1988. *Translation Studies*. London: Routledge.

Bassnet, S., and Harish Trivedi, eds. 1999. *Post-colonial Translation: Theory and Practice*. London: Routledge.

Bassnett-McGuire, Susan. 1980. *Translation Studies*. London: Methuen.

Batten, Alicia. 2000. Unworldly Friendship: The "Epistle of Straw" Reconsidered. Ph.D. diss., University of St. Michael's College, Toronto.

———. 2004. God in the Letter of James: Patron or Benefactor? *NTS* 50:257–72.

———. 2007. Ideological Strategies in James. Pages 6–26 in *Reading James with New Eyes: Methodological Reassessments of the Letter of James*. Edited by Robert L. Webb and John S. Kloppenborg. LNTS 342. London: T & T Clark.

Bauckham, Richard J. 1999. *James: Wisdom of James, Disciple of Jesus the Sage*. New Testament Readings. London: Routledge.

Bauer, W. 1979. *A Greek-English Lexicon of the New Testament and Other Early Chris-*

tian Literature. Translated and revised by W. F. Arndt, F. W. Gingrich, and F. W. Danker. 2d ed. Chicago: University of Chicago Press.

Baumgarten, Joseph. 1996. The "Halakha" in Miqsat Ma'ase ha-Torah MMT. *JAOS* 116:512–16.

————. 2003. Theological Elements in the Formulation of Qumran Law. Pages 33–41 in *Emanuel: Studies in Hebrew Bible, Septuagint, and Dead Sea Scrolls in Honor of Emanuel Tov*. Edited by Paul Shalom et al. SVTP 94. Leiden: Brill.

Baumgarten, Joseph, Esther Chazon, and Avital Pinnick, eds. 2000. *The Damascus Document, a Centennial of Discovery: Proceedings of the Third International Symposium of the Orion Center for the Study of the Dead Sea Scrolls and Associated Literature, 4–8 February 1998*. STDJ 34. Leiden: Brill.

Bechtel, Lyn M. 1994. What if Dinah Is Not Raped? (Genesis 34). *JSOT* 62:19–36.

Becker, A. L. 1995. *Beyond Translation. Essays Toward a Modern Philology*. Ann Arbor: University of Michigan Press.

Beker, J. Christiaan. 1980. *Paul the Apostle: The Triumph of God in Life and Thought*. Philadelphia: Fortress.

Berenbaum, Michael, and Fred Skolnik, eds. 2007. *Encyclopaedia Judaica*. 2nd ed. Vol. 18. Detroit: Macmillan Reference.

Berg, Ria. 2002. Wearing Wealth: Mundus Muliebris and Ornatus as Status Markers for Women in Imperial Rome. Pages 15–74 in *Women, Wealth, and Power in the Roman Empire*. Edited by Päivi Setälä, Ria Berg, and Rikka Hälikkä. Acta Instituti Romani Finlandiae 25. Rome: Säätiö Institutum Romanum Finlandiae.

Bernard, Jacques. 2001. Pour lire 4QMMT: Quelques-unes des mises en pratique de la Torah. Pages 79–100 in *Le judaïsme à l'aube de l'ere Chrétienne: XVIIIe congrès de l'ACFEB, Lyon, septembre 1999*. Edited by Philippe Abadie and Jean-Pierre. Lémonon. Paris: Cerf.

Bernstein, Moshe. 1994. Introductory Formulas for Citation and Re-citation of Biblical Verses in the Qumran Pesharim: Observations on a Pesher Technique. *DSD* 1:30–70.

————. 1996. Employment and Interpretation of Scripture in 4QMMT: Preliminary Observations. Pages 39–50 in *Reading 4QMMT: New Perspectives on Qumran Law and History*. Edited by John Kampen and Moshe Bernstein. SBLSymS 2. Atlanta: Scholars Press.

Bernstein, Moshe, Florentino García Martínez, and John Kampen, eds. 1997. *Legal Texts and Legal Issues: Proceedings of the Second Meeting of the International Organization for Qumran Studies, Published in Honour of Joseph M. Baumgarten*. STDJ 23. Leiden: Brill.

Bertholet, Katell. 2006. 4QMMT et la question du canon de la Hébraïque Bible. Pages 1–14 in *From 4QMMT to Resurrection: Mélanges qumraniens en homage à Émile Puech*. Edited by Florentino García Martínez, Annette Steudel, and Eibert J. C. Tigchelaar. STDJ 61. Leiden: Brill.

Betz, Hans Dieter. 1979. *Galatians: A Commentary on Paul's Letter to the Churches in Galatia*. Philadelphia: Fortress.

————, ed. 1986. *The Greek Magical Papyri in Translation, Including the Demotic Spells*. Chicago: University of Chicago Press.

Bibby, Reginald. 1987. *Fragmented Gods: The Poverty and Potential of Religion in Canada*. Toronto: Irwin.

Bigelow, Gordon. 2003. *Fiction, Famine, and the Rise of Economics in Victorian Britain and Ireland*. Cambridge Studies in Nineteenth Century Literature and Culture. Cambridge: Cambridge University Press.

————. 2005. Let There Be Markets: The Evangelical Roots of Economics. *Harper's Magazine* 310:33–38.

Black, Matthew. 1973. *Romans*. London: Oliphants.

Blenkinsopp, Joseph. 2002. *Isaiah 40–55: A New Translation with Introduction and Commentary*. AB 19A. Garden City, NY: Doubleday.

Bohren, Rudolf. 1952. *Das Problem der Kirchenzucht im Neuen Testament*. Zurich: Evangelischer Verlag.

Boling, Robert G. 1975. *Judges: Introduction, Translation, and Commentary*. AB 6A. Garden City, NY: Doubleday.

Booth, William James. 1994. Household and Market: On the Origins of Moral Economic Philosophy. *Review of Politics* 56:207–35.

Borgen, Peder, Kåre Fuglseth, and Roald Skarsten. 2000. *The Philo Index: A Complete Greek Word Index to the Writings of Philo of Alexandria*. Grand Rapids: Eerdmans.

Botterweck, G. J., and H. Ringgren, eds. 1970–. *Theologisches Wörterbuch zum Alten Testament*. Stuttgart: W. Kohlhammer.

Boyer, Paul. 1992. *When Time Shall Be No More: Prophecy and Belief in Modern American Culture*. Cambridge, MA: Belknap.

Boyle, Marjorie O'Rourke. 2001. The Law of the Heart: The Death of a Fool (1 Samuel 25). *JBL* 120:401–27.

————. 2005. Broken Hearts: The Violation of Biblical Law. *JAAR* 73:731–57.

Braund, D. C. 1984. *Rome and the Friendly King: The Character of the Client Kingship*. London: Croom Helm.

Brayford, Susan A. 1999. To Shame or Not to Shame: Sexuality in the Mediterranean Diaspora. *Semeia* 87:163–76.

Brenner, Athalya. 1993. On "Jeremiah" and the Poetics of (Prophetic?) Pornography. Pages 177–93 in *On Gendering Texts: Female and Male Voices in the Hebrew Bible*. Edited by Athalya Brenner and Fokkelien van Dijk-Hemmes. Leiden: Brill.

————. 1996. Pornoprophetics Revisited: Some Additional Reflections. *JSOT* 70:63–86.

Brooke, George. 1997. The Explicit Presentation of Scripture in 4QMMT. Pages 67–88 in *Legal Texts and Legal Issues: Proceedings of the Second Meeting of the International Organization for Qumran Studies, Published in Honour of Joseph M. Baumgarten*. Edited by Moshe Bernstein, Florentino García Martínez, and John Kampen. STDJ 23. Leiden: Brill.

Brower, R., ed. 1959. *On Translation*. Cambridge: Harvard University Press.

Brown, F., S. Driver, and C. A. Briggs. 1907. *A Hebrew and English Lexicon of the Old Testament*. Oxford: Clarendon.

Brun, Lyder. 1932. *Segen und Fluch im Urchristentum*. Norske Videnskaps-akademi i Oslo, historisk-filosofisk klasse, Skrifter 1932, 1st vol. (1933), no. 1. Oslo: Jacob Dybwad.

Buffon, Georges, Louis Leclerc, and M. A. Richard. 1935. *Oeuvres Completes De Buffon.* Paris: Pourrat Freres.

Byrne, Brendan. 1996. *Romans.* Collegeville, MN: Liturgical Press.

Cambier, J. 1968–69. La chair et l'esprit en I Cor. v.5. *NTS* 15:221–32.

Campbell, Barth. 1993. Flesh and Spirit in 1 Cor 5:5: An Exercise in Rhetorical Criticism of the NT. *JETS* 36:331–42.

Carroll, Robert P. 1985. Desire under the Terebinths: On Pornographic Representations in the Prophets—A Response. Pages 86–95 in *Feminist Interpretation of the Bible.* Edited by Letty T. Russell. Philadelphia: Westminster.

Cartlidge, Neil. 2001. *The Owl and the Nightingale: Text and Translation.* Exeter, England: Exeter University Press.

Cheyfitz, Eric. 1991. *The Poetics of Imperialism: Translation and Colonization from the Tempest to Tarzan.* New York: Oxford University Press.

Childs, Brevard S. 2001. *Isaiah.* OTL. Louisville: Westminster John Knox.

Collins, Adela Yarbro. 1980. The Function of "Excommunication" in Paul. *HTR* 73:251–63.

Collins, John J., and Robert A. Kugler, eds. 2000. *Religion in the Dead Sea Scrolls.* Grand Rapids: Eerdmans.

Collins, R. F. 1999. *First Corinthians.* Sacra Pagina 7. Collegeville, MN: Liturgical Press.

Conzelmann, Hans. 1975. *1 Corinthians: A Commentary on the First Epistle to the Corinthians.* Hermeneia. Philadelphia: Fortress.

Cousar, Charles B. 1993. The Theological Task of 1 Corinthians: A Conversation with Gordon D. Fee and Victor Paul Furnish. Pages 90–102 in *1 & 2 Corinthians.* Vol. 2 of *Pauline Theology.* Edited by David M. Hay. Minneapolis: Fortress.

Cox, Claude. 1983. Theory and Practice in Bible Translation. *EvQ* 3:159–67.

Cranfield, C. E. B. 1979. *A Critical and Exegetical Commentary on the Epistle to the Romans.* Vol. 2. Edinburgh: T & T Clark.

Crook, Zeba A. 2001–5. The Divine Benefactions of Paul the Client. *Journal of Greco-Roman Christianity and Judaism* 2:9–26.

———. 2004. *Reconceptualising Conversion: Patronage, Loyalty, and Conversion in the Religions of the Ancient Mediterranean.* Berlin: de Gruyter.

———. 2005a. Reciprocity: Covenantal Exchange as a Test Case. Pages 78–91 in *Ancient Israel: The Old Testament in Its Social Context.* Edited by Philip F. Esler. Minneapolis: Fortress.

———. 2005b. Reflections on Culture and Social-Scientific Models. *JBL* 124:515–20.

Dalton, George. 1965. Primitive, Archaic, and Modern Economies: Karl Polanyi's Contribution to Economic Anthropology and Comparative Economy. Pages 1–24 in *Essays in Economic Anthropology: Dedicated to the Memory of Karl Polanyi. Proceedings of the 1965 Annual Spring Meeting of the American Ethnological Society.* Edited by June Helm. Co-edited by Paul Bohannan and Marshall D. Sahlins. Seattle: University of Washington Press.

Danker, Frederick W., Walter Bauer, and William Arndt, eds. 2000. *A Greek-English*

Lexicon of the New Testament and Other Early Christina Literature. 3d ed. Chicago: University of Chicago Press.

Deissmann, Adolf. 1927. *Light from the Ancient East: The New Testament Illustrated by Recently Discovered Texts of the Graeco-Roman World.* Rev. ed. London: Hodder and Stoughton.

Deist, Ferdinand E. 2000. *The Material Culture of the Bible.* Sheffield: Sheffield Academic Press.

de la Mora, Gonzalo Fernández. 1987. *Egalitarian Envy: The Political Foundations of Social Justice.* Translated from *La envidia igualitaria* (Barcelona: Planeta, 1984) by Antonio T. de Nicholàs. New York: Paragon House

DeSilva, David A. 2000. *Honor, Patronage, Kinship, and Purity: Unlocking New Testament Culture.* Downers Grove, IL: InterVarsity.

de Ste. Croix, G. E. M. 1983. *The Class Struggle in the Ancient Greek World.* Corrected version. London: Duckworth.

de Vos, Craig S. 1998. Stepmothers, Concubines, and the Case of ΠΟΡΝΕΙΑ in 1 Corinthians 5. *NTS* 44:104–14.

De Witt Burton, E. 1921. *A Critical and Exegetical Commentary on the Epistle to the Galatians.* Edinburgh: T & T Clark.

Dibelius, Martin. 1966. *Die Formgeschichte des Evangeliums.* 5th ed. Edited by Günther Bornkamm. Tübingen: Mohr Siebeck.

Di Bella, Maria Pia. 1992. Name, Blood, and Miracles: The Claims to Renown in Traditional Sicily. Pages 153–65 in *Honor and Grace in Anthropology.* Edited by J. G. Peristiany and Julian Pitt-Rivers. Cambridge: Cambridge University Press.

Dickie, Matthew W. 1987. Lo phthonos degli dèi nella letteratura Greca del quinto secolo avanti Cristo. *Atene e Roma* n.r. 32:113–25.

Dingwaney, Anuradha, and Carol Maier, eds. 1995. *Between Languages and Cultures: Translation and Cross-Cultural Texts.* Pittsburgh: University of Pittsburgh Press.

Dittenberger, W., ed. 1903–5. *Orientis graeci inscriptiones selectae.* 2 vols. Leipzig.

Donfried, K. P. 1976. Justification and Last Judgment in Paul. *Int* 30:140–52.

Doskocil, Walter. 1958. *Der Bahn in der Urkirche: Eine Rechtsgeschichtliche Untersuchung.* Münchener Theologische Studien 3.11. Munich: Karl Zink.

Doughty, D. J. 1973. The Priority of ΧΑΡΙΣ: An Investigation of the Theological Language of Paul. *NTS* 19:163–80.

Douglas, Mary. 1966. *Purity and Danger: An Analysis of the Concepts of Pollution and Taboo.* London: Routledge & Kegan Paul.

———. 1970. *Natural Symbols: Explorations in Cosmology.* New York: Random House.

Dover, K. J. 1974. *Greek Popular Morality in the Time of Plato and Aristotle.* Berkeley: University of California Press.

Edelstein, Emma J., and L. Edelstein. 1975. *Asclepius: A Collection and Interpretation of the Testimonies.* 2 vols. New York: Arno Press.

Eichhorn, J. G. 1790. *Urgeschichte.* Edited by J. P. Gabler. 3 vols. Altdorf, Switzerland: Monat und Kussler.

Eisenstadt, S. N., and R. Roniger. 1984. *Patrons, Clients, and Friends: Interpersonal*

Relations and the Structure of Trust in Society. Cambridge: Cambridge University Press.

Elliott, John H. 1988. The Fear of the Leer: The Evil Eye from the Bible to Li'l Abner. *Forum* 4, no. 4: 42–71.

———. 1990. Paul, Galatians, and the Evil Eye. *CurTM* 17:262–73.

———. 1991. The Evil Eye in the First Testament: The Ecology and Culture of a Pervasive Belief. Pages 147–59 in *The Bible and the Politics of Exegesis: Essays in Honor of Norman K. Gottwald on His Sixty-fifth Birthday.* Edited by David Jobling et al. Cleveland: Pilgrim.

———. 1992. Matthew 20:1–15: A Parable of Invidious Comparison and Evil Eye Accusation. *BTB* 22, no. 2: 52–65.

———. 1994. The Evil Eye and the Sermon on the Mount. Contours of a Pervasive Belief in Social Scientific Perspective. *BibInt* 2, no. 1: 51–84.

———. 1996. Patronage and Clientage. Pages 142–56 in *The Social Sciences and New Testament Interpretation.* Edited by Richard L. Rohrbaugh. Peabody, MA: Hendrickson.

———. 2005a. Lecture socioscientifique: Illustration par l'accusation du Mauvais Oeil en Galatie. Pages 141–67 in *Guide des nouvelles lectures de la Bible.* Edited by André Lacocque. Translated by Jean-Pierre Prévost. Paris: Bayard.

———. 2005b. Jesus, Mark, and the Evil Eye. *LTJ* (Victor Pfitzner FS) 39, no. 2–3: 157–68.

———. 2007a. Envy and the Evil Eye: More on Mark 7:22 and Mark's "Anatomy of Envy." Pages 87–105 in *In Other Words: Essays in Honor of Jerome H. Neyrey, S.J.* Edited by Zeba Crook and Anselm Hagedorn. Sheffield: Sheffield University Press.

———. 2007b. Envy, Jealousy, and Zeal in the Bible: Sorting Out the Social Differences and Theological Implications—No Envy for YHWH. Pages 344–63 in *To Break Every Yoke: Essays in Honor of Marvin L. Chaney.* Edited by Robert Coote and Norman K. Gottwald. Sheffield: Sheffield Phoenix.

Engler, Steven, et al. 2007. Consider Translation: A Roundtable Discussion. *RSR* 33, no. 4: 299–316.

Eshel, E. 1995. 4QLev^d: A Possible Source for the Temple Scroll and *Miqsat ma'ase Ha-Torah. DSD* 2:1–13.

Esler, Philip. 1994. *The First Christians in Their Social Worlds: Social-Scientific Approaches to New Testament Interpretation.* London: Routledge.

———, ed. 2005. *Ancient Israel: The Old Testament in Its Social Context.* Minneapolis: Fortress.

———, ed. 2006. *Ancient Israel: The Old Testament in Its Social Context.* Minneapolis: Fortress.

Estévez Lopez, Elisa. 2003. *El Poder de una Mujer Creyente: Cuerpo, identidad y discipulado en Mc 5,24b–34. Un estudio desde las ciencias sociales.* Estella, Spain: Verbo Divino.

Fabry, Heinz-Josef. 1974. "*lēb.*" *TDOT* 7:399–437.

Fee, Gordon D. 1987. *The First Epistle to the Corinthians.* Grand Rapids: Eerdmans.

Fewell, Danna Nolan, and David M. Gunn. 1991. Tipping the Balance: Sternberg's Reader and the Rape of Dinah. *JBL* 110:193–211.

Finley, Moses. 1985. *The Ancient Economy*. 2nd ed. London: Hogarth Press.

Fischer, Georg. 1984. Die Redewendung דבר על־לב im AT—Ein Beitrag um Verständnis von Jes 40, 2." *Bib* 65:244–50.

Fitzmyer, Joseph A. 1960. The Use of Explicit Old Testament Quotations in Qumran Literature and in the New Testament. *NTS* 7:297–333.

―――. 1993. *Romans: A New Translation with Introduction and Commentary*. AB 33. New York: Doubleday.

Flint, Peter, Emanuel Tov, and James C. VanderKam, eds. 2006. *Studies in the Hebrew Bible, Qumran, and the Septuagint: Presented to Eugene Ulrich*. SVTP 101. Leiden: Brill.

Fogel, Joshua A. 1993. Recent Translation Theory and Linguistic Borrowing in the Modern Sino-Chinese Cultural Context. *Indiana East Asian Working Papers Series on Language and Politics in Modern China*. 1–6.

Forkman, Göran. 1972. *The Limits of the Religious Community: Expulsion from the Religious Community within the Qumran Sect, within Rabbinic Judaism, and within Primitive Christianity*. ConBNT 5. Lund, Sweden: Gleerup.

Foster, George M. 1965. Peasant Society and the Image of Limited Good. *AA* 67:293–315.

―――. 1972a. The Anatomy of Envy: A Study in Symbolic Behavior. *CA* 13:165–202.

―――. 1972b. A Second Look at Limited Good. *AQ* 45:57–64.

Fraade, Steven D. 1998. Looking for Legal Midrash at Qumran. Pages 59–79 in *Biblical Perspectives: Early Use and Interpretation of the Bible in Light of the Dead Sea Scrolls. Proceedings of the First International Symposium of the Orion Center for the Study of the Dead Sea Scrolls and Associated Literature, 12–14 May 1996*. Edited by Michael Stone and Esther Chazon. STDJ 28. Leiden: Brill.

―――. 2000. To Whom It May Concern: 4QMMT and Its Addressees. *RevQ* 19:507–26.

―――. 2003. Rhetoric and Hermeneutics in Miqsat Ma'ase ha-Torah (4QMMT): The Case of the Blessings and Curses. *DSD* 10:150–61.

Frazer, Sir James George. 1918. *Folk-Lore in the Old Testament: Studies in Comparative Religion, Legend, and Law*. London: Macmillan.

Friedrich, Paul. 1977. "Sanity and the Myth of Honor: The Problem of Achilles." *Ethos* 5, no. 3: 281–305.

Friesen, Steven J. 2004. Poverty in Pauline Studies: Beyond the So-Called New Consensus. *JSNT* 26:323–61.

―――. 2005. Injustice or God's Will: Explanations of Poverty in Proto-Christian Communities. Pages 240–60 in *A People's History of Christianity*. Vol. 1: *Christian Origins*. Edited by Richard A. Horsley. Minneapolis: Fortress.

Funk, Robert W., and Roy W. Hoover. 1993. *The Five Gospels: The Search for the Authentic Words of Jesus*. New York: Macmillan.

Furnish, Victor Paul. 1984. *II Corinthians*. AB 32A. Garden City, NY: Doubleday.

Garnsey, Peter. 1988. *Famine and Food Supply in the Graeco-Roman World: Responses to Risk and Crisis.* Cambridge: Cambridge University Press.

Gentzler, Edwin. 1993. *Contemporary Translation Theories.* London: Routledge.

Getty, Mary Ann. 1983. *First Corinthians, Second Corinthians.* Collegeville, MN: Liturgical Press.

Gill, Christopher. 2003. Is Rivalry a Virtue or a Vice? Pages 29–51 in *Envy, Spite, and Jealousy: The Rivalrous Emotions in Ancient Greece.* Edited by David Konstan and N. Keith Rutter. Edinburgh Leventis Studies 2. Edinburgh: Edinburgh University Press.

Gilmore, David D., ed. 1987. *Honor and Shame and the Unity of the Mediterranean.* Special Publication 22. Washington, DC: American Anthropological Association.

Ginsberg, Harold Louis. 1972. Heart. *EncJud* 8:508–10.

Good, E. M. 1962. Jealousy. *IDB* 2:806–7.

Goodwin, Daniel R. 1881. On the Use of לב and Καρδία in the Old and New Testaments. *Journal of the Society of Biblical Literature and Exegesis* 1:67–72.

Gore, Charles. 1889. "The Holy Spirit and Inspiration." In *Lux Mundi.* Edited by Charles Gore. New York: United States Book Company.

Gottwald, Norman K., and Robert Coote, eds. 2007. *To Break Every Yoke: Essays in Honor of Marvin L. Chaney.* Sheffield: Sheffield Phoenix.

Gould, Ezra P. 1975. *The Gospel according to St. Mark.* ICC. Edinburgh: T & T Clark.

Grabbe, Lester. 1996. 4QMMT and Second Temple Jewish Society. Pages 89–108 in *Reading 4QMMT: New Perspectives on Qumran Law and History.* Edited by John Kampen and Moshe Bernstein. SBLSymS 2. Atlanta: Scholars Press.

Grossman, Maxine. 2001. Reading *4QMMT*: Genre and History. *RevQ* 20:3–22.

Grundmann, Walter. 1972. ταπεινός ταπεινόω, ταπείνωσις ταπεινόφρων, ταπεινοφροσύνη *TDNT* 8:1–26.

Guelich, Robert A. *Mark 1–8:26.* Word Biblical Commentary 34a. Dallas: Word.

Guenthner, F., and M. Guenthner-Reutter, eds. 1978. *Meaning and Translation: Philosophical and Linguistic Approaches.* London: Duckworth.

Guillaume, Alfred. 1938. *Prophecy and Divination among the Hebrews and other Semites.* London: Hodder and Stoughton.

Gurknecht, Christoph, and Lutz J. Rolle. 1996. *Translating by Factors.* New York: State University of New York Press.

Hagedorn, Anselm C., and Jerome H. Neyrey. 1998. "It Was Out of Envy That They Handed Jesus Over" (Mark 15.10): The Anatomy of Envy and the Gospel of Mark. *JSNT* 69:15–56.

Halliday, M. A. K. 1976. Anti-languages. *AA* 78:570–84.

Hanson, K. C., and Douglas Oakman. 1998. *Palestine in the Time of Jesus.* Minneapolis: Fortress.

Harrelson, Walter. 2002. What Translation Is. *Religious Studies News/SBL Edition* 3/7: 5–6.

Harrington, Hannah. 1997. Holiness in the Laws of 4QMMT. Pages 109–28 in *Legal Texts and Legal Issues: Proceedings of the Second Meeting of the International Organization for Qumran Studies, Published in Honour of Joseph M. Baumgarten.*

Edited by Moshe Bernstein, Florentino García Martínez, and John Kampen. STDJ 23. Leiden: Brill.

Harrison, James R. 2003. *Paul's Language of Grace in Its Graeco-Roman Context.* Tübingen: Mohr Siebeck.

Hartin, Patrick J. 1991. *James and the "Q" Sayings of Jesus.* JSNTSup 47. Sheffield: Sheffield Academic Press.

———. 2003. *James.* Sacra Pagina 14. Collegeville, MN: Liturgical Press.

Harvey, William. 1628. *Exercitatio anatomica de motu cordis et sanquinis in animalibus.* Frankfurt: William Fitzer.

Hatim, B., and I. Mason. 1988. *Discourse and the Translator.* London: Longman.

Hays, Richard B. 1996. *The Moral Vision of the New Testament: Community, Cross, New Creation. A Contemporary Introduction to New Testament Ethics.* New York: HarperSanFrancisco.

———. 1997. *First Corinthians.* Louisville: John Knox Press.

Hemer, Colin J. 1986. Medicine in the New Testament World. Pages 43–83 in *Medicine and the Bible.* Edited by Bernard Palmer. Exeter, England: Paternoster.

Høgenhaven, Jesper. 2003. Rhetorical Devices in 4QMMT. *DSD* 10:187–204.

Hollenbach, Paul. 1987. Defining Rich and Poor Using Social Sciences. *SBLSP* 26:50–63.

Holman, Susan R. 2001. *The Hungry Are Dying: Beggars and Bishops in Roman Cappadocia.* Oxford Studies in Historical Theology. New York: Oxford.

Hooke, S. H. 1958. *Myth, Ritual, and Kingship: Essays on the Theory and Practice of Kingship in the Ancient Near East and in Israel.* Oxford: Clarendon.

Hoppe, Leslie J., OFM. 2004. *There Shall Be No Poor among You: Poverty in the Bible.* Nashville: Abingdon.

Horden, Peregrine, and Nicholas Purcell. 2000. *The Corrupting Sea: A Study of Mediterranean History.* Oxford: Blackwell.

Hort, F. J. A. 1909. *The Epistle of St. James: The Greek Text with Introduction, Commentary as Far as Chapter IV, Verse 7, and Additional Notes.* London: Macmillan.

Howard, J. Keir. 2001. *Disease and Healing in the New Testament: An Analysis and Interpretation.* Lanham, MD: University Press of America.

Hübner, Hans. 1987. Paulusforschung seit 1945: Ein kritischer Literaturbericht. *ANRW* 25.4:2649–3840. Part 2, *Principat,* 25.4. Edited by Wolfgang Haase. New York: de Gruyter.

Hughes, Philip E. 1962. *Paul's Second Letter to the Corinthians.* NICNT. Grand Rapids: Eerdmans.

Hui, C. Harry, and Harry C. Triandis. 1986. Individualism-Collectivism: A Study of Cross-Cultural Researchers. *Journal of Cross-Cultural Psychology* 17:225–48.

Humphreys, S. C. 1969. History, Economics, and Anthropology: The Work of Karl Polanyi. *History and Theory* 8:165–212.

Hutchinson Edgar, David. 2001. *Has God Not Chosen the Poor? The Social Setting of the Epistle of James.* JSNTSup 206. Sheffield: Sheffield Academic Press.

Inhorn, Marcia C. 1994. *Quest for Conception: Gender, Infertility, and Egyptian Medical Traditions.* Philadelphia: University of Pennsylvania Press.

————. 1996. *Infertility and Patriarchy: The Cultural Politics of Gender and Family Life in Egypt.* Philadelphia: University of Pennsylvania Press.

Inhorn, Marcia C., and Frank van Balen, eds. 2002. *Infertility around the Globe: New Thinking on Childlessness, Gender, and Reproductive Technologies.* Berkeley: University of California Press.

Irvine, Judith. 1989. When Talk Isn't Cheap: Language and Political Economy. *AE* 16:248–67.

Johnson, A. R. 1964. *The Vitality of the Individual in the Thought of Ancient Israel.* Cardiff: University of Wales.

Johnson, Luke Timothy. 1995. *The Letter of James.* AB 37A. New York: Doubleday.

————. 1998. *Religious Experience in Early Christianity: A Missing Dimension in New Testament Studies.* Minneapolis: Fortress.

————. 2004. James 3:13–4:10 and the *Topos peri phthonou.* Pages 182–201 in *Brother of Jesus, Friend of God: Studies in the Letter of James.* Grand Rapids: Eerdmans.

Jordan, Clarence. 2004. *Cotton Patch Gospel: Luke and Acts.* Macon: Smyth & Helwys.

Joy, N. George. 1988. Is the Body Really to Be Destroyed? (1 Corinthians 5:5). *BT* 39:429–36.

Kampen, John, and Moshe Bernstein, eds. 1996. *Reading 4QMMT: New Perspectives on Qumran Law and History.* SBLSymS 2. Atlanta: Scholars Press.

Käsemann, Ernst. 1969. Sentences of Holy Law in the New Testament. Pages 66–81 in *New Testament Questions of Today.* Philadelphia: Fortress.

————. 1980. *Commentary on Romans.* Translated by Geoffrey William Bromiley. Grand Rapids: Eerdmans.

Kelly L. G. 1979. *The True Interpreter: A History of Translation Theory and Practice in the West.* Oxford: Basil Blackwell.

Kennedy, George A. 1984. *New Testament Interpretation through Rhetorical Criticism.* Studies in Religion. Chapel Hill: University of North Carolina Press.

Kim, S. (1978). "The Grace That Was Given to Me . . .": Paul and the Grace of His Apostleship. Pages 50–59 in *Die Hoffnung festhalten.* Edited by Gerhard Maier. Neuhausen-Stuttgart, Germany: Hänssler-Verlag.

Kister, Menahem. 1999. Studies in 4QMiqsat Ma'ase Ha-Torah and Related Text. *Tarbiz* 68, no. 3: 317–71.

Kloppenborg, John S. 1999. Patronage Avoidance in James. *HTS* 55:755–94.

————. 2007. The Emulation of the Jesus Tradition in the Letter of James. Pages 121–50 in *Reading James with New Eyes: Methodological Reassessments of the Letter of James.* Edited by Robert L. Webb and John S. Kloppenborg. LNTS 342. London: T & T Clark.

Konstan, David. 2006. *The Emotions of the Ancient Greeks: Studies in Aristotle and Classical Literature.* Robson Classical Lectures. Toronto: University of Toronto Press.

Konstan, David, and N. Keith Rutter, eds. 2003. *Envy, Spite, and Jealousy: The Rivalrous Emotions in Ancient Greece.* Edinburgh Leventis Studies 2. Edinburgh: Edinburgh University Press.

Kugler, Robert A. 1997. Halakhic Interpretive Strategies at Qumran: A Case Study. Pages 131–40 in *Legal Texts and Legal Issues: Proceedings of the Second Meeting of the International Organization for Qumran Studies, Published in Honour of Joseph M. Baumgarten.* Edited by Moshe Bernstein, Florentino García Martínez, and John Kampen. STDJ 23. Leiden: Brill.

————. 2000. Rewriting Rubrics: Sacrifice and Religion at Qumran. Pages 90–112 in *Religion in the Dead Sea Scrolls.* Edited by John J. Collins and Robert A. Kugler. Grand Rapids: Eerdmans.

Lampe, G. W. H. 1967. Church Discipline and the Interpretation of the Epistles to the Corinthians. Pages 337–61 in *Christian History and Interpretation: Studies Presented to John Knox.* Edited by W. R. Farmer, C. F. D. Moule, and R. R. Niebuhr. Cambridge: Cambridge University Press.

Lane, William L. 1974. *The Gospel according to St. Mark.* Grand Rapids: Eerdmans.

Laws, Sophie. 1980. *The Epistle of James.* HNTC. San Francisco: Harper & Row.

Leclerc, Jean Louis (Comte de Buffon). 1749. *Histoire Naturelle, Générale et Particulière, avec La Description du Cabinet du Roi.* Vol. 2, 429. Paris: L'imprimerie Royale.

Leeb, Carolyn S. 2000. *Away from the Father's House: The Social Location of na'ar and na'arah in Ancient Israel.* JSOTSup 301. Sheffield: Sheffield Academic.

Lefevere, Andre. 1977. *Translating Literature: The German Tradition from Luther to Rosenzweig.* Assen, Netherlands: Van Gorcum.

Lewis, C. S. 1962. *The Problem of Pain: How Human Suffering Raises Almost Intolerable Intellectual Problems.* New York: Macmillan.

Lewis, John G. 2005. *Looking for Life: The Role of "Theo-Ethical Reasoning" in Paul's Religion.* JSNTSup 291. London: T & T Clark.

Liddell, Henry George, and Robert Scott, eds. 1996. *A Greek-English Lexicon.* New York: Oxford University Press.

Limberis, Vasiliki. 1991. The Eyes Infected by Envy: Basil of Caesarea's Homily, On Envy. *HTR* 84:163–84.

Lindsey, Hal. 1970. *Late Great Planet Earth.* HarperCollins Canada.

Lipinski, Edward. 2007. Sin. Pages 621–25 in *Encyclopaedia Judaica.* Edited by Michael Berenbaum and Fred Skolnik. Vol. 18. 3rd ed. Detroit: Macmillan Reference.

Loewen, J. A. 1970. The Social Context of Guilt and Forgiveness. *PA* 17, no. 2: 80–96. Oklahoma City: Society for Applied Anthropology.

Louw, Johannes P. 1988. The Function of Discourse in a Sociosemiotic Theory of Translation. *BT* 3:329–35.

Malina, Bruce J. 1978. Limited Good and the Social World of Early Christianity. *BTB* 8:162–76.

————. 1981. *The New Testament World: Insights from Cultural Anthropology.* Louisville: Westminster John Knox.

————. 1986. Wealth and Poverty in the New Testament and Its World. *Int* 41:354–67.

————. 1991. Reading Theory Perspective. Pages 3–23 in *The Social World of Luke-Acts.* Edited by Jerome H. Neyrey. Peabody, MA: Hendrickson.

————. 1993. *The New Testament World: Insights from Cultural Anthropology*. Louisville: Westminster John Knox.

————. 1996. Patron and Client: The Analogy behind Synoptic Theology. Pages 143–75 in *The Social World of Jesus*. London: Routledge.

————. 2001. *The New Testament World: Insights from Cultural Anthropology*. 3rd ed. Louisville: Westminster John Knox.

Malina, Bruce J., and Jerome H. Neyrey. 1996. *Portraits of Paul*. Louisville: Westminster John Knox.

————. 1998. *Calling Jesus Names: The Social Value of Labels in Matthew*. Sonoma, CA: Polebridge Press.

Malina, Bruce J., and Richard L. Rohrbaugh. 1992. *Social-Science Commentary on the Synoptic Gospels*. Minneapolis: Fortress.

————. 1998. *Social-Science Commentary on the Gospel of John*. Minneapolis: Fortress.

————, eds. 2003. *Social-Science Commentary on the Synoptic Gospels*. 2nd ed. Minneapolis: Fortress.

Manson, William. 1932. Grace in the New Testament. Pages 33–60 in *The Doctrine of Grace*. Edited by W. T. Whitley. London: SCM Press.

Martin, Dale. 1995. *The Corinthian Body*. New Haven: Yale University Press.

Martínez, Florentio García, Annette Steudel, and Eibert J. C. Tigchelaar, eds. 2006. *From 4QMMT to Resurrection: Mélanges qumraniens en homage à Émile Puech*. STDJ 61. Leiden: Brill.

Matera, Frank J. 1992. *Galatians*. Collegeville, MN: Liturgical Press.

Matthews, Victor H., and Don C. Benjamin, eds. 1994. Honor and Shame in the World of the Bible. *Semeia* 68.

Maynard-Reid, Pedrito U. 1987. *Poverty and Wealth in James*. Maryknoll, NY: Orbis.

Mayor, Joseph B. 1892. *The Epistle of St. James*. London: Macmillan.

Mays, James Luther. 1969. *Hosea: A Commentary*. OTL. Philadelphia: Westminster.

Mazid, Bahaa-Eddin. 2007. *Politics of Translation: Power, Culture, Ideology, and X-phemism in Translation between Arabic and English*. Lincom Studies in Translation 2. Munich: LINCOM.

McLuhan, Marshall. 1962. *The Gutenberg Galaxy: The Making of Typographic Man*. Toronto: University of Toronto Press.

Meeks, Wayne A., ed. 1972. *The Writings of St. Paul*. Norton Critical Editions in the History of Ideas. New York: Norton.

Meikle, Scott. 2002. Modernism, Economics, and the Ancient Economy. Pages 233–50 in *The Ancient Economy*. Edited by Walter Scheidel and Sitta Von Reden. New York: Routledge.

Meyer, Paul W. 1997. Pauline Theology: A Proposal for a Pause in Its Pursuit. Pages 140–60 in *Pauline Theology*. Vol. 4: *Looking Back, Pressing On*. Edited by E. Elizabeth Johnson and David M. Hay. SBLSymS 4. Atlanta: Scholars Press.

Milobenski, Ernst. 1964. *Der Neid in der Griechischen Philosophie*. Klassich-Philologische Studien 29. Wiesbaden, Germany: Otto Harrassowitz.

Mitchell, Margaret M. 1991. *Paul and the Rhetoric of Reconciliation: An Exegetical*

Investigation of the Language and Composition of 1 Corinthians. HUT 28. Tübingen: Mohr Siebeck.

Moerman, Daniel E. 1979. Anthropology of Symbolic Healing. *CA* 20:59–80.

———. 2002. *Meaning, Medicine, and the "Placebo Effect."* Cambridge: Cambridge University Press.

Moffatt, James. 1932. *Grace in the New Testament.* New York: Ray Long and R. R. Smith.

Molière, (Jean-Baptiste Poquelin). *Le Bougeois Gentilhomme.* Act 1, scene 5.

Most, W. G. 2002. Grace (in the Bible). Pages 380–83 in *New Catholic Encyclopedia.* Detroit: Gale.

Moulton, J. M., W. F. Howard, and N. Turner. 1906–76. *A Grammar of New Testament Greek.* 4 vols. Edinburgh: T & T Clark.

Murphy-O'Connor, Jerome. 1979. *1 Corinthians.* New Testament Message 10. Wilmington, DE: Glazier.

———. 1998. *1 Corinthians.* New York: Doubleday.

Neufeld, Dietmar. 2006. Barreness: Trance as Protest a Strategy. Pages 128–41 in *Ancient Israel: The Old Testament in Its Social Context.* Edited by Philip F. Esler Minneapolis: Fortress.

Neusner, Jacob, Ernest S. Frerichs, and Nahum M. Sarna, eds. 1989. *From Ancient Israel to Modern Judaism: Intellect in Quest of Understanding, Essays in Honor of Marvin Fox.* BJS 159. Atlanta: Scholars Press.

Neyrey, Jerome H. 1990. *Paul, in Other Words: A Cultural Reading of His Letters.* Louisville: Westminster John Knox.

———. 1998. *Honour and Shame in the Gospel of Matthew.* Louisville: Westminster John Knox.

———. 2005. God, Benefactor, and Patron: The Major Cultural Model for Interpreting the Deity in Greco-Roman Antiquity. *JSNT* 27, no. 4: 465–92.

———. 2007a. Jesus the Broker in the Fourth Gospel. *CBQ* 69, no. 2: 271–91.

———. 2007b. Lost in Translation: The Leper Did Not "Give Thanks" to God. Paper presented at the annual meeting of the Context Group, Philadelphia, March 17.

———, ed. 1991. *The Social World of Luke-Acts: Models for Interpretation.* Peabody, MA: Hendrickson.

Neyrey, Jerome H., and Richard L. Rohrbaugh. 2001. "He Must Increase, I Must Decrease" (John 3:30): A Cultural and Social Interpretation. *CBQ* 63, no. 3: 464–83.

Nichols, Anthony. 1988. Explicitness in Translation and the Westernization of Scripture. *RTR* 3:78–88.

Nida, Eugene A. 1964. *Toward a Science of Translating.* Leiden: Brill.

———. 1975. *Language Structure and Translation.* Stanford, CA: Stanford University Press.

———. 1979a. Translating Means Communicating: A Sociolinguistic Theory of Translation I. *BT* 3:101–7.

———. 1979b. Translating Means Communicating: A Sociolinguistic Theory of Translation II. *BT* 3:318–25.

————. 1992. *Lexical Semantics of the Greek New Testament: A Supplement to the Greek-English Lexicon of the New Testament Based on Semantic Domains*. Atlanta: Scholars Press.

————. 1994. *Towards a Science of Translating*. Leiden: Brill.

————. 1995. *The Sociolinguistics of Interlingual Communication*. Brussels: Editions du Hazard.

Nida, Eugene A., and Johannes P. Louw, eds. 1992. *The Lexical Semantics of the Greek New Testament: A Supplement to the Greek-English Lexicon of the New Testament Based on Semantic Domains*. Atlanta: Scholars Press.

Nida, Eugene A., and Charles R. Taber. 1969. *The Theory and Practice of Translation*. Leiden: Brill.

Nida, Eugene A., and Jan de Waard. 1986. *From One Language to Another: Functional Equivalence in Bible Translation*. Nashville: Nelson.

Nord, C. 2002. Bridging the Cultural Gap: Bible Translation as a Case in Point. *AcT* 98–116.

Northwest Environment Watch. 2002. *This Place on Earth 2002: Measuring What Matters*. Seattle: Northwest Environment Watch.

Oakes, Peter. 2004. Constructing Poverty Scales for Graeco-Roman Society: A Response to Steven Friesen's "Poverty in Pauline Studies." *JSNT* 26:367–71.

Oakman, Douglas E. 1991a. The Ancient Economy in the Bible. *BTB* 21:34–39.

————. 1991b. The Countryside in Luke-Acts. Pages 151–70 in *The Social World of Luke-Acts: Models for Interpretation*. Edited by Jerome H. Neyrey, S.J. Peabody, MA: Hendrickson.

————. 2002. Money in the Moral Universe of the New Testament. Pages 335–48 in *The Social Setting of Jesus and the Gospels*. Edited by Wolfgang Stegemann, Bruce J. Malina, and Gerd Theissen. Minneapolis: Fortress.

O'Meara, Thomas F. 1987. Grace. Pages 84–88 in *The Encyclopedia of Religion*. Edited by M. Eliade. New York: Collier Macmillan.

Opperwall, N. J., and R. J. Wyatt. 1982. Jealous. *ISBE* 2:971–73.

Orr, William Fridell, and James Arthur Walther. 1976. *I Corinthians: A New Translation*. AB 32. Garden City, NY: Doubleday.

Osiek, Carolyn, and David L. Balch. 1997. *Families in the New Testament World: Households and House Churches*. Louisville: Westminster John Knox.

Pagan, Samuel. 1996. Poor and Poverty: Social Distance and Bible Translation. *Semeia*: 69–79.

Parker, Robert. 1983. *Miasma: Pollution and Purification in Early Greek Religion*. Oxford: Clarendon Press.

Parrott, W. Gerrod, and Richard H. Smith. 1993. Distinguishing the Experiences of Envy and Jealousy. *JPSP* 64:906–20.

Parry, D. 1997. Notes on Divine Name Avoidance in Scriptural Units of the Legal Texts of Qumran. Pages 437–49 in *Legal Texts and Legal Issues: Proceedings of the Second Meeting of the International Organization for Qumran Studies, Published in Honour of Joseph M. Baumgarten*. Edited by Moshe Bernstein, Florentino García Martínez, and John Kampen. STDJ 23. Leiden: Brill.

Parsons, Michael. 2002. Luther and Calvin on Rape: Is the Crime Lost in the Agenda? *EvQ* 74, no. 2: 123–42.

Pascuzzi, Maria. 1997. *Ethics, Ecclesiology, and Church Discipline: A Rhetorical Analysis of 1 Corinthians 5.* Tesi Gregoriana, Serie Teologia 32. Rome: Editrice Pontificia Università Gregoriana.

Penner, Todd C. 1996. *The Epistle of James and Eschatology: Re-reading an Ancient Letter.* JSNTSup 121. Sheffield: Sheffield Academic Press.

Peristiany, J. G., ed. 1966. *Honour and Shame: The Values of Mediterranean Society.* Chicago: University of Chicago Press.

Piepkorn, A. C. 1965. Grace. Pages 947–58 in *The Encyclopedia of the Lutheran Church.* Edited by J. Bodensieck. Minneapolis: Augsburg.

Pilch, John J. 1983. *Galatians and Romans.* Collegeville, MN: Liturgical Press.

———. 1991. Sickness and Healing in Luke-Acts. Pages 181–209 in *The Social World of Luke-Acts: Models for Interpretation.* Edited by Jerome H. Neyrey. Peabody, MA: Hendrickson.

———. 1998. Appearances of the Risen Jesus in Cultural Context: Experiences of Alternate Reality. *BTB* 28:52–60.

———. 2000a. Improving Bible Translations: The Example of Sickness and Healing. *BTB* 30:129–34.

———. 2000b. *Healing in the New Testament: Insights from Medical and Mediterranean Anthropology.* Minneapolis: Fortress.

———. 2002. Altered States of Consciousness in the Synoptics. Pages 103–15 in *The Social Setting of Jesus and the Gospels.* Edited by Wolfgang Stegemann, Bruce J. Malina, and Gerd Theissen. Minneapolis: Fortress.

———. 2004. A Window into the Biblical World: The Evil Eye. *TBT* 42:48–53.

———. 2007. Flute Players, Death, and Music in the Afterlife (Matthew 9:18–19, 23–26). *BTB* 37:12–19.

Pilch, John J., and Bruce J. Malina, eds. 1998. *Handbook of Biblical Social Values.* Peabody, MA: Hendrickson.

Pleins, J. David. 1987. Poverty in the Social World of the Wise. *JSOT* 37:61–78.

Pöchhacker, Franz, and Miriam Schlesinger, eds. 2002. *The Interpreting Studies Reader.* London: Routledge.

Polanyi, Karl. 1944. *The Great Transformation.* New York: Rinehart.

———. 1957. Aristotle Discovers the Economy. Pages 64–94 in *Trade and Market in the Early Empires: Economies in History and Theory.* Edited by Karl Polanyi, Conrad M. Arensberg, and Harry W. Pearson. New York: Free Press.

Popkes, W. 1991. *Zêlos* etc. *EDNT* 2:100–101.

Porter, Stanley E. 1999. Mark 1:4, Baptism, and Translation. Pages 81–98 in *Baptism, the New Testament, and the Church: Historical and Contemporary Studies in Honour of R. E. O. White.* Edited by S. F. Porter and A. R. Cross. Sheffield: Sheffield Academic Press.

———. 2001. Some Issues in Modern Translation Theory and the Study of the Greek New Testament. *CurBS*: 350–82.

———. 2005. Eugene Nida and Translation. *BT* 1:8–19.

Porter, Stanley E., and R. S. Hess. 1999. *Translating the Bible: Problems and Prospects.* JSNTSup 173. Sheffield: Sheffield Academic Press.

Preisendanz, Karl. 1973–74. *Papyri graecae magicae: Die griechischen Zauberpapyri.* 2nd ed. Sammlung Wissenschaftlicher Commentare. Stuttgart: Teubner.

Prickett, Stephen. 1986. *Words and the Word: Language, Poetics and Biblical Interpretation.* Cambridge: Cambridge University Press.

Pritchard, James Bennett, ed. 1969. *Ancient Near Eastern Texts Relating to the Old Testament.* 3rd ed. Princeton: Princeton University Press.

Prothero, Stephen R. 2003. *American Jesus: How the Son of God Became a National Icon.* New York: Farrar, Straus and Giroux.

Quell, Gottfried. 1964. "ἁμαρτάνω, ἁμάρτημα, ἁμαρτία." *TDNT* 1:267–86.

Qimron, Elisha. 1996. The Nature of the Reconstructed Composite Text of 4QMMT. Pages 9–13 in *Reading 4QMMT: New Perspectives on Qumran Law and History.* Edited by John Kampen and Mosche Bernstein. SBLSymS 2. Atlanta: Scholars Press.

Qimron, Elisha, and John Strugnell. 1994. *Qumran Cave 4, V. Miqsat Ma'aseh ha-Torah.* DJD 10. Oxford: Clarendon.

Rakoczy, Thomas. 1996. *Böser Blick, Macht des Auges und Neid der Götter: Eine Untersuchung zur Kraft des Blickes in der griechischen Literatur.* Classica Monacensia 13. Tübingen: Gunter Narr.

Rashkow, Ilona 1990. Hebrew Bible Translation and the Fear of Judaization. *Sixteenth Century Journal* 21:217–33.

Regev, Eyal. 2003. Abominated Temple and Holy Community: The Formation of the Notions of Purity and Impurity in Qumran. *DSD* 10:243–78.

———. 2005. Were the Priests All the Same? Qumranic Halakha in Comparison with Sadducean Halakha. *DSD* 12:158–88.

Rener, Frederick M. 1989. *Interpretatio: Language and Translation from Cicero to Tyler.* Atlanta: Rodopi.

Robinson, Douglas. 1997. *Western Translation Theory from Herodotus to Nietzsche.* Manchester, England: St. Jerome.

Roetzel, Calvin J. 1969. The Judgment Form in Paul's Letters. *JBL* 88:305–12.

———. 1998. *The Letters of Paul: Conversations in Context.* 4th ed. Louisville: Westminster John Knox.

Rohrbaugh, Richard L. 2007. *The New Testament in Cross-cultural Perspective.* Eugene, OR: Cascade Books.

———, ed. 1996. *The Social Sciences and New Testament Interpretation.* Peabody, MA: Hendrickson.

Rosner, Brian S. 1991. Temple and Holiness in 1 Corinthians 5. *TynBul* 42:137–45.

———. 1992. "ΟΥΞΙ ΜΑΛΛΟΝ ΕΠΕΝΘΗΣΑΤΕ": Corporate Responsibility in 1 Corinthians 5. *NTS* 38:470–73.

Sakenfeld, Katherine Doob, ed. 2006. *New Interpreter's Dictionary of the Bible.* Nashville: Abingdon.

Salevsky, Heidemarie. 1991. Theory of Bible Translation and General Theory of Translation. *BT* 1:101–14.

Salillas, Raphael. 1905. *La Fascinación en España.* Madrid: Eduardo Arias.

Saller, Richard P. 1982. *Personal Patronage under the Early Empire*. Cambridge: Cambridge University Press.

————. 2002. Framing the Debate over Growth in the Ancient Economy. Pages 251–69 in *The Ancient Economy*. Edited by Walter Scheidel and Sitta Von Reden. New York: Routledge.

Salom, A. P. 1958. The Imperatival Use of *hina* in the New Testament. *ABR* 6:125–41.

Sandys-Wunsch, John. 2005. *What Have They Done to the Bible? A History of Modern Biblical Interpretation*. Collegeville, MN: Liturgical Press.

Sapir, Edward. 1956. *Culture, Language, and Personality*. Berkeley: University of California Press.

Sauer, G. 1976. ηανθ *qin'ā* Eifer. *THAT* 2:647–50.

Schiffman, Lawrence H. 1985. Exclusion from the Sanctuary and the City of the Sanctuary in the *Temple Scroll*. *HAR* 9:308–9.

————. 1989. Architecture and Law: The Temple and Its Courtyards in the *Temple Scroll*. Pages 267–84 in *From Ancient Israel to Modern Judaism: Intellect in Quest of Understanding, Essays in Honor of Marvin Fox*. Edited by Jacob Neusner, Ernest S. Frerichs, and Nahum M. Sarna. 2 vols. BJS 159. Atlanta: Scholars Press.

————. 1990. *Miqsat Ma'aseh Ha-Torah* and the *Temple Scroll*. *RevQ* 14:448–51.

————. 1993. The Prohibition of Skins of Animals in the *Temple Scroll* and *Miqsat ma'aseh Ha-Torah*. Proceedings of the Tenth World Congress of Jewish Studies Division A. Jerusalem: World Union of Jewish Studies.

————. 1994. *Reclaiming the Dead Sea Scrolls*. Philadelphia: JPS.

————. 1996. The Place of 4QMMT in the Corpus of Qumran Manuscripts. Pages 81–98 in *Reading 4QMMT: New Perspectives on Qumran Law and History*. Edited by John Kampen and Mosche Bernstein. SBLSymS 2. Atlanta: Scholars Press.

————. 2000. The Relationship of the Zadokite Fragments and the Temple Scroll. Pages 133–45 in *The Damascus Document, a Centennial of Discovery: Proceedings of the Third International Symposium of the Orion Center for the Study of the Dead Sea Scrolls and Associated Literature, 4–8 February, 1998*. Edited by Joseph Baumgarten, Esther Chazon, and Avital Pinnick. STDJ 34. Leiden: Brill.

————. 2001. The Pharisees and Their Legal Traditions according to the Dead Sea Scrolls. *DSD* 8:262–77.

Schmidt, W. H. 1973. דבר. *ThWAT* 2:101–33.

Schneemelcher, Wilhelm. 1991. *New Testament Apocrypha*. Edited by R. McL. Wilson. Louisville: Westminster John Knox.

Schniedewind, William. 1999. Qumran Hebrew as Antilanguage. *JBL* 118:235–52.

Schoeck, Helmut. 1987. *Envy: A Theory of Social Behavior*. Indianapolis: Liberty.

Schreiner, Thomas R. 1998. *Romans*. Grand Rapids: Baker.

Schulte, Rainer, and John Biguenet, eds. 1992. *Thories of Translation: An Anthology of Essays from Dryden to Derrida*. Chicago: University of Chicago Press.

Scott, James C. 1976. *The Moral Economy of the Peasant: Rebellion and Subsistence in Southeast Asia*. New Haven: Yale University Press.

Sellin, Gerhard. 1987. Hauptprobleme des Ersten Korintherbriefes. *ANRW* 25.4:2940–3044. Part 2, *Principat*, 25.4. Edited by Wolfgang Haase. New York: de Gruyter.

Seneca, Lucius Annaeus. 1928. *Moral Essays*. Translated by John W. Basore. LCL. Cambridge: Harvard University Press.

Setel, T. Drorah. 1985. Prophets and Pornography: Female Sexual Imagery in Hosea. Pages 143–55 in *Feminist Interpretation of the Bible*. Edited by Letty T. Russell. Philadelphia: Westminster.

Sharp, Carolyn. 1997. Phinehan Zeal and Rhetorical Strategy in 4QMMT. *RevQ* 18:207–22.

Shemesh, Aharon, and C. Werman, eds. 2003. Halakhah at Qumran: Genre and Authority. *DSD* 10:121–22.

Singh Avadhesh K., ed. 1996. *Translation: Its Theory and Practice*. New Delhi: Creative Books.

Smith, Adam. 1776. *An Inquiry into the Nature and Causes of the Wealth of Nations*. Edited by Edwin Cannan. New York: Modern Library, 1994.

Smith, Mark. S. 1998. The Heart and Innards in Israelite Emotional Expressions: Notes from Anthropology and Psychobiology. *JBL* 117, no. 3: 427–36.

Smith, William Robertson. 1889. *Lectures on the Religion of the Semites*. Edinburgh: Black.

Smyth, Herbert Weir. 1920. *Greek Grammar*. Cambridge: Harvard University Press.

———. 1956. *Greek Grammar*. Rev. ed. Cambridge: Harvard University Press.

Snell-Hornby, Mary. 1990. Linguistic Transcoding or Cultural Transfer: A Critique of Translation Theory in Germany. Pages 81–82 in *Translation, History, and Culture*. Edited by Susan Bassnett and Andre Lafevre. New York: Pinter.

———. 1988. *Translation Studies: An Integrated Approach*. Amsterdam: John Benjamins.

Snell-Hornby, Mary, Zuzana Jettmarova, and Klaus Kaindl, eds. 1995. *Translation as Intercultural Communication*. Amsterdam: John Benjamins.

Soggin, J. Alberto. 1981. *Judges: A Commentary*. OTL. Philadelphia: Westminster.

South, James T. 1992. *Disciplinary Practices in Pauline Texts*. Lewiston, NY: Mellen.

Speiser, E. A. 1964. *Genesis: Introduction, Translation, and Notes*. AB 1. Garden City, NY: Doubleday.

Stambaugh, John E., and David L. Balch. 1986. *The New Testament in Its Social Environment*. Library of Early Christianity 2. Philadelphia: Westminster Press.

Stegemann, Ekkehard W., and Wolfgang Stegemann. 1995. *The Jesus Movement. A Social History of Its First Century*. Translated by O. C. Dean. Minneapolis: Fortress.

Sternberg, Meir. 1992. Biblical Poetics and Sexual Politics: From Reading to Counterreading. *JBL* 111, no. 3: 463–88.

Steudel, Annette. 2006. 4Q448: The Lost Beginning of MMT? Pages 247–63 in *From 4QMMT to Resurrection: Mélanges qumraniens en homage à Émile Puech*. Edited by Florentino García Martínez, Annette Steudel, and Eibert J. C. Tigchelaar. STDJ 61. Leiden: Brill.

Stevenson, T. R. 1992. The Ideal Benefactor and the Father Analogy in Greek and Roman Thought. *CQ* 42, no. 2: 421–36.

Stone, Michael, and Esther Chazon, eds. 1998. *Biblical Perspectives: Early Use and Interpretation of the Bible in Light of the Dead Sea Scrolls. Proceedings of the First*

International Symposium of the Orion Center for the Study of the Dead Sea Scrolls and Associated Literature, 12–14 May 1996. STDJ 28. Leiden: Brill.

Stritof, Sheri, and Bob Stritof. 2007. Is Marital Rape a Crime? *About.com.* http://marriage.about.com/cs/maritalrape/f/maritalrape10.htm.

Strupp, H. H., and S. W. Hadley. 1979. Specific vs. Nonspecific Factors in Psychotherapy: A Controlled Study of Outcome. *AGP* 36:1125–36.

Stuart, Douglas K. 1987. *Hosea–Jonah.* WBC 31. Waco, TX: Word.

Stumpf, A. *Zêlos* etc. 1964. *TDNT* 2:877–88.

Swartz, Marcus J. 1988. Shame, Culture, and Status among the Swahili of Mombasa. *Ethos* 16:21–51.

Tacitus. 1925–37. *The Histories, the Annals.* Translated by C. H. Moore and J. Jackson. 4 vols. LCL. Cambridge: Harvard University Press.

Taylor, Charles. 2004. *Modern Social Imaginaries.* Durham, NC: Duke University Press.

Theissen, G. 1983. *The Miracle Stories of the Early Christian Tradition.* Edinburgh: T & T Clark.

Thiselton, Anthony C. 2000. *The First Epistle to the Corinthians: A Commentary on the Greek Text.* NIGTC. Grand Rapids: Eerdmans.

Thornton, Timothy C. G. 1972. Satan—God's Agent for Punishing. *ExpTim* 83:151–52.

Thrall, Margaret E. 1994. *Introduction and Commentary on II Corinthians I–VII.* Vol. 1 of *The Second Epistle to the Corinthians.* ICC 8. Edinburgh: T & T Clark.

Triandis, Harry C. 1990. Cross-cultural Studies of Individualism and Collectivism. Pages 41–133 in *Cross-cultural Perspectives: Nebraska Symposium on Motivation 1989.* Edited by John J. Berman. Nebraska Symposium on Motivation 37. Lincoln: University of Nebraska Press.

Twain, Mark. 1935. *The Family Mark Twain.* New York: Harper Brothers.

Ulrich, Eugene. 2003. The Non-attestation of a Tripartite Canon in 4QMMT. *CBQ* 65:202–14.

Unamuno, Miguel de. 1942. La envidia hispánica. In *Ensayos*, vol. 2. Madrid: Aguilar. (Orig. pub. 1909.)

———. 1980. *Abel Sánchez, una historia de pasión.* Austral ed. (Orig. pub. 1917.)

Unnik, W. C. van. 1971. *Aphthonos Metadidomi.* Brussels: Paleis der Academien.

———. 1973. *De aphthonia van God in de oudchristelijke literatuur.* Pages 17–55 in *Mededelingen der koninlijke Nederlandse Akademi van Wetenschappen.* Afd. Letterk. n.r. 36/2. Amsterdam: Noord-Hollandsche Uitgevers Maatschapij.

Vanderkam, James C. 1997. The Calendar, 4Q327, and 4Q394. Pages 179–94 in *Legal Texts and Legal Issues: Proceedings of the Second Meeting of the International Organization for Qumran Studies, Published in Honour of Joseph M. Baumgarten.* Edited by Moshe Bernstein, Florentino García Martínez, and John Kampen. STDJ 23. Leiden: Brill.

———. 1998a. *Calendars in the Dead Sea Scrolls: Measuring Time.* London: Routledge.

———. 1998b. Authoritative Literature in the Dead Sea Scrolls. *DSD* 5:382–402.

————. 2006. To What End? Functions of Scriptural Interpretation in Qumran Texts. Pages 302–20 in *Studies in the Hebrew Bible, Qumran, and the Septuagint Presented to Eugene Ulrich*. Edited by Peter Flint, Emanuel Tov, and James C. VanderKam. SVTP 101. Leiden: Brill.

van Dijk-Hemmes, Fokkelien. 1989. The Imagination of Power and the Power of Imagination: An Intertextual Analysis of Two Biblical Love Songs. The Song of Songs and Hosea 2. *JSOT* 44:75–88.

van Wolde, Ellen. 2002. Does *'Innâ* Denote Rape? A Semantic Analysis of a Controversial Word. *VT* 42, no. 4: 528–44.

Venuti, Lawrence. 1993. Translation as Cultural Politics: Regimes of Domestication in English. *Textual Practice* 7, no. 2: 208–23.

————. 1995. *The Translator's Invisibility: A History of Translation*. London: Routledge.

————. 1998. *The Scandals of Translation: Towards an Ethic of Difference*. London: Routledge.

Verboven, Koenraad. 2002. *The Economy of Friends: Economic Aspects of Amicitia and Patronage in the Late Republic*. Collection Latomus. Brussels: Éditions Latomus.

Versnel, H. S. 1982. Religious Mentality in Ancient Prayer. Pages 1–64 in *Faith, Hope, and Worship: Aspects of Religious Mentality in the Ancient World*. Edited by H. S. Versnel. Leiden: Brill.

Viano, Christina. 2003. Competitive Emotions and *Thumos* in Aristotle's Rhetoric. Pages 85–97 in *Envy, Spite, and Jealousy: The Competitive Emotions in Ancient Greece*. Edited by David Konstan and N. Keith Rutter. Edinburgh Leventis Studies 2. Edinburgh: Edinburgh University Press.

von Rad, Gerhard. 1972. *Genesis: A Commentary*. Rev. ed. Translated by John H. Marks. OTL. Philadelphia: Westminster.

Vorländer, H. 1967. "ἀφίημι." Pages 697–703 in vol. 1 of *The New International Dictionary of New Testament Theology*. Edited by Colin Brown. 3 vols. Grand Rapids: Zondervan.

Wachob, Wesley H. 2000. *The Voice of Jesus in the Social Rhetoric of James*. SNTSMS 106. Cambridge: Cambridge University Press.

Walcot, Peter. 1978. *Envy and the Greeks: A Study of Human Behavior*. Warminster, England: Aris & Phillips.

Waltke, Bruce, and M. O'Connor. 1990. *An Introduction to Biblical Hebrew Syntax*. Winona Lake, IN: Eisenbrauns.

Watts, John D. W. 1987. *Isaiah 34–66*. WBC 25. Waco, TX: Word.

Weems, Renita J. 1995. *Battered Love: Marriage, Sex, and Violence in the Hebrew Prophets*. Minneapolis: Fortress.

Weiser, Artur. 1949. *Das Buch der zwölf kleinen Propheten*. Vol. 1. ATD 24. Göttingen: Vandenhoeck & Ruprecht.

Weissenberg, Hanne von. 2003. *4QMMT*—Towards an Understanding of the Epilogue. *RevQ* 21:29–45.

Wenham, Gordon J. 1994. *Genesis 16–50*. WBC 2. Dallas: Word.

Whybrow, Peter C. 2005. *American Mania: When More Is Not Enough.* New York: Norton.

Wiles, Gordon P. 1974. *Paul's Intercessory Prayers: The Significance of the Intercessory Prayer Passages in the Letters of St Paul.* SNTSMS 24. Cambridge: Cambridge University Press.

Wittenberg, G. H. 1987. The Situational Context of Statements Concerning Poverty and Wealth in the Book of Proverbs. *Scriptura* 21:1–23.

Wolff, Hans Walter. 1973. *Anthropologie des Alten Testaments.* Munich: C. Kaiser.

———. 1974a. *Anthropology of the Old Testament.* London: SCM.

———. 1974b. *Hosea: A Commentary on the Book of the Prophet Hosea.* Hermeneia. Philadelphia: Fortress.

Yadin, Azzan. 2003. 4QMMT, Rabbi Ishmael, and the Origins of Legal Midrash. *DSD* 10:130–49.

Yarbrough, O. Larry. 1995. Parents and Children in the Letters of Paul. Pages 126–41 in *The Social World of the First Christians: Essays in Honor of Wayne A. Meeks.* Edited by L. M. White and O. L. Yarbrough. Minneapolis: Fortress.

Contributors

ALICIA BATTEN
Associate Professor of Religion, Pacific Lutheran University

ZEBA A. CROOK
Assistant Professor of Religion, Carleton University

RICHARD E. DEMARIS
Associate Professor of Theology, Valparaiso University

JOHN H. ELLIOTT
Professor Emeritus, Theology and Religious Studies, University of San Francisco

ROBERT A. KUGLER
Paul S. Wright Professor of Christian Studies, Lewis and Clark College

CAROLYN LEEB
Assistant Professor of Theology, Valparaiso University

DIETMAR NEUFELD
Associate Professor of Christian Origins, University of British Columbia

JOHN J. PILCH
Professor Emeritus, Christian Studies, Georgetown University

RICHARD L. ROHRBAUGH
Professor Emeritus, Christian Studies, Lewis and Clark College

JOHN SANDYS-WUNSCH
Centre for Studies in Religion and Society, Thornloe University

INDEX OF ANCIENT WRITINGS

Index of Modern Authors

van Wolde, Ellen, 116, 117
Venuti, Lawrence, 11, 12, 13, 14, 23
Verboven, Koenraad, 68, 74
Versnel, H. S., 32
Viano, Christina, 75
von Rad, Gerhard, 117
Vorländer, H., 52, 53

Wachob, Wesley H., 74, 77
Walcott, Peter, 84
Walther, James Arthur, 35
Waltke, Bruce, 137
Weems, Renita, J., 115

Weiser, Artur, 113
Weissenberg, Hanne von, 127.
Wenham, Gordon J., 117
Werman, C., 131
Wettstein, J. J., 92
Wiles, Gordon P., 42
Wittenberg, G. H., 77
Wolff, Hans Walter, 111, 113
Wyatt, R. J., 81

Yadin, Azzan, 128, 138
Yarborough, Larry O., 42

Subject Index

Printed in the United States
205246BV00002B/1-150/P

9 781589 833470